Francis Schaeffer Study Center

Western Civilization – Year Four
The Modern World from 1865 – 1990

Source Book

Readings for the period from 1865 – 1920

Compiled by Robert G. W. Shearer

Internet: www.greenleafpress.com
3761 Highway 109N, Unit D
Lebanon, Tennessee 37087
615-449-1617

Published by Greenleaf Press

Copyright © 2008 Robert G. W. Shearer.

Permission is granted to copy, distribute and/or modify this document under the terms of the GNU Free Documentation License, Version 1.2 or any later version published by the Free Software Foundation; with no Invariant Sections, no Front-Cover Texts, and no Back-Cover Texts. A copy of the license is included in the section entitled "GNU Free Documentation License".

Table of Contents

Syllabus		pages 4-5
Week 2:	Reconstruction	page 7
Week 3:	The Franco-Prussian War	page 33
Week 4:	The New Imperialism	page 53
Week 5:	Anarchism	page 63
	Proudon, Czołgosz, and **The Propaganda of the Deed**	
Week 6:	The Spanish-American War	page 89
Week 7:	The Boxer Rebellion	page 105
Week 8:	Teddy Roosevelt	page 115
Week 9	The Russo-Japanese War	page 143
Week 10:	The Great War	page 163
Appendix:	Text of the GNU Free Documentation License	page 200

A note about Wikipedia articles:

Wikipedia has been a controversial source of information. Its great strength (and its great weakness) is that articles can be edited and improved by users. This works well on many topics, but is subject to abuse on contemporary or controversial issues. I have carefully reviewed the articles included in this sourcebook and satisfied myself that the information presented is trustworthy.

In general, Wikipedia is not a bad place to start, but one should test and verify the information and analysis of any article against other sources before deciding that it can be trusted.

- Rob Shearer
  Director, Schaeffer Study Center

Course Syllabus
Western Civilization - Year 4
The Modern World from 1865 to 1990

The Francis Schaeffer Study Center

Class: Western Civilization - Year 4
The Modern World from 1865 to 1990

Instructor: Rob Shearer
Email: Rob@greenleafpress.com

Tuition: $256

Western Civilization – Four Year Sequence:

Year 1: Israel, Egypt, Greece, & Rome
Year 2: Middle Ages, Renaissance & Reformation
Year 3: The Age of Revolution (1580-1865)
Year 4: Modern Times (1865-1990)

Class: Western Civilization - Year 4 - Modern Times (1865-1990)

Text: *Modern Times*, by Paul Johnson ISBN=006-092-2834, $20.00

Overview: The purpose of the course is to acquaint students with our rich cultural heritage in the west. In year four, we cover the period from 1865 to 1990 AD. I am passionately committed to the idea that our focus should be on biography and on those events and ideas which have had an on-going, continuing impact on western civilization. There will be much more biography and far less narrative history than a typical survey course - the intent of the course is to lay a foundation that later study (college or independent reading) can build upon.

Western Civ 4 is intended as a course for High School Seniors. As such, the assigned reading load is a bit heavier, and the subject matter is a bit more advanced than any of the previous courses. Students will need to devote more time and attention, especially to Modern Times. Johnson's text is provocative and should prompt some interesting discussions.

My approach to history begins with the assumption that all history is providential - that God is actively involved and not a passive, detached observer. We will deal explicitly with issues of character and morality as we study selected famous men.

I will begin each class with a 5 minute quiz so that students can demonstrate their reading comprehension skills and then we will discuss the issues from the week's reading. There will be two take-home tests and two in-class semester exams which will have some short answer and some essay questions that will require students to analyze and reflect on the issues of each era that we study. The grade I assign (which is always subject to review & alteration by parents) will be based 40% on quiz average, 40% on semester tests, and 20% on class participation.

Parents are invited and encouraged to attend any or all class sessions as they wish.

Average study time for this class: 4-6 hours weekly

Class: Western Civilization - Year 4 - Modern Times (1865-1990)

Class/Seminar Title	Reading Assignment
Week 1: The World of Vladimir Lenin (1870-1924)	
Week 2: Reconstruction and its discontents	
Week 3: The Franco-Prussian War	
Week 4: The New Imperialism	
Week 5: Proudhon and Anarchism	
Week 6: The Spanish American War 1898	
Week 7: The Boxer Rebellion	
Week 8: Teddy Roosevelt 1901-1909	
Week 9: Russo-Japanese War 1904-1905	
Week 10: The Great War	
Week 11: A Relativistic World	pp 1-48
Week 12: The First Despotic Utopias	pp. 49-103
Week 13: Waiting for Hitler	pp. 104-137
Thanksgiving	
Week 14: Legitimacy in Decadence	pp. 138-175
Week 15: An Infernal Theocracy, a Celestial Chaos	pp. 176-202
Week 16: The Last Arcadia	pp 203-229
Christmas Break	
Week 17: Degringolade	pp 230-260
Week 18: The Devils	pp 261-308
Week 19: The High Noon of Aggression	pp 309-340
Week 20: The End of Old Europe	pp 341-371
Week 21: The Watershed Year	pp 372-397
Week 22: Superpower and Genocide	pp 398-431
Week 23: Peace by Terror	pp 432-465
Week 24: The Bandung Generation	pp 466-505
Spring Break	
Week 25: Caliban's Kingdoms	pp 506-543
Week 26: Experimenting with Half Mankind	pp 544-574
Week 27: The European Lazarus	pp 575-612
Week 28: America's Suicide Attempt	pp 613-658
Week 29: The Collectivist Seventies	pp 659-696
Week 30: The Recovery of Freedom	pp 697-744
Week 31: The 1990's & Beyond	tba
Week 32: Final in-class exam	

This Page is intentionally blank

(actually, it **WAS** blank, but then I added this text, so now it's not blank anymore, but it had to be inserted so that the next chapter will start on a right-hand page – aren't you glad you asked?)

Francis Schaeffer Study Center
Mt. Juliet, Tennessee

Western Civilization, Year Four

From 1865 to 1990, Reconstruction to Modern Times

Rob Shearer, Tutor

Week Two Reading

Reconstruction

Reconstruction

From Wikipedia, the free encyclopedia

Contents

- 1 Loyalty Issue
- 2 Suffrage issue
- 3 Wartime plans and legislation
- 4 Presidential Reconstruction: 1865–66
    - 4.1 Black Codes
    - 4.2 Moderate responses
    - 4.3 Johnson vetoes; Democrats regroup
- 5 Radical Reconstruction: 1866–77
    - 5.1 Radicals win 1866 election
    - 5.2 Constitutional Amendments
    - 5.3 Military reconstruction
    - 5.4 Black Reconstruction
    - 5.5 Public schools and Railroads
    - 5.6 Views of the Conservatives in the South
- 6 Redemption and the end of Reconstruction in 1870s
    - 6.1 Republicans split: election of 1872
    - 6.2 Democrats try a "New Departure"
    - 6.3 Panic of 1873 weakens GOP
    - 6.4 1876 Election
    - 6.5 South under Redeemers
- 7 Legacy and Historiography
- 8 Significant dates
- 9 See also
- 10 Primary Sources & Collections of Primary Sources
    - 10.1 Newspapers and Magazines
    - 10.2 Laws passed by Congress
- 11 Secondary sources
    - 11.1 Surveys
- 12 National politics; Constitutional issues
- 13 South: regional, state & local studies
- 14 External links
    - 14.1 Notes

Summary

Reconstruction was the period in United States history, 1865–77, that resolved the issues of the American Civil War when both the Confederacy and its system of slavery were destroyed. The period of Reconstruction addressed the return of the southern states that had seceded, the status of ex-Confederate leaders, and the integration of the African-American Freedmen into the legal, political, economic and social system. Violent controversy arose over how to accomplish those tasks.

During the was Republican leaders agreed that slavery and the Slave Power had to be permanently destroyed, and all forms of Confederate nationalism had to be suppressed. Moderates said this could be easily accomplished as soon as Confederate armies surrendered and the southern states repealed secession and ratified the 13th Amendment — all of which happened by September 1865. However the Radical Republicans were much more skeptical of southern intentions and demanded far more stringent federal action. Presidents Abraham Lincoln and Andrew Johnson were the leaders of the moderate Republicans; Thaddeus Stevens and Charles Sumner led the Radical Republicans. Radicals judged the moderate policies to be a failure, especially Johnson's opposition to civil rights for the Freedmen.

Winning the election of 1866, the Radicals took full control in Washington. The House of Representatives impeached Johnson, who was subsequently acquitted by a single vote in the Senate. They used the Army to give the vote to black men, who had never been permitted to vote or attend school under antebellum Southern governments, and briefly took the vote away from an estimated 10 or 15,000 white men who had been Confederate officials or had not yet sworn to uphold the government of the United States. The Radical stage lasted for varying lengths in the different states, where a Republican coalition of Freedmen, Scalawags and Carpetbaggers took control and promoted modernization through railroads and public schools. They were charged with corruption by their opponents, the conservative–Democratic coalition, calling themselves "Redeemers" after 1870. Violence sponsored by the Ku Klux Klan was countered by federal intervention.

By 1877, however, Redeemers regained control of every state, and President Rutherford Hayes withdrew federal troops, causing the collapse of the remaining three Republican state governments. The 13th, 14th and 15th amendments were permanent legacies. Bitterness from the heated partisanship of the era lasted a century.

The Opening Political Issues of Reconstruction

Loyalty Issue

The loyalty issue emerged in the debate over the Wade-Davis Act of 1864, which Lincoln vetoed. Wade-Davis required voters to take the "Ironclad Oath," swearing that in the past they never had supported the Confederacy or been one of its soldiers. Lincoln ignored the past and asked voters to swear that in the future they would support the Union. The Radical lost support following Lincoln's pocket veto, but they regained strength in 1866.

Suffrage issue

Suffrage was a central issue. On the one hand was the question of allowing some or all ex-Confederates to vote. The moderates wanted virtually all of them to vote, but the Radicals wanted restrictions on ex-Confederate leaders. Thaddeus Stevens proposed, unsuccessfully, that ex-Confederates lose the vote for five years. No one knew how many Confederate leaders temporarily lost the vote but one estimate was 10,000 to 15,000.[1]. Second was the issue of whether blacks should vote. Conservatives who included ex-Confederate and Northern Democrats opposed black voting while Abraham Lincoln and Andrew Johnson wanted some blacks to vote, especially army veterans. Lincoln proposed giving the vote to "the very intelligent, and especially those who have fought gallantly in our ranks" [2], while Governor Johnson said, "The better class of them will go to work and sustain themselves, and that class ought to be allowed to vote, on the ground that a loyal negro is more worthy than a disloyal white man" [3]. As President Johnson wrote the governor of Mississippi recommending, "If you could extend the elective franchise to all persons of color who can read the Constitution in English and write their names, and to all persons of color who own real estate valued at not less than two hundred and fifty dollars, and pay taxes thereon, you would completely disarm the adversary [Radicals in Congress], and set an example the other states will follow." [4]

Senator Charles Sumner of Massachusetts, leader of the Radical Republicans, was initially hesitant to enfranchise the largely illiterate ex-slave population. However Sumner decided it was necessary for blacks to vote for three reasons: [5]

1. for their own protection;
2. for the protection of white Unionists (i.e. "scalawags");
3. for the peace of the country.

The Radicals said the only way to get experience was to get the vote first, and they passed laws allowing all male freedmen to vote. In 1867, black men voted for the first time and, over the course of Reconstruction, more than 1,500 African Americans held public office. (The question of women's suffrage was debated, but rejected.)

Though former Confederates — the South's pre-Civil War political leaders — renounced secession and gave up slavery, they were angered in 1867 when their previously all-white state governments were ousted by federal military forces, and replaced by lawmakers elected for the first time by black and white voters.

"No more than 137 officeholders lived outside the South before the Civil War," Eric Foner wrote in the introduction to *Freedom's Lawmakers*, a biographical directory, with many photographs, of more than 1500 black officeholders during Reconstruction.

Of the less than 10 percent of more than 1,500 black officeholders listed in the directory who lived outside the South before the Civil War, Foner wrote, "Most were individuals born in the North (where about 220,000 free blacks lived in 1860), but their numbers also included free Southerners whose families moved to the North, free blacks and a few privileged slaves sent North for education, several immigrants from abroad, and fugitives from bondage."

Wartime plans and legislation

Planning for Reconstruction began in 1861, at the onset of the war. The Radical Republicans, seeking strict policies, used as their base the Congressional Joint Committee on Reconstruction. Abraham Lincoln pursued a lenient plan for reconstruction, especially in Louisiana, Tennessee, and Arkansas. In those states, he proposed a ten percent plan that required 10 percent of the voters from the 1860 election to swear an oath of future loyalty to the Union. He never succeeded in getting compliance with his plan [6].

Lincoln opposed the Radicals on Reconstruction issue, and vetoed their key legislation, the Wade–Davis Act. It would allow a state to be rehabilitated only if a majority of voters swore the "Ironclad Oath" which stated they had never in the past supported the Confederacy. Observers at the time--and historians since--agree that probably no state would have qualified, leaving them under military control indefinitely. By vetoing the act (which had been passed by Congress on July 2, 1864), Lincoln blocked the Radicals from a dominant role. (They became dominant again in 1866.) Historian William Gienapp explains Lincoln's veto:[7]

> Lincoln, in contrast, shrank from inaugurating a fundamental upheaval in southern society and mores, and by stressing future over past loyalty, he was willing to allow recanting Rebels to dominate the new southern governments. Moreover, Lincoln believed that the best strategy was to introduce black suffrage in the South by degrees in order to accustom southern whites to blacks voting. How far he was willing to go in extending rights to former slaves remained unclear, but his gradualist approach to social change remained intact, just as when he had tried to get the border states in 1862 to adopt gradual emancipation. Finally, the radicals and Lincoln held quite different views of the relationship of Reconstruction to the war effort. By erecting impossibly high standards that no southern state could meet, the Wade–Davis bill sought to postpone Reconstruction until the war was over. For Lincoln, in contrast, a lenient program of Reconstruction would encourage southern whites to abandon the Confederacy and thus was integral to his strategy for winning the war.

Lincoln thus wanted to bring the Southern states back into good standing as fast as possible and with a minimum of vengeance. Insisting as well that there be new rights for the Freedmen, he created the Bureau of Refugees, Freedmen and Abandoned Lands, known as the Freedmen's Bureau. In one experiment in the Sea Islands of South Carolina, Freedmen were allowed to farm plantations seized by the Army; they never received ownership [8].

Presidential Reconstruction: 1865–66

Northern anger over the Confederate John Wilkes Booth's assassination of Lincoln and the immense human cost of the war led to demands for harsh policies. Vice President Andrew Johnson had taken a hard line, and spoke of hanging rebel Confederates but when he succeeded Lincoln as President, Johnson took a much softer line, pardoning many Confederate leaders and allowing ex-Confederates to maintain their control of Southern state governments, Southern lands, and black people [9]. Jefferson Davis was held in prison for two years, but not the other Confederate leaders; there were no treason trials. Only one person — Captain Henry Wirz, the commandant of the prison camp in Andersonville, Georgia — was executed for war crimes.

Black Codes

The Johnson governments quickly enacted "black codes", effectively giving freedmen only a limited set of second-class civil rights, and no voting rights. Southern plantation owners feared they would lose their labor force, making the cotton lands worthless. Many Southern whites feared that blacks would consider themselves their equals. Mississippi and South Carolina black codes have been described:[10]

> "Negroes must make annual contracts for their labor in writing; if they should run away from their tasks, they forfeited their wages for the year. Whenever it was required of them they must present licenses (in a town from the mayor; elsewhere from a member of the board of police of the beat) citing their places of residence and authorizing them to work. Fugitives from labor were to be arrested and carried back to their employers. Five dollars a head and mileage would be allowed such negro catchers. It was made a misdemeanor, punishable with fine or imprisonment, to persuade a freedman to leave his employer, or to feed the runaway. Minors were to be apprenticed, if males until they were twenty-one, if females until eighteen years of age. Such corporal punishment as a father would administer to a child might be inflicted upon apprentices by their masters. Vagrants were to be fined heavily, and if they could not pay the sum, they were to be hired out to service until the claim was satisfied. Negroes might not carry knives or firearms unless they were licensed so to do. It was an offense, to be punished by a fine of $50 and imprisonment for thirty days, to give or sell intoxicating liquors to a negro. When negroes could not pay the fines and costs after legal proceedings, they were to be hired at public outcry by the sheriff to the lowest bidder....
> "In South Carolina persons of color contracting for service were to be known as "servants," and those with whom they contracted, as "masters." On farms the hours of labor would be from sunrise to sunset daily, except on Sunday. The negroes were to get out of bed at dawn. Time lost would be deducted from their wages, as would be the cost of food, nursing, etc., during absence from sickness. Absentees on Sunday must return to the plantation by sunset. House servants were to be at call at all hours of the day and night on all days of the week. They must be "especially civil and polite to their masters, their masters' families and guests," and they in return would receive "gentle and kind treatment." Corporal and other punishment was to be administered only upon order of the district judge or other civil magistrate. A vagrant law of some severity was enacted to keep the negroes from roaming the roads and living the lives of beggars and thieves."

The Black codes outraged northern opinion and apparently were never put into effect in any state.

Moderate responses

In response to the Black codes and worrisome signs of Southern recalcitrance, the Radical Republicans blocked the readmission of the ex-rebellious states to the Congress in fall 1865. Congress also renewed the Freedman's Bureau, but Johnson vetoed it. Senator Lyman Trumbull of Illinois, leader of the moderate Republicans, took affront at the black codes. He proposed the first **Civil Rights Law** because, he explained:[11]

> Of what avail, he asked, is the Thirteenth Amendment "if in the late slaveholding States laws are to be enacted and enforced depriving persons of African descent of privileges which are essential to freemen?" The legislatures of the Southern States have by law discriminated against the negroes. "They deny them certain rights and subject them to severe penalties. ...Although they do not make a man an absolute slave they yet deprive him of the rights of a freeman; and it is perhaps difficult to draw the precise line to say where freedom ceases and slavery begins but a law that does not allow a colored person to go from one county to another, and one that does not allow him to hold property, to teach, to preach, are certainly laws in violation of the rights of a freeman.... The purpose of this bill is to destroy all these discriminations and to carry into effect the constitutional amendment;" it is to give the negro "the right to acquire property, to go and come at pleasure, to enforce rights in the courts, to make contracts, and to inherit and dispose of property." The constitutional warrant for the bill was the second section of the Thirteenth Amendment, "Congress shall have power to enforce this article [abolishing slavery] by appropriate, legislation."

The key to the bill was the opening section:

> "All persons born in the United States and not subject to any foreign Power, excluding Indians not taxed, are hereby declared to be citizens of the United States; and such citizens of every race and color, without regard to any previous condition of slavery or involuntary servitude, except as punishment for crime whereof the party shall have been duly convicted, shall have the same right in every State and Territory in the United States, to make and enforce contracts, to sue, be parties, and give evidence, to inherit, purchase, lease, sell, hold, and convey real and personal property, and to full and equal benefit of all laws and proceedings for the security of person and property, as is enjoyed by white citizens, and shall be subject to like punishment, pains, and penalties and to none other, any law, statute, ordinance, regulation, or custom to the Contrary notwithstanding."

Congress quickly passed the Civil Rights bill; the Senate on February 2 voted 33–12; the House on March 13 voted 111–38.

Johnson vetoes; Democrats regroup

Although strongly urged by moderates in Congress to sign the Civil Rights bill, Johnson broke decisively with them by vetoing it on March 27. His veto message objected to the measure because it conferred citizenship on the Freedmen at a time when eleven out of thirty-six States were unrepresented and attempted to fix by Federal law "a perfect equality of the white and black races in every State of the Union." Johnson said it was an invasion by Federal authority of the rights of the States; it had no warrant in the Constitution and was contrary to all precedents. It was a "stride toward centralization and the concentration of all legislative power in the national government." [12]

"The national debate over reconstruction, and in particular, the Freedman's Bureau, is evident in a campaign broadside from Pennsylvania's gubernatorial campaign of 1866. "This cartoon's racist imagery played upon public fears that government assistance would benefit indolent freedmen at the expense of white workers."

The Democratic party, proclaiming itself the party of white men, north and south, supported Johnson. [13] However the Republicans in Congress overrode his veto (the Senate by the close vote of 33:15, the House by 122:41) and the Civil Rights bill became law. The last moderate proposal was the Fourteenth Amendment, also authored by moderate Trumbull. It was designed to put the key provisions of the Civil Rights Act into the Constitution, but it went much further. It extended citizenship to everyone born in the United States (except visitors and Indians on reservations), penalized states that did not give the vote to Freedmen, and most importantly, created new federal civil rights that could be protected by federal courts. It guaranteed the Federal war debt (and promised the Confederate debt would never be paid). Johnson used his influence to block the amendment in the states, as three-fourths of the states were required for ratification. (The Amendment was later ratified.) The moderate effort to compromise with Johnson had failed and an all-out political war broke out between the Republicans (both Radical and moderate) on one side, and on the other Johnson and his allies in the Democratic party in the North, and the conservative groupings (which used different names) in each southern state.

Radical Reconstruction: 1866–77

Radicals win 1866 election

The Congressional elections of 1866 were fought over the issue of Reconstruction. The Southern states were not allowed to vote, having not yet been re-admitted to the Union; the result was solid Republican gains in Congress [14]. The Radicals under Stevens and Sumner, for the first time now took full control of Congress and passed the first Reconstruction Act in March 1867.

Constitutional Amendments

Three new Constitutional Amendments were adopted in the wake of the Civil War. The 13th abolishing slavery was ratified in 1865. The 14th was rejected in 1866 but ratified in 1868, granting federal civil rights. The 15th passed in 1870, decreeing that the right to vote could not be denied because of race, color, or previous condition of servitude. (It did not grant the right to vote, as electoral policies are defined by the states.)

Military reconstruction

The first Reconstruction Act placed ten Confederate states under military control, grouping them into five military districts: [15]

- First Military District: Virginia, under General John Schofield
- Second Military District: The Carolinas, under General Daniel Sickles
- Third Military District: Georgia, Alabama and Florida, under General John Pope
- Fourth Military District: Arkansas and Mississippi, under General Edward Ord
- Fifth Military District: Texas and Louisiana, under Generals Philip Sheridan and Winfield Scott Hancock

Tennessee, which had been readmitted to full status on July 24, 1866, was not made part of a military district, and federal controls did not apply.

The ten Southern state governments were re-constituted under the direct control of the US Army. There was little or no fighting, but rather a state of martial law in which the military closely supervised local government, supervised elections, and protected office holders from violence [16]. Blacks, for the first time in history, and whites were enrolled as voters; former Confederate leaders were excluded.[Foner 1988 p 274–5] No one state was representative. Here is what happened in Texas:[17]

> The first critical step ... was the registration of voters according to guidelines established by Congress and interpreted by Generals Sheridan and Griffin. The Reconstruction Acts called for registering all adult males, white and black, except those who had ever sworn an oath to uphold the Constitution of the United States and then engaged in rebellion.... Sheridan interpreted these restrictions stringently, barring from registration not only all pre-1861 officials of state and local governments who had supported the Confederacy but also all city officeholders and even minor functionaries such as sextons of cemeteries. In May Griffin ... appointed a three-man board of registrars for each county, making his

choices on the advice of known Unionists and local Freedmen's Bureau agents. In every county where practicable a freedman served as one of the three registrars.... Final registration amounted to approximately 59,633 whites and 49,479 blacks. It is impossible to say how many whites were rejected or refused to register (estimates vary from 7,500 to 12,000), but blacks, who constituted only about 30 percent of the state's population, were significantly overrepresented at 45 percent of all voters.

Elections in 1867 returned a Republican victory in every state (except Virginia, where Conservative Democrats won). These governments then agreed to the Congressional conditions for readmission to the Union, including ratification of the Constitutional Amendments. With most ex-Confederates ineligible because they could not take the Ironclad oath, the majority of delegates in every state but South Carolina were African Americans.

Race of delegates to 1867 state conventions

	Black	White	% Black
Virginia	80	25	76%
North Carolina	107	13	89%
South Carolina	48	76	39%
Georgia	133	33	80%
Florida	28	18	61%
Alabama	92	16	85%
Mississippi	68	17	80%
Texas	81	9	90%
Louisiana	"great majority"		

Source: Rhodes (1920) v 6 p. 199

All Southern states were readmitted to the Union by the end of 1870, the last being Georgia, gaining re-admission on July 15, 1870. All but 500 top Confederate leaders were pardoned when President Ulysses Grant signed the Amnesty Act of 1872.

Black Reconstruction

1 Harper's Weekly magazine Nov 14, 1867, celebrates the first black voters: farmer, politician, soldier

One by one, the Southern states held new elections in which Freedmen voted. In most cases, the result was a Republican state government; the state was readmitted, the Congressional delegation was seated, and most soldiers were removed. Most Republicans were organized into clubs called Union Leagues. The Republican coalition in each state comprised Freedmen (the largest group) and local white Republicans (called "scalawags"), the second largest group. In addition two groups of northerners were important, African Americans and whites (called "carpetbaggers", The black politicians were not unlettered slaves, but free blacks, especially from the North — "mostly freeborn urban mulattoes." [18]

The old political élite of the Democratic Party, mostly former Confederates, were (temporarily) frozen out of power (although some, like General James Longstreet, joined the Republicans).

Republicans took control of all Southern state

2 Hiram Revels (center), the first Black Senator, replaces Jefferson Davis (left) in Senate. Harper's Weekly Feb 19, 1870

governorships and state legislatures, leading to the election of numerous African-Americans to state and national office, as well as to the installation of African-Americans into other positions of power [19].

Public schools and Railroads

As modernizers the Republicans believed that education was a long-term solution to the economic poverty and ignorance of the South. They created a system of public schools, which were segregated by race everywhere except New Orleans. Most blacks approved the segregated schools because they provided jobs for black teachers. In general elementary and a few secondary schools were built in the cities. But the South had few cities and in the rural areas the public school was a one-room affair that attracted about half the younger children. The teachers were poorly paid and their pay was often in arrears [20].

Conservatives contended the rural schools were too expensive and unnecessary for a region where the vast majority of people were cotton or tobacco farmers. John Hope Franklin found that the schools were not very effective, because of "poverty, the inability of the states to collect taxes, and inefficiency and corruption in many places prevented successful operation of the schools." [21]

Year Four Sourcebook, page 17

3 1868 Republican cartoon identifies Democratic candidate Seymour (right panel) with KKK violence and with the Confederate soldiers

Numerous private academies and colleges for Freedmen were established by northern missionaries. Every state created state colleges for Freedmen, such as Alcorn State University in Mississippi; in 1890 the black state colleges started receiving federal funds as land grant schools [22]. They received state funds after Reconstruction ended because, as Lynch explains, "there are very many liberal, fair-minded and influential Democrats in the State who are strongly in favor of having the State provide for the liberal education of both races." [23]

Every state (and many localities) subsidized railroads, which modernizers felt could haul the South out of isolation and poverty. Millions of dollars in bonds and subsidies were fraudulently pocketed. One ring in North Carolina spent $200,000 in bribing the legislature and obtained millions in state money for its railroads. Instead of building new track, however, it used the funds to speculate in bonds, reward friends with extravagant fees, and enjoy lavish trips to Europe [24]. Taxes were quadrupled across the South to pay off the railroad bonds and the school costs, leading to intense complaints among taxpayers [25]. Nevertheless thousands of miles of lines were built as the Southern system expanded from 11,000 miles in 1870 to 29,000 in 1890. The lines were owned and directed overwhelmingly by Northerners. Railroads helped create a mechanically skilled group of craftsmen, and indeed broke the isolation of much of the region. Passengers were few, however, and apart from hauling the cotton crop when it was harvested, there was little freight traffic [26]. As Franklin explains, "numerous railroads fed at the public trough by bribing legislators...and through the use and misuse of state funds." The effect, according to one businessman, "was to drive capital from the State, paralyze industry, and demoralize labor." [27]

The new spending on schools and especially on railroad subsidies, combined with fraudulent spending and a collapse in state credit because of huge deficits, forced the states to dramatically increase tax rates — up to ten times higher — despite the poverty of the region. Angry taxpayers revolted, as the conservatives shifted their focus away from race to taxes [28]. Former Congressman John Lynch, a black Republican leader from Mississippi, concluded, "The argument made by the taxpayers, however, was plausible and it may be conceded that, upon the whole, they were about right; for no doubt it would have been much easier upon the taxpayers to have increased at that time the interest-bearing debt of the State than to have increased the tax rate. The latter course, however, had been adopted and could not then be changed." [29]

Views of the Conservatives in the South

The white Southerners who lost power reformed themselves into "Conservative" parties that battled the Republicans throughout the South. The party names varied, and by the late 1870s they called themselves simply "Democrats." Their views on national policy were reflected later by the historians of the Dunning School.

Historian Walter Lynwood Fleming was representative of the Dunning School in that he was sympathetic to southern conservatives and contemptuous of Radical corruption, and paternalistic toward the African Americans: he wrote:

> The Negro troops, even at their best, were everywhere considered offensive by the native whites. General Grant, indeed, urged that only white troops be used to garrison the interior. But the Negro soldier, impudent by reason of his new freedom, his new uniform, and his new gun, was more than Southern temper could tranquilly bear, and race conflicts were frequent. A New Orleans newspaper thus states the Southern point of view: "Our citizens who had been accustomed to meet and treat the Negroes only as respectful servants, were mortified, pained, and shocked to encounter them ... wearing Federal uniforms and bearing bright muskets and gleaming bayonets.... They are jostled from the sidewalks by dusky guards, marching four abreast. They were halted, in rude and sullen tones, by Negro sentinels. ... The lawlessness of the Negroes in parts of the Black Belt and the disturbing influences of the black troops, of some officials of the Bureau, and of some of the missionary teachers and preachers, caused the whites to fear insurrections and to take measures for protection. Secret semi-military organizations were formed which later developed into the Ku Klux orders. [3]

Representative also of the Dunning School is the analysis of Ellis Oberholtzer (a northern scholar) in 1917: [30]

> Outrages upon the ex-slaves in the South there were in plenty. Their sufferings were many. But white men, too, were victims of lawless violence, and in all portions of the North as well as in the late "rebel" states. Not a political campaign passed without the exchange of bullets, the breaking of skulls with sticks and stones, the firing of rival club-houses. Republican clubs marched the streets of Philadelphia, amid revolver shots and brickbats, to save the negroes from the "rebel" savages in Alabama. The "very spirit of Cain," the New York *Nation* said in the summer of 1866, seemed to stalk over the land. Noble motives which earlier had governed men were swept aside and were lost in the general saturnalia of malignity. The troops serving in the South were there not so much to protect the negroes as to punish their old masters; not so much to guard the imperiled interests of the Southern "loyalists," of whom a deal had been said, as to exasperate the President and the members of his party in the North. The project to make voters out of black men was not so much for their social elevation as for the further punishment of the Southern white people —for the capture of offices for Radical scamps and the entrenchment of the Radical party in power for a long time to come in the South and in the country at large. One Northern state had followed another in refusing to give the ballot to its own negroes.

Reaction by conservatives included the formation of violent secret societies especially the Ku Klux Klan. Violence occurred in cities and in the countryside between white former Confederates, Republicans, African-Americans, representatives of the federal government, and Republican-organized armed Loyal Leagues.

Redemption and the end of Reconstruction in 1870s

Republicans split: election of 1872

As early as 1868 Supreme Court Chief Justice Salmon P. Chase, a leading Radical during the war, concluded that:

> "Congress was right in not limiting, by its reconstruction acts, the right of suffrage to whites; but wrong in the exclusion from suffrage of certain classes of citizens and all unable to take its prescribed retrospective oath, and wrong also in the establishment of despotic military governments for the States and in authorizing military commissions for the trial of civilians in time of peace. There should have been as little military government as possible; no military commissions; no classes excluded from suffrage; and no oath except one of faithful obedience and support to the Constitution and laws, and of sincere attachment to the constitutional Government of the United States."[31]

By 1872, President Grant had alienated large numbers of leading Republicans, including many Radicals by the wanton corruption of his administration and his use of federal soldiers to prop up Radical state regimes. The opponents, called "Liberal Republicans", included founders of the party who expressed dismay that the party had succumbed to corruption. Leaders included editors of some of the most powerful newspapers. Charles Sumner, embittered by Grant's corruption, joined the new party, which nominated editor Horace Greeley. The badly disorganized Democratic party supported Greeley.

Grant made up for the defections by new gains among Union veterans, as well as strong support from the "Stalwart" faction of his party (which depended on his patronage), and the Southern Republican parties. Grant won a smashing landslide, as the Liberal Republican party vanished and many former supporters — even ex-abolitionists — abandoned the cause of Reconstruction [32].

Likewise in the South political–racial tensions built up inside the Republican party. In 1868, Georgia Democrats, with support from some Republicans, expelled all 28 black Republican members (arguing blacks were eligible to vote, but not to hold office.) In state after state the more conservative scalawags fought for control with the more radical carpetbaggers, and usually lost. Thus in Mississippi the conservative faction led by scalawag James Luck Alcorn was decisively defeated by the radical faction led by Carpetbagger Adelbert Ames. The party lost support steadily as many scalawags left it; few new recruits were acquired. Meanwhile the Freedmen were demanding a much larger share of the offices and patronage, and thus squeezing out their carpetbagger allies [33]. Finally some of the more prosperous Freedmen were joining the Democrats, angered at the failure of the Republicans to help them acquire land [34]. Although some Marxist historians, especially W.E.B. DuBois, looked for and celebrated a cross-racial coalition of poor whites and poor blacks, such a coalition rarely formed, Congressman Lynch explains that, "While the colored men did not look with favor upon a political alliance with the poor whites, it must be admitted that, with very few exceptions, that class of whites did not seek, and did not seem to desire such an alliance." Lynch explains that poor whites resented the job competition from Freedmen. Furthermore the poor whites "with a few exceptions, were less efficient, less capable, and knew less about matters of state and governmental administration than many of the ex-slaves.... As a rule, therefore, the whites that came into the leadership of the Republican party between 1872 and 1875 were representatives of the most substantial families of the land." [35] Thus the poor whites became Democrats and bitterly opposed the black Republicans.

Democrats try a "New Departure"

By 1870, the Democratic–Conservative leadership across the South decided it had to end its opposition to Reconstruction as well as to black suffrage in order to survive and move on to new issues. The Grant administration had proven by its crackdown on the KKK that it would use as much federal power as necessary. The Democrats in the North concurred. They wanted to fight the GOP on economic grounds rather than race. The New Departure offered the chance for a clean slate without having to refight the Civil War every election. Furthermore many wealthy landowners thought they could control part of the newly enfranchised black electorate to their own advantage. Not all Democrats agreed; a hard core element wanted to resist Reconstruction no matter what. Eventually a group called Redeemers took control of the party in state after state [36]. They formed coalitions with conservative Republicans, including scalawags and carpetbaggers, emphasizing the need for economic modernization. Railroad building was seen as a panacea, for northern capital was needed. The new tactics were a success in Virginia as William Mahone built a winning coalition. In Tennessee the Redeemers formed a coalition with Republican governor DeWitt Senter. Across the South Democrats switched from the race issue to taxes and corruption — charging that Republican governments were corrupt and inefficient, as taxes began squeezing cash-poor farmers who rarely saw $20 in currency a year, but had to pay taxes in currency or lose their farm.

In North Carolina, Republican governor William Woods Holden used state troops against the Klan, but the prisoners were released by federal judges, Holden became the first governor in American history to be impeached and removed from office. Republican political disputes in Georgia split the party and enabled the Redeemers to take over [37]. Violence was a factor in neutralizing Republican leaders in the deep South, with its larger black Republican population. In the North a live-and-let-live attitude made elections more like a sporting contest. But in the deep South it was life or death. Explained an Alabama scalawag, "Our contest here is for life, for the right to earn our bread ... for a decent and respectful consideration as human beings and members of society." [38]

Panic of 1873 weakens GOP

The Panic of 1873 hit the Southern economy hard, and disillusioned many Republicans who had gambled that railroads would pull the South out of its poverty. The price of cotton fell by half; many small landowners, local merchants and cotton factors (wholesalers) went bankrupt. Sharecropping, for both black and white farmers, became more common as a way to spread the risk of owning land. The old abolitionist element in the North was aging away, or had lost interest, and was not replenished. Many carpetbaggers returned to the North or joined the Redeemers. Blacks had an increased voice in the Republican party, but across the South it was divided by internal bickering and was rapidly losing its cohesion. Many local black leaders started emphasizing individual economic progress in cooperation with white elites, rather than racial political progress in opposition to them, a conservative attitude that foreshadowed Booker T. Washington. [39]

Nationally, President Grant took the blame for the depression, as his Republican party lost 96 seats in all parts of the country in the 1874 elections. The Bourbon Democrats took control of the House and were confident of electing Samuel J. Tilden president in 1876. President Grant was not running for re-election and seemed to be losing interest in the South. State after state fell to the Redeemers, with only four in Republican hands in 1873, Arkansas, Louisiana, Mississippi and South Carolina; Arkansas then fell after the Brooks–Baxter War in 1874. Political violence was endemic in Louisiana, but efforts to seize the state government were repulsed by federal troops who entered the state legislature and hauled away several Democratic legislators. The violation of tradition embarrassed Grant, and some of his cabinet recommended against further intervention [40]. By now all Democrats and most northern Republicans agreed that Confederate nationalism and slavery were dead — the war goals were achieved — and further federal military interference was an undemocratic violation of historic republican values. The victory of Rutherford Hayes in the hotly contested Ohio gubernatorial election of 1875 indicated his "let alone" policy toward the South would become Republican policy, as indeed happened when he won the 1876 GOP nomination for president. The last explosion of violence came in Mississippi's 1875 election, in which Democratic rifle clubs, operating in the open and without disguise, threatened or shot enough Republicans to decide the election for the Redeemers. The Republican governor Adelbert Ames asked Grant for federal troops to fight back; Grant refused, saying public opinion was "tired out" of the perpetual troubles in the South. Ames fled the state as the Democrats took over Mississippi [41].

1876 Election

Reconstruction continued in South Carolina, Louisiana and Florida until 1877. After Republican Rutherford Hayes won the disputed U.S. Presidential election of 1876 the South agreed to accept Hayes's victory if the President withdrew the last Federal troops from the South. By this point everyone had agreed that slavery and Confederate nationalism were dead, and the war goals had been achieved. However, the African-Americans who wanted their legal rights guaranteed by the Federal government were repeatedly frustrated for another 75 years; they considered Reconstruction a failure [42]

The end of Reconstruction marked the beginning of a period, 1877–1900, that saw the steady reduction of many civil and political rights for African-Americans, and ushered in the nadir of American race relations. The exact process varied state by state and town by town. In Virginia, the Redeemers gerrymandered cities to minimize Republican seats; reduced the number of polling places in black precincts; made local officials appointees of the state legislature; and did not allow the vote to felons or to people who failed to pay their annual poll tax; *see Jim Crow laws*. Blacks would legally and socially remain second-class citizens until Jim Crow was abolished by the Civil Rights Act of 1964 and the Voting Rights Act of 1965.

South under Redeemers

The initial flurry of Reconstruction civil rights measures was eroded and converted into laws that expanded racial segregation and discrimination throughout Southern institutions and everyday life. In exchange for its acceptance of reintegration into the Union, the South (along with the rest of the country) was allowed to reestablish a segregated, race-discriminatory society.

Much of the civil rights legislation was overturned by the Supreme Court. Most notably, the court suggested in the *Slaughterhouse Case* (1873), then held in the *Civil Rights Cases* (1883), that the 14th amendment only gave Congress the power to outlaw public, rather than private, discrimination. *Plessy v. Ferguson* (1896) went even further, announcing that state-mandated segregation was legal as long as the law provided for "separate but equal" facilities.

The Supreme Court maintained "separate but equal" as the "law of the land" for another six decades, until finally reversing it in the landmark case of *Brown v. Board of Education* of *Topeka* (1954). Congress also belatedly restored the eroded rights of the descendants of Freedman. With the backing of President Lyndon Johnson, it passed the Civil Rights Act of 1964, which outlawed discrimination in "public accommodations" (i.e., restaurants, hotels and businesses open to the public, as well as in private schools and workplaces), terminology which originated in the Civil Rights Act of 1875.

Legacy and Historiography

Reconstruction was initially viewed as a failure by most observers North and South because of its corruption.[43] Booker T. Washington, who grew up in West Virginia during Reconstruction, concluded that, "the Reconstruction experiment in racial democracy failed because it began at the wrong end, emphasizing political means and civil rights acts rather than economic means and self-determination." [44] His solution was to concentrate on building the economic infrastructure of the black community.

Two novels by Thomas R. Dixon — *The Clansman* and *The Leopard's Spots: A Romance of the White Man's Burden — 1865–1900* — romanticized white resistance to Northern/black coercion, hailing vigilante action by the Ku Klux Klan. Other authors romanticized the benevolence and happiness of the antebellum plantation regarding to the treatment and disposition of African-Americans. These sentiments were expressed on the screen in D.W. Griffith's anti-Republican 1915 movie *The Birth of a Nation*.

The Dunning School of scholars based at the history department of Columbia University analyzed Reconstruction as a failure, at least after 1866, for quite different reasons. They claimed that it took freedoms and rights from qualified whites and gave them to unqualified blacks who were being duped by corrupt carpetbaggers and scalawags. As one scholar notes, for the Dunning School, "Reconstruction was a battle between two extremes: the Democrats, as the group which included the vast majority of the whites, standing for decent government and racial supremacy, versus the Republicans, the Negroes, alien carpetbaggers, and renegade scalawags, standing for dishonest government and alien ideals. These historians wrote literally in terms of white and black."[45]

In the 1930s, "revisionism" became popular among scholars. As disciples of Charles A. Beard, they focused on economic causation. They argued that the Radical rhetoric of equal rights was mostly a smokescreen hiding the true motivation of Reconstruction's real backers. While conceding that a few men like Stevens and Sumner were thoroughly idealistic, Howard Beale argued Reconstruction was primarily a successful attempt by financiers, railroad builders and industrialists in the Northeast, using the Republican party, to control the national government for its own selfish economic ends. Those ends were to continue the wartime high protective tariff, the new network of national banks, and to guarantee a "sound" currency. To succeed the business class had to remove the old ruling agrarian class of Southern planters and Midwestern farmers. This it did by inaugurating Reconstruction, which made the South Republican, and by selling its policies to the voters wrapped up in such attractive vote-getting packages as northern patriotism or the bloody shirt. Historian William Hesseltine added the point that the Northeastern businessmen wanted to control the South economically, which they did through ownership of the railroads.[46] However, historians in the 1950s and 1960s refuted Beale's economic causation by demonstrating that Northern businessmen were widely divergent on monetary or tariff policy, and seldom paid attention to Reconstruction issues.[47]

In the 1960s, neoabolitionist historians emerged, led by John Hope Franklin, Kenneth Stampp and Eric Foner. Strongly aligned with the Civil Rights Movement, they rejected the Dunning school and found a great deal to praise in Radical Reconstruction. The primary advocate of this view, Eric Foner, argued that it was never truly completed, and that a Second Reconstruction was needed in the late 20th century to complete the goal of full equality for African-Americans. The neo-abolitionists followed the revisionists in minimizing or the corruption and waste created by Republican state governments, saying it was no worse than Tweed's Ring in New York City.[48] Instead they emphasized that poor treatment of Freedmen was a worse scandal and a grave corruption of America's republican ideals. They argued that the real tragedy of Reconstruction was not that it failed because blacks were incapable of governing, but that it failed because the civil rights and equalities granted during this period were but a passing, temporary development. These rights were suspended in the South from the 1880s through 1964, but were restored by the Civil Rights Movement that is sometimes referred to as the "Second Reconstruction."

Significant dates

State	Seceded from Union	Joined Confederacy	Readmitted into Union	Democratic Party Re-Establishes Control
South Carolina	December 20, 1860	February 4, 1861	July 9, 1868	November 28, 1876
Mississippi	January 9, 1861	February 4, 1861	February 23, 1870	January 4, 1876
Florida	January 10, 1861	February 4, 1861	June 25, 1868	January 2, 1877
Alabama	January 11, 1861	February 4, 1861	July 14, 1868	November 16, 1874
Georgia	January 19, 1861	February 4, 1861	July 15, 1870	November 1, 1871
Louisiana	January 26, 1861	February 4, 1861	June 25 (July 9), 1868	January 2, 1877
Texas	February 1, 1861	March 2, 1861	March 30, 1870	January 14, 1873
Virginia	April 17, 1861	May 7, 1861	January 26, 1870	October 5, 1869
Arkansas	May 6, 1861	May 18, 1861	June 22, 1868	November 10, 1874
North Carolina	May 21, 1861	May 16, 1861	July 4, 1868	November 28, 1876
Tennessee	June 8, 1861	May 16, 1861	July 24, 1866	October 4, 1869

Primary Sources & Collections of Primary Sources

- Barnes, William H., ed. *History of the Thirty-ninth Congress of the United States.* (1868) useful summary of Congressional activity.
- Berlin, Ira, ed. *Freedom: A Documentary History of Emancipation, 1861–1867* (1982)
- Blaine, James. *Twenty Years of Congress: From Lincoln to Garfield. With a review of the events which led to the political revolution of 1860* (1886). By Republican leader, from Maine, who served both as a U.S. Representative and U.S. Senator.
- Fleming, Walter L. *Documentary History of Reconstruction: Political, Military, Social, Religious, Educational, and Industrial*(1906). Uses broad collection of primary sources.
- *Memoirs of W. W. Holden* (1911), North Carolina Scalawag governor
- Hyman, Harold M., ed. *The Radical Republicans and Reconstruction, 1861-1870.* (1967), collection of long political speeches and pamphlets.
- Lynch, John R. *The Facts of Reconstruction.* (New York: 1913)Full text online, courtesy of Project Gutenberg EBook One of first black congressmen during Reconstruction presents alternate view to white historian Fleming.
- Edward McPherson. *The Political History of the United States of America During the Period of Reconstruction (1875)* large collection of speeches and primary documents, 1865-1870, complete text online. [The copyright has expired.]
- Pike, James Shepherd, *The prostrate state: South Carolina under negro government* (1874)
- Reid, Whitelaw. *After the war: a southern tour, May 1, 1865 to May 1, 1866.* (1866) by Republican editor
- Charles Sumner, "Our Domestic Relations: or, How to Treat the Rebel States" *Atlantic Monthly* September 1863, early Radical manifesto

Laws passed by Congress

- Reconstruction Act March 2, 1867
- Reconstruction Act March 23, 1867
- Reconstruction Act July 19, 1867
- Reconstruction Act March 11, 1868

Secondary sources

Surveys

- Du Bois, W. E. Burghardt. *Black Reconstruction in America 1860-1880* (1935), ISBN 0689708203 (1998 edition with introduction by David Levering Lewis ISBN 0684856573.) Counterpoint to Dunning School of historiography, explores role of Freedmen and their economic challenges.
- Du Bois, W. E. Burghardt "The Freedmen's Bureau," (1901)
- Du Bois, W.E.B. "Reconstruction and its Benefits," *American Historical Review*, 15 (July, 1910), 781—99 JSTOR
- Dunning, William Archibald. *Reconstruction: Political & Economic, 1865-1877* (1905), by Dunning School founder, argues that black voters were duped by Carpetbaggers into supporting wholesale corruption.
- Finkelman, Paul, (editor). Encyclopedia of African American History, 1896 to the Present: From the Age of Segregation to the Twenty-first Century (Oxford Univ Pr, 2006) ISBN 0195167791.

- Fleming, Walter Lynwood, *The Sequel of Appomattox, A Chronicle of the Reunion of the States*(1918) short survey from Dunning School
- Foner, Eric and Mahoney, Olivia. *America's Reconstruction: People and Politics After the Civil War.* ISBN 0-8071-2234-3
- Foner, Eric. *Reconstruction: America's Unfinished Revolution, 1863-1877* (1988), history of Reconstruction emphasizing Black and abolitionist perspective
- Foner, Eric. "Reconstruction Revisited" in *Reviews in American History*, Vol. 10, No. 4, The Promise of American History: Progress and Prospects (Dec., 1982), pp. 82-100, review of the historiography
- Franklin, John Hope. *Reconstruction after the Civil War* (1961), short survey
- Hamilton, Peter Joseph. *The Reconstruction Period* (1906), history of era using Dunning School 570 pp; chapter on each state
- Henry, Robert Selph. *The Story of Reconstruction* (1938).
- Litwack, Leon. *Been in the Storm So Long* (1979). Pulitzer Prize. Narrative based on interviews with ex-slaves and diaries and accounts written by former slaveholders.
- Oberholtzer, Ellis Paxson. *A History of the United States since the Civil War.* Vol 1 and vol 2 (1917) Detailed narrative based on turn of the twentieth century neoconfederate Dunning School viewpoint.
- Perman, Michael. *Emancipation and Reconstruction* (2003), a short survey.
- Randall, James G. and David Donald, *The Civil War and Reconstruction* (2nd ed. 1961)
- Rhodes, James G. *History of the United States from the Compromise of 1850 to the McKinley-Bryan Campaign of 1896. Volume: 6.* (1920). 1865-72; Neoconfederate Dunning School narrative stresses national politics; also vol 7: 1872-77 (1920)
- Stalcup, Brenda. ed. *Reconstruction: Opposing Viewpoints* (Greenhaven Press: 1995). Using primary documents, clearly presents opposing viewpoints. Text suitable for students and adult readers.
- Stampp, Kenneth M. *The Era of Reconstruction, 1865-1877* (1967); short survey that begins to overturn the formerly dominant Dunning School analysis.
- Stampp, Kenneth M. and Leon M. Litwack, eds. *Reconstruction: An Anthology of Revisionist Writings," (1969), reprinted essays.*
- Trefousse, Hans L. *Historical Dictionary of Reconstruction* Greenwood (1991), 250 entries
- Williams, T. Harry. "An Analysis of Some Reconstruction Attitudes" *The Journal of Southern History,* Vol. 12, No. 4. (Nov., 1946), pp. 469-486. JSTOR
- Wilson, Woodrow. *The Reconstruction of the Southern States (1901)*; interpretive essay by Wilson; elected President in 1912, he grew up in South Carolina during Reconstruction

National politics; Constitutional issues

- Belz, Herman. *Emancipation and Equal Rights: Politics and Constitutionalism in the Civil War Era* (1978) pro-moderate.
- Belz, Herman. *A New Birth of Freedom: The Republican Party and Freedman's Rights, 1861-1866* (2000) pro-moderate.
- Benedict, Michael Les. *The Impeachment and Trial of Andrew Johnson* (1999), pro-Radical.
- Benedict, Michael Les. *A Compromise of Principle: Congressional Republicans and Reconstruction* (1974) pro-Radical
- Benedict, Michael Les. "Preserving the Constitution: The Conservative Bases of Radical Reconstruction," *Journal of American History* vol 61 #1 (1974) pp 65-90

- Benedict, Michael Les. "Constitutional History and Constitutional Theory: Reflections on Ackerman, Reconstruction, and the Transformation of the American Constitution." *Yale Law Journal* Vol: 108. Issue: 8. 1999. pp 2011-2038.
- Blight, David. *Race and Reunion: The Civil War in American Memory* (2000). Examines national memory of Civil War, Reconstruction, and Redemption, North-South reunion, and the retreat from equality for African Americans.
- Brandwein, Pamela; "Slavery as an Interpretive Issue in the Reconstruction Congresses" *Law & Society Review*. Volume: 34. Issue: 2. 2000. pp 315+ shows Democratic party history, grounded on white supremacy was crucial in legitimating the Court's narrow doctrinal interpretations of the Fourteenth Amendment.
- Burg, Robert W. "Amnesty, Civil Rights, And The Meaning Of Liberal Republicanism, 1862-1872". *American Nineteenth Century History* 2003 4(3): 29-60.
- Donald, David Herbert. *Charles Sumner and the Rights of Man* (1970), Pulitzer prize winning biography
- Dunning, William A. "The Constitution of the United States in Reconstruction" in *Political Science Quarterly* Vol. 2, No. 4 (Dec., 1887), pp. 558-602 JSTOR
- Dunning, William A. "Military Government in the South During Reconstruction" *Political Science Quarterly* Vol. 12, No. 3 (Sep., 1897), pp. 381-406 JSTOR
- Gambill, Edward. *Conservative Ordeal: Northern Democrats and Reconstruction, 1865-1868.* (1981). Political history of Democratic Party unable to shed its Civil War label of treason and defeatism, even as it successfully blocked a few elements of Radical Reconstruction.
- Gillette, William. *Retreat from Reconstruction, 1869-1879.* Louisiana State University Press: 1979. Traces failure of Reconstruction to the power of Democrats, administrative inefficiencies, racism, and lack of commitment by northern Republicans.
- Hyman, Harold M. *A More Perfect Union* (1975), constitutional history of Civil War & Reconstruction.
- Kaczorowski, Robert, *The Politics of Judicial Interpretations: The Federal Courts, Department of Justice and Civil Rights, 1866-1876.* Justice Department fight against KKK
- McAfee, Ward. *Religion, Race, and Reconstruction: The Public School in the Politics of the 1870s* SUNY Press, 1998.
- McLaughlin, Andrew. *A Constitutional History of the United States* (1935) Pulitzer Prize; ch 45-47 are on Reconstruction online version
- McKitrick, Eric L. *Andrew Johnson and Reconstruction* (1961) portrays Johnson as weak politician unable to forge coalitions.
- McPherson, James M. *The Abolitionist Legacy: From Reconstruction to the NAACP* (1975) (ISBN 069110039X)
- Montgomery, David. *Beyond Equality: Labor and the Radical Republicans, 1862-1872* (1981). Emphasis on labor unions in North.
- Nicolay, John and John Hay, "First Plans for Emancipation," *Century* (Dec 1888): pp 276-94; Online Authors were Lincoln's top aides in the White House
  - Nicolay, John and John Hay, "The Wade-Davis Manifesto" *Century* (July 1889): pp 414-21 online version
- Simpson, Brooks D. *Let Us Have Peace: Ulysses S. Grant and the Politics of War and Reconstruction, 1861-1868* (1991).
- Stryker, Lloyd Paul; *Andrew Johnson: A Study in Courage* 1929. pro-Johnson
- Summers, Mark Wahlgren.*The Press Gang: Newspapers and Politics, 1865-1878* (1994)
- Trefousse, Hans L. *Andrew Johnson: A Biography* (1989)
- Trefousse, Hans L. *Thaddeus Stevens: Nineteenth-Century Egalitarian* (1997)

- Trelease, Allen W. *White Terror: The Ku Klux Klan Conspiracy and Southern Reconstruction*, (Louisiana State University Press: 1995). First published in 1971 and based on massive research in primary sources, this is the most comprehensive treatment of the Klan and its relationship to post-Civil War Reconstruction. Includes narrative on other night-riding groups. Details close link between terrorism by Klan and Democratic Party.

South: regional, state & local studies

- Brown, Canter Jr. *Florida's Black Public Officials, 1867-1924*
- Campbell. Randolph B. *Grass-Roots Reconstruction in Texas, 1865-1880* (1998)
- Coulter, E. Merton. *The Civil War and Readjustment in Kentucky* (1926)
- Coulter, E. Merton. *The South During Reconstruction, 1865-1877* (1947). Dunning School. region-wide history
- Crouch, Barry A. *The Freedmen's Bureau and Black Texans.* University of Texas Press, (1992).
- David Ebner and Larry Langman, eds. *Hollywood's Image of the South: A Century of Southern Films* Greenwood Press. 2001. Ch 9-10 on Reconstruction and KKK.
- David H. Donald. "The Scalawag in Mississippi Reconstruction," *The Journal of Southern History* Vol. 10, No. 4 (Nov., 1944), pp. 447-460 JSTOR
- Fields, Barbara Jean, *Slavery and Freedom on the Middle Ground: Maryland* (1985)
- Fischer, Roger. *The Segregation Struggle in Louisiana, 1862-1877. (University of Illinois Press: 1974) Study of free persons of color in New Orleans who provided leadership in the unsuccessful fight against segregation of schools and public accommodations.*
- Fitzgerald, Michael W. *Urban Emancipation: Popular Politics in Reconstruction Mobile, 1860–1890.* (Baton Rouge: Louisiana State University Press, 2002. 301 pp. ISBN 0-8071-2837-6.)
- Fitzgerald, Michael R. "Radical Republicanism and the White Yeomanry During Alabama Reconstruction, 1865-1868." *Journal of Southern History* 54 (November 1988): 565-96. Online at JSTOR
- Fleming, Walter L. *Civil War and Reconstruction in Alabama* 1905. Dunning School
- Foner, Eric. *Freedom's Lawmakers: A Directory of Black Officeholders During Reconstruction* (Revised edition, LSU Press, 1996) Unique directory with biographies of more than 1,500 officeholders.
- Garner, James Wilford. *Reconstruction in Mississippi* (1901), Dunning School
- Hadden, Sally E., *Slave Patrols: Law and Violence in Virginia and the Carolinas* (Harvard Univ Press, 2001) ISBN 0674004701 Epilogue explores Black Freedom, White Violence: Patrols, Police, and role of Klan
- Hahn, Steven. *A Nation under Our Feet: Black Political Struggles in the Rural South from Slavery to the Great Migration* (2003)
- Hamilton, Peter Joseph. *The Reconstruction Period* (1906), full length history of era; Dunning School approach; 570 pp; chapters on each state
- Harris, William C. *The Day of the Carpetbagger: Republican Reconstruction in Mississippi* (1979)
- Holt, Thomas. *Black over White: Negro Political Leadership in South Carolina During Reconstruction.* (University of Illinois Press: 1977). Black elected officials, their divisions, and battles with white governors who controlled patronage and their ultimate failure.
- Kolchin, Peter. *First Freedom: The Responses of Alabama's Blacks to Emancipation and Reconstruction.* (Greenwood Press: 1972) Explores black migration, labor, and social structure in the first five years of Reconstruction.

- A. B. Moore, "Railroad Building in Alabama During the Reconstruction Period" *The Journal of Southern History*, Vol. 1, No. 4. (Nov., 1935), pp. 421-441. JSTOR
- Olsen, Otto H. ed., *Reconstruction and Redemption in the South* (1980), state by state, neoabolitionist
- Patton; James Welch. *Unionism and Reconstruction in Tennessee, 1860-1869* 1934
- Perman, Michael. *The Road to Redemption: Southern Politics, 1869-1879* University of North Carolina Press. 1984. detailed state-by-state narrative of Conservatives
- Rabinowitz, Howard N. editor. *Southern Black Leaders of the Reconstruction Era* (University of Illinois Press: 1982) ISBN 0252009290. Examines how Southern Black leaders functioned during Reconstruction and within the Republican Party.
- Ramsdell, Charles W., "Presidential Reconstruction in Texas ", *Southwestern Historical Quarterly*, (1907) v.11#4 277 - 317.
- Ramsdell, Charles William. *Reconstruction in Texas* Columbia University Press, 1910. Dunning school
- Reynolds, John S. *Reconstruction in South Carolina, 1865—1877,* Negro Universities Press, 1969
- Rose, Willie Lee . *Rehearsal for Reconstruction: The Port Royal Experiment* (1967) Blacks given land in 1863 in coastal South Carolina
- Rubin, Hyman III. *South Carolina Scalawags* (2006)
- Russ, Jr., William A. "The Negro and White Disfranchisement During Radical Reconstruction" *The Journal of Negro History* Vol. 19, No. 2 (Apr., 1934), pp. 171-192
- Russ, Jr., William A. "Registration and Disfranchisement Under Radical Reconstruction," *The Mississippi Valley Historical Review* Vol. 21, No. 2 (Sep., 1934), pp. 163-180
- Simkins, Francis Butler, and Robert Hilliard Woody. *South Carolina during Reconstruction* (1932), revisionist (Beardian) school
- Stover, John F. *The Railroads of the South, 1865-1900: A Study in Finance and Control* (1955)
- Summers, Mark Wahlgren. *Railroads, Reconstruction, and the Gospel of Prosperity: Aid Under the Radical Republicans, 1865-1877* (1984)
- Taylor, Alrutheus A., *Negro in Tennessee 1865-1880* (Reprint Co, June 1, 1974) ISBN 0871521652
- Taylor, Alrutheus, *Negro in South Carolina During the Reconstruction* (AMS Press: 1924) ISBN 0404002161
- Taylor, Alrutheus, *The Negro in the Reconstruction Of Virginia* (The Association for the Study of Negro Life and History: 1926)
- Taylor, A. A. "The Negro in South Carolina During the Reconstruction" *The Journal of Negro History*, Vol. 9-11 (1924-1926) (multi-part article) JSTOR full text
- Wiener, Jonathan M. *Social Origins of the New South; Alabama, 1860-1885.* (1978) new social history
- Wharton, V. L. "The Race Issue in the Overthrow of Reconstruction in Mississippi," *Phylon* (1940-1956) Vol. 2, No. 4 (4th Qtr., 1941), pp. 362-370 JSTOR
- Wiggins, Sarah Woolfolk. *The Scalawag in Alabama Politics, 1865-1881* (1991)

Notes

1. ^ Foner 1988 pp 273-6
2. ^ Gienapp, p. 155
3. ^ Patton p126
4. ^ President Andrew Johnson to Gov. William L. Sharkey of Mississippi, August 1865 in Franklin 1961, p. 42
5. ^ Randall and Donald 581

6. ^ Harris 1997
7. ^ Gienapp p167
8. ^ Rose 1967
9. ^ Trefousse 1989
10. ^ Oberholtzer 1:128–9
11. ^ Rhodes, *History* 6:65-66
12. ^ Rhodes, *History* 6:68
13. ^ Trefousse 1989
14. ^ Foner 261-71
15. ^ Foner 1988 ch 6
16. ^ Foner 1988, ch 6–7
17. ^ Randolph Campbell, *Gone to Texas* 2003 p. 276.
18. ^ Foner 1988 p 285-6
19. ^ Foner 1988 ch 7
20. ^ Foner 365–8
21. ^ Franklin 139
22. ^ McAfee 1998
23. ^ Lynch 1913
24. ^ Foner 387
25. ^ Franklin p141-48; Summers 1984
26. ^ Stover 1955
27. ^ Franklin p147–8
28. ^ Foner 415–16
29. ^ Lynch 1913
30. ^ Oberholtzer, vol 1 p 485
31. ^ J. W. Schuckers, *The Life and Public Services of Salmon Portland Chase,* (1874). p. 585; letter of May 30, 1868 to August Belmont
32. ^ McPherson 1975
33. ^ Foner 537-41
34. ^ Foner 374-5
35. ^ Lynch 1915
36. ^ Perman 1984, ch 3
37. ^ Foner, ch 9
38. ^ Foner p 443
39. ^ Foner p545–7
40. ^ Foner 555–56
41. ^ Foner ch 11
42. ^ Foner 604
43. ^ McPherson 1965
44. ^ Louis R. Harlan, *Booker T. Washington in Perspective* (1988) p. 164
45. ^ Williams 1946 p473
46. ^ Williams 1946 p470
47. ^ Foner 1982; Montgomery, *vii–ix*)
48. ^ Williams, 469; Foner p. *xxii*

Retrieved from "http://en.wikipedia.org/wiki/Reconstruction"

- This page was last modified 19:49, 15 July 2006.

This Page is intentionally blank

(actually, it **WAS** blank, but then I added this text, so now it's not blank anymore, but it had to be inserted so that the next chapter will start on a right-hand page – aren't you glad you asked?)

Francis Schaeffer Study Center
Mt. Juliet, Tennessee

Western Civilization, Year Four
From 1865 to 1990, Reconstruction to Modern Times
Rob Shearer, Tutor

Week Three Reading
The Franco-Prussian War

Franco-Prussian War

From Wikipedia, the free encyclopedia

Franco-Prussian War			
Part of the wars of German unification		France	Prussia allied with German states (later German Empire)
		Commanders	
		Napoleon III	Helmuth von Moltke
		Strength	
		500,000	550,000
		Casualties	
		150,000 dead or wounded 284,000 captured 350,000 civilian	100,000 dead or wounded 200,000 civilian
The Prussian 7th Cuirassiers charge the French guns at the Battle of Mars-La-Tour, August 16, 1870			
		Franco-Prussian War	
Date:	July 19, 1870 - May 10, 1871	Wissembourg – Spicheren – Worth – Borny-Colombey – Strasbourg – Mars-La-Tour – Gravelotte – Metz – Beaumont – Noiseville – Sedan – Bellevue – Coulmiers – Amiens – Beaune-La-Rolande – Hallue – Bapaume – Le Mans – Lisaine – St. Quentin – Paris – Belfort	
Location:	France and Germany		
Result:	Decisive German victory		
Casus belli:	Spanish succession dispute		
Territory changes:	Prussia and other German states unite to form German Empire; Germany annexes Alsace-Lorraine		
Combatants			

Summary

The **Franco-Prussian War** (July 19, 1870 – May 10, 1871) was declared by France on Prussia, which was backed by the North German Confederation and the south German states of Baden, Württemberg and Bavaria. The conflict marked the culmination of tension between the two powers following Prussia's rise to dominance in Germany, which before 1866 was still a loose federation of quasi-independent territories.

The war began over the possible ascension of a candidate from the Catholic branch of the Hohenzollern royal family to the vacant Spanish throne as Isabella II had abdicated in 1868. This was strongly opposed by France who issued an ultimatum to King Wilhelm I of Prussia to have the candidacy withdrawn, which was done. Aiming to humiliate Prussia, Emperor Napoleon III of

France then required Wilhelm to apologize and renounce any possible further Hohenzollern candidature to the Spanish throne. King Wilhelm, surprised at his holiday resort by the French ambassador, declined as he was not informed yet. Prussia's Chancellor, Otto von Bismarck, edited the King's account of his meeting with the French ambassador to make the encounter more heated than it really was. Known as the Ems Dispatch, it was released to the press and and had the intended effect on the German public.

The French people and their parliament reacted with outrage, Napoleon III mobilized and declared war, on Prussia only, but effectively also on the states of southern Germany. The German armies quickly mobilized and within a few weeks controlled large amounts of land in Eastern France. Their success was due in part to rapid mobilization by train, to Prussian General staff leadership and to modern Krupp artillery made of steel. Napoleon III was captured with his whole army at the Battle of Sedan, yet this did not end the war, as a republic was declared in Paris on September 4, 1870, marking the creation of the Third Republic of France under the Government of National Defense and later the "Versaillais government" of Adolphe Thiers. The immediate result was an extension to the war as the Republic proclaimed a continuation of the fight.

Over a five-month campaign, the German armies defeated the newly recruited French armies in a series of battles fought across northern France. Following a prolonged siege, the French capital Paris fell on January 28, 1871. Ten days earlier, the German states had proclaimed their union under the Prussian King, uniting Germany as a nation-state, the German Empire. The final peace Treaty of Frankfurt was signed May 10, 1871, during the time of the bloody Paris Commune of 1871.

In France and Germany the war is known as the Franco-German War (French: *Guerre franco-allemande de 1870* German: *Deutsch-Französischer Krieg*), which perhaps more accurately describes the combatants rather than simply France and Prussia alone.

- Contents 1 **Causes of the war**
    - 1.1 The Luxembourg Crisis
    - 1.2 French prestige and domestic politics
    - 1.3 Bismarck and German nationalism
    - 1.4 Crisis and the outbreak of war
    - 1.5 Alliances and diplomacy
- 2 Opposing forces
- 3 French incursion
    - 3.1 Occupation of Saarbrücken
- 4 German advance
    - 4.1 Battle of Wissembourg
    - 4.2 Battle of Wœrth
    - 4.3 Battle of Spicheren
    - 4.4 Battle of Mars-La-Tour
    - 4.5 Battle of Gravelotte
    - 4.6 Siege of Metz
    - 4.7 Battle of Sedan
- 5 Overthrow of the French monarchy and armistice negotiations
- 6 The war is continued
    - 6.1 Siege of Paris
    - 6.2 The Loire Campaign
    - 6.3 Northern Campaign
    - 6.4 Eastern Campaign
- 7 Naval blockade
- 8 Armistice
- 9 Aftermath
- 10 References
- 11 External links

Causes of the war

Tensions had long been running high between Prussia and France following the Prussian victory in the Austro-Prussian War and its subsequent annexation of almost all Northern Germany. The humbling of Austria and Prussia's new territorial gains had shattered the European balance of power that had existed since the end of the Napoleonic Wars.

Prussian Prime Minister Otto Von Bismarck, after proving Prussia to be the most powerful of German States in the Austro-Prussian War, wanted to once again unite the German States under the Prussian banner. This would allow a Prussian Emperor to rule all of the German States in a united German Empire. It would also lead to a more prosperous age in which the might of the German Empire would be unparalleled in Europe.

Following the end of the Austro-Prussian War, Prussian prime minister Otto von Bismarck and the French emperor Napoleon III had attempted to reach a private agreement regarding the balance of power in Europe. Napoleon III wished to realise French aspirations for "natural borders," a long term goal of French foreign policy since the Middle Ages — to annex all land west of the Rhine river and the Alps including the German state of Palatinate-on-Rhine, Belgium, the southern Netherlands, Luxembourg, Savoy, and parts of Hesse and Rhenish Prussia. A solid defensible border was also insurance against the possibility of a united Germany unfriendly to France. However in 1840 the French politician Adolphe Thiers had sparked a Franco-German diplomatic crisis (the Rhine crisis, 1840) over a mention of "natural borders" on the west bank of the Rhine, reminding many Germans of Napoleonic efforts to establish a border on the Rhine.

Savoy had been obtained from Italy following French support for Italian independence from Austria. Now Napoleon III sought Prussian neutrality when attempting to acquire Luxembourg and Wallonia (the French-speaking part of Belgium), while expecting Prussian neutrality as "compensation" for French neutrality during the Austro-Prussian War and for Prussian territorial gains. Bismarck was non-committal at best, but to the French government, Bismarck appeared to agree to or at least agreed not to obstruct any French moves against the Low Countries.

The Luxembourg Crisis

Thus in 1867, France began by negotiating the purchase of Luxembourg from the Dutch government, as Luxembourg was then in personal union with the Netherlands. Assuming that Bismarck would honour his part of the agreement, the French government was shocked to learn that instead Bismarck, Prussia and the North German Confederation were threatening war should the sale be completed. Luxembourg lay astride one of the principal invasion routes an army would use to invade either France or Germany. The city of Luxembourg's formidable fortifications, constructed by the famous military engineer Marshal Vauban, were considered "the Gibraltar of the North", and neither side could tolerate the other controlling such a strategic location. To mediate the dispute, the United Kingdom hosted the London Conference (1867) attended by all European great powers. It confirmed Luxembourg's independence from the Netherlands and guaranteed its independence from all other powers. War appeared to have been averted, at the cost of thwarting French desires.

French prestige and domestic politics

France's position in Europe was now in danger of being overshadowed by the emergence of a powerful Prussia, and France looked increasingly flat-footed following Bismarck's successes. In addition, French ruler Napoleon III was on increasingly shaky ground in domestic politics. Having successfully overthrown the Second Republic and established the Bonapartist Second Empire, Napoleon III was confronted with ever more virulent demands for democratic reform from leading republicans such as Jules Favre, along with constant rumours of impending revolution. In addition, French aspirations in Mexico had suffered a final defeat with the execution of the Austrian-born, French puppet Emperor of Mexico Maximilian in 1867.

The French imperial government now looked to a diplomatic success to stifle demands for a return to either a republic or a Bourbon monarchy — the Empress Eugénie, wife of Napoleon III, was quoted as saying, "If there is no war, my son will never be emperor." A war with Prussia and resulting territorial gains in the Rhineland and later Luxembourg and Belgium seemed the best hope to unite the French nation behind the Bonapartist dynasty. With the resulting prestige from a successful war, Napoleon III could then safely suppress any lingering republican or revolutionary sentiment behind reactionary nationalism and return France to the center of European politics.

Bismarck and German nationalism

Prussia in turn was also beset with problems. While revolutionary fervour was far more muted than in France, Prussia had in 1866 acquired millions of new, suspect citizens as a result of the Austro-Prussian War which was also a civil war among German states. The remaining German kingdoms and principalities maintained a steadfastly parochial attitude towards Prussia and German unification. The German princes insisted upon their independence and balked at any attempt to create a federal state that would be dominated by Berlin. Their suspicions were heightened by Prussia's quick victory and her subsequent annexations. Before the war, only some Germans, inspired by the recent unification of Italy, accepted and supported what the princes began to realise: That Germany must unite in order to preserve the fruit of an eventual victory.

The Prussian premier Otto von Bismarck had an entirely different view. He was interested only in strengthening Prussia and the power of her king. Uniting Germany appeared immaterial to him unless it improved Prussia's position. Bismarck considered the conflict with France inevitable, knowing that France would not quietly tolerate a powerful state to its east. He also viewed the war as a means to end the influence which France had long since exercised over Germany. The defeated South German states had to sign mutual defense treaties with the North German Confederation, but only a clear aggression from outside could make sure they would ally with Prussia, rather than against her once more.

Crisis and the outbreak of war

Napoleon III and Bismarck independently sought a suitable crisis to forment, and in 1870 one arose. The Spanish throne had been vacant since the revolution of September 1868. The Spanish offered the throne to the German prince Leopold of Hohenzollern-Sigmaringen, a Catholic as well as a distant cousin of King Wilhelm of Prussia. Fearing that a Hohenzollern king in Prussia and another one in Spain would put France into a two-front situation, Napoleon III was determined this time to stand up to the expansion of Prussian influence. He successfully forced King Wilhelm to urge the prince's withdrawal from his Spanish candidacy. Disappointed that the Prussians had backed down so easily, the French government tried to prolong the crisis. In a newspaper interview, Napoleon III announced that a renewal of the Hohenzollern candidature would result in France going to war, and the secretary of foreign affairs, Duc de Gramont, did the same in a speech in front of the *Chambre législative*. The French ambassador in Prussia Vincent Benedetti was then ordered to require Wilhelm I to guarantee that no Hohenzollern would ever again be a candidate for the Spanish throne. When the French ambassador bypassed diplomatic channels and directly confronted the king at his holiday resort, King Wilhelm was "very polite but cooly categorical." His message to Berlin (the Ems Dispatch) reporting this event with the French ambassador reached the desk of Bismarck. Bismarck edited the telegram in such a way as to arouse French indignation, and then released it for publication. France officially declared war on July 19, 1870.

Alliances and diplomacy

Diplomatically and militarily, Napoleon III looked for support from Austria, Denmark, Bavaria, Baden, and Württemberg, as all had recently lost wars against Prussia. However, Napoleon III inexplicably failed to conduct any diplomacy to secure revanchist alliances from these states. Denmark had twice fought Prussia (a stalemate victory in 1846, and a defeat 1864 against a confederation of north German states and Austria under the leadership of Prussia) during the First and Second Wars of Schleswig and was unwilling to confront Prussia again. Austria also refused to risk confronting Prussia again so soon after the near disaster of the Austro-Prussian War.

To make matters worse, acts by Napoleon III and his governments had isolated France from the other European powers. Russia remained neutral, unwilling to aid France after French participation in Russia's humiliation during the Crimean War. Italy was also disinclined to assist France, having been forced to surrender claims to Savoy to France as the price for assistance against Austria during the Italian wars for unification. In addition, Napoleon III had made himself protector of the Papal States, infuriating Italian nationalists who wanted Italy united with Rome as the capital.

Bismarck had also worked assiduously to diplomatically isolate France from the other European powers. As part of the settlement of the Austro-Prussian War, secret treaties of mutual defense were signed between Prussia and Bavaria, Baden, and Württemberg. Bismarck also added the threat that should the south German monarchs refuse to honour their treaty commitments, he would personally appeal to pan-German nationalists in southern Germany to overthrow their royal houses. Bismarck then made public French correspondence demanding Belgium and Luxembourg as the price for remaining neutral during the Austro-Prussian War. The United Kingdom in particular took a decidedly cool attitude to these French demands — which they called 'tipping policy' — and showed no inclination to aid France. Though it had enjoyed some time as the leading power of continental Europe, the French Empire found itself dangerously isolated in the face of the allied German states.

According to the secret treaties signed with Prussia and in response to popular opinion, Bavaria, Baden, and Württemberg mobilised their armies and joined the war against France. While not prepared to join a united Germany, the south German monarchs could not ignore public opinion which would not stand for another Bonapartist invasion of Germany.

Opposing forces

The French Army comprised approximately 400,000 regular soldiers, some veterans of previous French campaigns in the Crimean War, Algeria, Franco-Austrian War in Italy, and in Mexico supporting the Second Mexican Empire. The infantry were equipped with the breech-loading Chassepot rifle, one of the most modern mass-produced firearms in the world at the time. With a rubber ring seal and a smaller bullet, the Chassepot had a maximum effective range of some 750 yards (685 meters) with a rapid reload time. [1] The artillery was equipped with rifled, muzzle-loaded Lahitte '4-pounder' (actual weight of shot: 4 kg / 8.4l lb) guns. In addition, the army was equipped with the precursor to the machine-gun — the mitrailleuse, which was mounted on an artillery gun carriage and grouped in batteries in a similar fashion to cannon. The army was nominally led by Napoleon III with Marshals François Achille Bazaine, Patrice MacMahon and Jules Trochu among others.

The Prussian Army was composed not of regulars but reserves. Service was compulsory for all men of military age, thus Prussia and its North and South German allies could mobilise and field some 1.2 million soldiers in time of war. The sheer number of soldiers available made mass-encirclement and destruction of enemy formations advantageous. The army was still equipped with the "needle-gun" Dreyse rifle of fame from the Battle of Königgrätz which was by this time showing the age of its 25 year old design. The deficiencies of the needle-gun were more than compensated for by the famous Krupp 6 pounder (3 kg) breech-loading cannons being issued to Prussian artillery batteries. Firing a contact-detonated shell filled with zinc balls and explosive, the Krupp gun had a range of 4,500 meters and blistering rate of fire compared to muzzle loading cannon. The Prussian army was commanded by Field-Marshal Helmuth von Moltke and the Prussian General Staff. The Prussian army was unique in Europe for having the only General Staff in existence, whose sole purpose was to direct operational movement, organise logistics and communications and develop the overall war strategy. In practice, a chief of staff was a much more important figure in the Prussian Army than in any other army, because he had the right to appeal against his superior to the commander of the next highest formation. Thus, for example, the Crown Prince was unable to contradict the advice of his Chief of Staff, General Leonhard, Count von Blumenthal, for fear of a direct appeal (in this case) to his father the King.

Given that France maintained a strong standing army, and that Prussia and the other German states would need weeks to mobilise their irregular armies, the French held the initial advantage of troop numbers and experience. French tactics emphasised the defensive use of the Chassepot rifle in trench-warfare style fighting; however, German tactics emphasised encirclement battles and using artillery offensively whenever possible.

French incursion

Battle of Bazelles, 1870

On 28 July 1870, Napoleon III left Paris for Metz and assumed command of the newly titled Army of the Rhine, some 100,000 strong and expected to grow as the French mobilisation progressed. Marshal MacMahon took command of I Corps (4 divisions) near Wissembourg, Marshal François Canrobert brought VI Corps (4 divisions) to Châlons-sur-Marne in northern France as a reserve and to guard against a Prussian advance through Belgium. A pre-war plan laid out by the late Marshal Adolphe Niel called for a strong French offensive from Thionville towards Trier and into the Prussian Rhineland. This plan was discarded in favour of a defensive plan by

Generals Charles Frossard and Bartélemy Lebrun, which called for the Army of the Rhine to remain in a defensive posture near the German border and repel any Prussian offensive. As Austria along with Bavaria, Württemberg and Baden were expected to join in a revenge war against Prussia, I Corps would invade the Bavarian Palatinate and proceed to "liberate" the south German states in concert with Austro-Hungarian forces. VI Corps would reinforce either army as needed.

Unfortunately for General Frossard's plan, the Prussian army was mobilising far more rapidly than expected. Against all expectations, the south German states had come to Prussia's aid and were mobilising their armies against France. The Austro-Hungarians, still smarting after their defeat by Prussia, seemed content to wait until a clear victor emerged before committing to France's cause.

Already, by August 3, 1870 some 320,000 German soldiers were now massed near the French border. A 40,000 strong French offensive into southern Germany would run into superior numbers and be rapidly cut off and destroyed. Napoleon III, however, was under immense domestic pressure to launch an offensive before the full might of Moltke's forces were mobilised and deployed. Reconnaissance by General Frossard had identified only one Prussian division guarding the border town of Saarbrücken, right before the entire Army of the Rhine. Accordingly, on July 31 Napoleon III ordered the Army forward across the Saar River to seize Saarbrücken.

Occupation of Saarbrücken

The war soon heated up.

General Frossard's II Corps and Marshal Bazaine's III Corps crossed the German border on August 2, 1870 and began to force the Prussian 40th Regiment of the 16th Division from the town of Saarbrücken with a series of direct attacks. The Chassepot rifle proved its worth against the Dreyse rifle, with French riflemen regularly outdistancing their Prussian counterparts in the skirmishing around Saarbrücken. However the Prussians resisted strongly, and the French suffered 86 casualties to the Prussian 83 casualties. Saarbrücken also proved to be a dead-end in terms of logistics — only one single railway there led from the border to the German hinterland which could be easily defended by a single force, and the only river systems in the region ran along the border instead of inland.

While the French hailed the invasion as the first step towards the Rhineland and later Berlin, General Frossard was receiving alarming reports from foreign news sources of Prussian and Bavarian armies massing to the southeast in addition to the forces to the north and northeast.

Moltke had indeed massed three armies in the area — the Prussian First Army commanded by General Karl von Steinmetz (50,000 soldiers) opposite Saarlouis, the Prussian Second Army commanded by Prince Friedrich Karl (134,000 soldiers) opposite the line Forbach — Spicheren, and the Prussian Third Army commanded by Crown Prince Friedrich Wilhelm (125,000 soldiers) poised to cross the border at Wissembourg. Cavalry reconnaissance had identified a French division of MacMahon's corps at Wissembourg. The Third Army moved forward to engage this division. The Second Army moved forward towards the border and Forbach and Spicheren beyond. The First Army marched to Saarlouis, to catch in the flank and rear any French forces moving to reinforce Spicheren. Moltke planned for the First Army in concert later with the Third Army to envelop the entire French army against the Second Army and destroy the entire force.

German advance

Battle of Wissembourg

On learning that the Second Army was just 30 miles from Saarbrücken and was moving towards the border, General Frossard hastily withdrew the elements of Army of the Rhine in Saarbrücken back to Spicheren and Forbach. Marshal MacMahon however was unaware of Prussian movements beyond vague rumours from newspapers, and left his four divisions spread 20 miles apart in depth to react to any Prussian invasion. At Wissembourg on August 4, MacMahon's 2nd Division commanded by General Abel Douay was the first to make contact with leading elements of the Prussian Third Army, beginning the Battle of Wissembourg.

The first action of the Franco-Prussian War (excluding the push into Saarbrücken by elements of Frossard's French II Corps on 2nd August) took place on 4th August 1870. This bloody little battle saw the unsupported division of General Douay of I Corps, with some attached cavalry, which was posted to watch the border, attacked in overwhelming but poorly coordinated fashion by the German 3rd Army. As the day wore on elements of one Bavarian and two Prussian Corps became embroiled in the fight which was notable for the complete lack of higher direction by the Prussians and blind offensive haste by their low level officers.

Douay held a very strong position but his force was too thinly stretched to hold it and his division was driven south by way of Riedseltz at dusk. Douay himself was killed in the early afternoon when a caisson of the divisional mitrailleuse battery exploded near him. General Pelle took up command and withdrew the remnants of the division.

Although Failly's V Corps was just a few miles away at Bitsche and the other three divisions of MacMahon's I Corps were a similar distance away to the south at Worth, neither moved to assist, despite the clear rumble of guns.

The Prussians seemed poise to capatalize on these happenings, and the French appeared still woefully unaware of the now forming Prussian juggernaut.

Battle of Wœrth

The two armies clashed again only two days later (August 6, 1870) near Wœrth, less than ten miles from Wissembourg. The German 3rd army had drawn reinforcements which brought its strength up to 140,000 troops. The French had also been reinforced, but their recruitment was slow, and their force numbered only 35,000. Although badly outnumbered, the French bravely defended their position along a ridge at the western outskirts of Woerth. By afternoon, both sides had suffered about 10,000 casualties, and the French army was too battered to continue resisting. To make matters even more dire for the French, the Germans had taken the town of Froeschwiller which sat on a hilltop in the center of the French line. Having lost any outlook for victory and facing a massacre, the French army broke off the battle and retreated in a western direction, hoping to join other French forces on the other side of the Vosges mountains. The German 3rd army did not pursue the withdrawing French. It remained in Alsace and moved slowly south, attacking and destroying the French defensive garrisons in the vicinity.

The battle of Woerth was the first major one of the Franco-German war, with more than 100,000 troops in the battlefield. It was also one of the first clashes where troops from various German states (Prussians, Badeners, Bavarians, Saxons, etc.) fought jointly. These facts have led some historians to call the battlefield of Woerth the 'cradle of Germany'.

Battle of Spicheren

The Battle of Spicheren, on August 5, was the second of three critical French defeats. The French were able to stall the German I Army until the German II Army under Prince Friedrich Karl of Prussia came to the aid of their compatriots and routed the French in a blazing attack. Together with the Battle of Worth, on the following day, the Prussians succeeded in separating the northern and southern flanks of the French army. The German victory compelled the French to withdraw to the defenses of Metz.

Battle of Mars-La-Tour

With the Prussian army now steamrolling, 130,000 French soldiers were bottled up in the Fortress of Metz following several defeats at the front. Four days after their retreat, on the 16th, the ever-present Prussian forces, here a group of grossly outnumbered 30,000 men of the advanced III Corps (of the 2nd Army) under General Konstantin von Alvensleben, found the French Army near Vionville, east of Mars-la-Tour. Despite odds of four to one, the III Corps launched a risky attack and routed the French, allowing them to then capture Vionville, blocking any further escape attempts to the west. Once blocked from retreat, the French in the fortress of Metz had no choice but to engage in a fight that would see the last major cavalry engagement in Western Europe. The battle soon erupted, and III corps was decimated by the incessant cavalry charges, losing over half its soldiers. Meanwhile, French suffered equivalent numerical loses of 16,000 soldiers, but still held on to overwhelming numerical superiority.

On August 16, 1870 the French had a chance to sweep away the key Prussian defence and escaped. Two Prussian corps attacked the French advanced guard thinking that it was the rearguard of the retreat of the French Army of the Meuse. Despite this misjudgment the two Prussian corps held the entire French army for the whole day. Outnumbered 5:1 the extraordinary self-belief of the Prussians prevailed over gross indecision by the French.

Battle of Gravelotte

The Battle of Gravelotte, or Gravelotte-St. Privat, was the largest battle during the Franco-Prussian War. It was fought about six miles west of Metz, Lorraine, France where on the previous day, having intercepted the French army's retreat to the west at the Battle of Mars-La-Tour, the Prussians were now closing in to complete the destruction of the French forces.

The combined German forces, under Field Marshal Count Helmuth von Moltke, were the Prussian First and Second Armies of the North German Confederation numbering about 210 infantry battalions, 133 cavalry squadrons, and 732 heavy cannons totaling 188,332 officers and men. The French Army of the Rhine, commanded by Marshal François-Achille Bazaine, numbering about 183 infantry battalions, 104 cavalry squadrons, backed by 520 heavy cannons, totaling 112,800 officers and men, dug in along high ground with their southern left flank at the town of Rozerieulles, and their northern right flank at St. Privat.

On August 18, 1870, the battle began when at 08:00 Moltke ordered the First and Second Armies to advance against the French positions. By 12:00, General Manstein opened up the battle before the village of Amanvillers with artillery from the 25th Infantry Division. But the French had spent the night and early morning digging trenches and rifle pits while placing their artillery and their *mitrailleuses*, an early type of machine gun, in concealed positions. With them finally aware of the Prussian advance, the French opened up a massive return fire against the mass of advancing Germans. The battle at first appeared in favour of the French with their superior Chassepot rifle. However, the Prussian artillery was superior with the all-steel Krupps breech-loading gun.

By 14:30, General Steinmetz, the commander of the First Army, unilaterally launched his VIII Corps across the Mance Ravine in which the Prussian infantry were soon pinned down by murderous rifle and *mitrailleuse* fire from the French positions. At 15:00, the massed guns of the VII and VIII Corps opened fire to support the attack. But by 16:00, with the attack in danger of stalling, Steinmetz ordered the VII Corps forward, followed by the 1st Cavalry Division.

By 16:50, with the Prussian southern attacks in danger of breaking up, the 3rd Prussian Guards Brigade of the Second Army opened an attack against the French positions at St-Privat which were commanded by General Canrobert. At 17:15, the 4th Prussian Guards Brigade joined the advance followed at 17:45 by the 1st Prussian Guards Brigade. All of the Prussian Guard attacks were too pinned down by lethal French gunfire from the rifle pits and trenches. At 18:15 the 2nd Prussian Guards Brigade, the last of the Guards Division, was committed to the attack on St Privat while Steinmetz committed the last of the reserves of the First Army across the Mance Ravine. By 18:30, a considerable portion of the VII and VIII Corps disengaged from the fighting and withdrew towards the Prussian positions at Rezonville.

With the defeat of the First Army, Crown Prince Frederick Charles ordered a massed artillery attack against Canrobert's position at St. Privat to prevent the Guards attack from failing too. At 19:00 the 3rd Division of Fransecky's II Corps of the Second Army advanced across Ravine while the XII Corps cleared out the nearby town of Roncourt and with the survivors of the Guards Division launched a fresh attack against the ruins of St. Privat. At 20:00, the arrival of the Prussian 4th Division of the II Corps and with the Prussian right flank on Mance Ravine, the line stabilised. By then, the Prussians of the Guards Division and the XII and II Corps captured St. Privat forcing the decimated French forces to withdraw. But with the Prussians exhausted from the fighting, the French were now able to mount a counter-attack. But then General Bourbaki refused to commit the reserves of the French Old Guard to the battle because he considered it a 'defeat'.

By 22:00, firing largely died down across the battlefield for the night. The next morning, the French Army of the Rhine, rather than resume the battle with an attack of its own against the battle-weary German armies, retreated to Metz where they were besieged and forced to surrender two months later.

The casualties were horrible, especially for the attacking Prussian forces. A grand total of 20,163 German troops were killed, wounded or missing in action during the August 18 battle. The French losses were 7,855 killed and wounded along with 4,420 prisoners of war (half of them were wounded) for a total of 12,275. While most of the Prussians fell under the French Chassepot rifles, most French fell under the Prussian Krupp shells. In a breakdown of the casualties, Frossard's II Corps of the Army of the Rhine suffered 621 casualties while inflicting 4,300 casualties on the Prussian First Army under Steinmetz before the Pointe du Jour. The Prussian Guard Division losses were even more staggering with 8,000 casualties out of 18,000 men. The Special Guard Jäger lost 19 officers, a surgeon and 431 men out of a total of 700. The 2nd Guards Brigade lost 39 officers and 1,076 men. The 3rd Guards Brigade lost 36 officers and 1,060 men. On the French side, the units holding St Privat lost more than half their number in the village.

Siege of Metz

With the defeat of Marshal Bazaine's Army of the Rhine at Gravelotte, the French were forced to retire to Metz where they were besieged by over 150,000 Prussian troops of the First and Second Armies. The further crushing French loss was sealed when he surrendered 180,000 soldiers on October 27.

Battle of Sedan

Emperor Napoleon III, along with Field Marshal MacMahon, formed the new French Army of Châlons to march on to Metz to rescue Bazaine. With Napoleon III personally leading the army with Marshal MacMahon in attendance, they led the Army of Chalons in a left-flanking march northeast towards the Belgian border in an attempt to avoid the Prussians before striking south to link up with Bazaine.

Napoleon III and Bismarck after the battle of Sedan

The Prussians, under the command of Field Marshal Count Helmuth von Moltke, took advantage of this incompetent manoeuvre to catch the French in a pincer grip. Leaving the Prussian First and Second Armies besieging Metz, Moltke took the Prussian Third Army and the Army of the Meuse northward where they caught up with the French at Beaumont on August 30. After a hard-fought battle with the French losing 5,000 men and 40 cannons in a sharp fight, they withdrew toward Sedan. Having reformed in the town, the Army of Chalons was immediately isolated by the converging Prussian armies. Napoleon III ordered the army to break out of the encirclement immediately. With MacMahon wounded on the previous day, General Auguste Ducrot took command of the French troops in the field.

On September 1, 1870, the battle opened with the Army of Châlons, with 202 infantry battalions, 80 cavalry squadrons and 564 artillery guns, attacking the surrounding Prussian Third and Meuse Armies totaling 222 infantry battalions, 186 cavalry squadrons and 774 artillery guns. General De Wimpffen, the commander of the French V Corps in reserve, hoped to launch a combined infantry and cavalry attack against the Prussian XI Corps. But by 11:00, Prussian artillery took a toll on the French while more Prussian troops arrived on the battlefield. The French cavalry, commanded by General Marguerite, launched three desperate attacks on the nearby village of Floing where the Prussian XI Corps was concentrated. Marguerite was killed leading the very first charge and the two additional charges led to nothing but heavy losses.

By the end of the day, with no hope of breaking out, Napoleon III called off the attacks. The French lost over 17,000 men killed and wounded with 21,000 captured. The Prussians reported their losses at 2,320 killed, 5,980 wounded and 700 captured or missing.

By the next day, on September 2, Napoleon III surrendered and was taken prisoner with 104,000 of his soldiers. It was an overwhelming victory for the Prussians, for they not only captured an entire French army, but the leader of France as well. The defeat of the French at Sedan had decided the war in Prussia's favour. One French army was immobilised and besieged in the city of Metz, and no other forces stood French ground against the Germans, yet the war would not end within the next five months to come.

Overthrow of the French monarchy and armistice negotiations

When news hit Paris of Emperor Napoleon's III capture, the French Second Empire was overthrown in a bloodless and successful coup d'etat which was launched by General Trochu, Jules Favre, and Léon Gambetta at Paris on September 4. They removed the second Bonapartist monarchy and proclaimed [1] a republic led by a Government of National Defense, leading to the Third Republic. Napoleon III was taken to Germany, and released later. He went into exile in the United Kingdom, dying in 1873.

After the German victory at Sedan, most of France's standing forces were out of combat, one army was immobilised and besieged in the city of Metz, and the army led by Emperor Napoleon III himself had surrendered to the Germans. Under these circumstances, the Germans hoped for an armistice which would put an official end to the hostilities and lead to peace. Especially Prussia's Prime Minister von Bismarck entertained that hope for he wanted to end the war as soon as possible. To a nation with as many neighbours as Prussia, a prolonged war meant the growing risk of intervention by another power, and von Bismarck was determined to limit that risk.

At first, the outlook for peace seemed fair. The Germans estimated that the new government of France could not be interested in continuing the war that had been declared by the monarch they had quickly deposed of. Hoping to pave the road to peace, Prussia's Prime Minister von Bismarck invited the new French Government to negotiations held at Ferrières and submitted a list of moderate conditions, including limited territorial demands in Alsace. This area west of the Rhine, inhabited by Germans for over thousand years (bi-lingual Oaths of Strasbourg 842), had been annexed by Louis XIV in 1681. Further claims of a French border along the Rhine in Palatinate had been made since (Adolphe Thiers, Rhine crisis 1840), while the Germans vowed to defend both banks of the Rhine (Die Wacht am Rhein, Deutschlandlied). As Prussia had recently acquired large areas populated by Catholics, further extensions were not considered desirable by Bismarck, though.

But while the republican government was amenable to reparation payments or transfer of colonial territories in Africa or in South East Asia to Prussia, Jules Favre on behalf of the Government of National Defense declared on September 6 that

> "We are not going to cede a single inch of our territory and not a single stone of our (Vauban-built) fortresses"
> *Nous ne céderons ni un pouce de notre territoire ni une pierre de nos forteresses.* [2] [3] [4]

The republic renewed the declaration of war, called for recruits in all parts of the country, and pledged to drive the enemy troops out of France.

Under these circumstances, the Germans had to continue the war, yet couldn't pin down any proper military opposition in their vicinity. As the bulk of the remaining French armies were digging-in near Paris, the German leaders decided to put pressure upon the enemy by attacking the capital of France. In October 1870, German troops reached the outskirts of Paris, a heavily fortified city. The Germans surrounded it and erected a blockade, as already established and ongoing at Metz.

Bismarck's demand for Alsace caused a dramatic change in European public opinion, which was best exemplified by the reaction of Giuseppe Garibaldi.

> "On 7 September [1870], within three days of the revolution of 4 September in Paris, he wrote to the *Movimento* of Genoa: 'Yesterday I said to you: war to the death to Bonaparte. Today I say to you: rescue the French Republic by every means.'" [Jasper Ridley, *Garibaldi*, Viking Press, New York (1976) p 602].

Subsequently, Garibaldi went to France and assumed command of the Army of the Vosges, an army of volunteers that was never defeated by the Germans.

The war is continued

The French republican government's decision to continue the war changed public opinion in Germany for most Germans did not understand why France would not accept the German peace offer. Germans generally agreed that the outcome of the war was certain and that France could not reverse the military situation in her favor. Continued warfare would only lead to more bloodshed.

In the autumn of 1870, many Germans accepted the opinion that not only French leaders, but the French people itself, regarded by many as a role model in their previous fight for the French Revolution, were aggressive and would not accept defeat. Germans, now also dropping republican hopes in favor of the successful Prussian monarchy, began to view France as an 'hereditary enemy' (*Erbfeind*, French-German enmity), whom their ancestors had been made to fight for over 200 years since the Thirty Years' War, and who would continue to assault Germany if left unchecked. Many Germans demanded that:

- Germany should be strengthened and France should be weakened in order to rule out any future war [5]
- France should be occupied by German troops after the war
- France should be made to pay a high sum in reparations
- And most important, the German-speaking areas in eastern France should be annexed by a new, strong German Empire which was to be founded in order to unite the Germans against France

Prussia's prime minister von Bismarck had little respect for such plans. He refused to consider France an *Erbfeind* and aimed to appease France, like prior adversaries, by moderate conditions for peace which included only minor annexations. He was also sceptical about incorporating more of the South German Catholics, especially Austria, into a united Germany for it might weaken protestant Prussia's dominant position. But finally, when the German nobility began to accept the new popular opinion, von Bismarck reluctantly began to prepare to unite Germany.

Siege of Paris

The Siege of Paris lasting from September 19, 1870 – January 28, 1871 brought about the final defeat of the French Army during the Franco-Prussian War. On January 18, 1871 the new German Empire was proclaimed at the Palace of Versailles.

Faced with the German blockade of Paris, the new French government called for the establishment of several large armies in France's provinces. These new bodies of troops were to march towards Paris and attack the Germans there from various directions at the same time. In addition, armed French civilians were to create a guerilla force - the so-called Francs-tireurs - for the purpose of attacking German support lines.

The Loire Campaign

Dispatched from Paris as the republican government's emissary, Léon Gambetta passed over the German lines in a hot air balloon and organized the recruitment of new French armies.

News about an alleged German 'extermination' plan infuriated the French and strengthened their support to their new government. Within a few weeks, five new armies totaling more than 500,000 troops were recruited.

The Germans noticed this development and dispatched some of their troops to the French provinces in order to detect, attack, and disperse the new French armies before they could become a menace, for the blockade of Paris or elsewhere. The Germans were not prepared for an occupation of the whole of France. This would stretch them out, and they would become vulnerable.

On October 10, fighting erupted between German and French republican forces near Orléans. At first, the Germans were victorious, but the French drew reinforcements and defeated the Germans at Coulmiers on November 9. But after the surrender of Metz, more than 100,000 well-trained and battle-experienced German troops joined the German 'Southern Army'. With these reinforcements, the French were forced to abandon Orléans on December 4, to be finally defeated near Le Mans between January 10 and 12, 1871.

A second French army which operated north of Paris was turned back near Amiens (November 27, 1870), Bapaume (January 3, 1871) and St. Quentin (January 19).

Northern Campaign

Following the Army of the Loire's defeats, Gambetta turned to General Faidherbe's Army of the North. The Army of the North had achieved several small victories at towns such as Ham, La Hallue, and Amiens, and was well-protected by the belt of fortresses in northern France, allowing Faidherbe's men to launch quick attacks against isolated Prussian units, then retreat behind the belt of fortresses. Despite the army's access to the armaments factories of Lille, the Army of the North suffered from severe supply difficulties which kept the soldiers' already poor morale at a permanently low level. In January 1871, Gambetta forced Faidherbe to march his army beyond the fortresses and engage the Prussians in open battle. The army was severely weakened by low morale, supply problems, the terrible winter weather, and low troop quality, whilst General Faidherbe himself was unable to direct battles effectively due to his terrible health, the result of decades of campaigning in West Africa. At the Battle of St Quentin, the Army of the North suffered a crushing defeat and was scattered, releasing thousands of Prussian soldiers to be relocated to the East.

Eastern Campaign

Following the destruction of the French Army of the Loire, remnants of the Loire army gathered in eastern France to form the Army of the East, commanded by General Charles Bourbaki. In a final attempt to cut the German supply lines in northeast France, Bourbaki's army marched north to attack the Prussian siege of Belfort and relieve the beleaguered French defenders.

In the battle of the Lisaine, Bourbaki's men failed to break through German lines commanded by General August von Werder. Bringing in the German 'Southern Army', General von Manteuffel then drove Bourbaki's army into the mountains near the Swiss border. Facing annihilation, this last intact French army crossed the border and was disarmed and imprisoned by the neutral Swiss near Pontarlier (February 1, 1871).

Naval blockade

At the outset of the war, elements of the 470-ship French Navy were put to sea and to attempt a blockade of the north German coasts, which the relatively small north German navy (Norddeutsche Bundesmarine) could do little to oppose. Despite this, the blockade was only partially successful as the French navy suffered chronic shortages of coal and the lack of a forward military base in the North Sea and especially the Baltic Sea.

To take pressure from the expected German attack into Alsace-Lorraine, Napoleon III and others in the French high command planned at the outset of the war to launch a seaborne invasion of northern Germany. It was hoped that the invasion would not only divert German troops from the front, but also inspire Denmark to assist with its 50,000 strong army and the substantial Danish Navy. However it was discovered that Prussia had recently installed formidable coastal defenses around the major north German ports, including coastal artillery batteries consisting of Krupp heavy artillery tubes made of steel. The French Navy lacked the necessary heavy weaponry to deal with these coastal defences, while the difficult topography of the Prussian coastline, made a seaborne invasion of northern Germany impossible.

The French Marines and naval infantry tasked with the invasion of northern Germany were subsequently dispatched to bolster the French Army of Châlons, where they were captured at the Battle of Sedan along with Napoleon III. Suffering a severe shortage of officers following the capture of most of the professional French army at the Siege of Metz and the battle of Sedan, naval officers were taken from their ships to officer the hastily assembled *gardes mobiles* or French reserve army units.

As also the autumn storms of the North Sea took their toll on the remaining patrolling French ships, the blockade became less and less effective. By September 1870 the blockade was finally abandoned altogether for the winter, and the French Navy retired to ports along the English Channel, remaining in port for the rest of the war.

Isolated engagements took place between French and German ships in other theaters, such as the blockade by FS *Dupleix* of the German ship *Hertha* in Nagasaki, Japan.

Armistice

On January 28, 1871, the Government of National Defense based in Paris negotiated an armistice with the Prussians. With Paris starving, and Gambetta's provincial armies reeling from one disaster after another, French Premiere Jules Ferry was permitted to leave Paris and arrived at Versailles on January 24th to discuss peace terms with Bismarck.

Bismarck agreed to end the siege and allow food convoys to immediately enter Paris (including trains carrying millions of German army rations), on condition that the Government of National Defence surrendered several key fortresses outside Paris to the Prussians. Without the forts, the French Army would no longer be able to defend Paris. Although public opinion in Paris was strongly against any form of surrender of concession to the Prussians, the Government realised that it could not hold the city for much longer, and that Gambetta's provincial armies would probably never break through to relieve Paris. President Jules Trochu resigned on January 25th and was replaced by Jules Favre, who signed the surrender on January 27th at Versailles, with the armistice coming into effect at midnight on the night of the 27th/28th. Several sources claim that in his carriage on the way back to Paris, Favre broke into tears, and collapsed into his daughter's arms as the guns around Paris fell silent at midnight.

At Tours, Gambetta received word from Paris on January 30th that the Government had surrendered. Furious, he refused to surrender and launched an immediate attack on German forces at Orleans which, predictably, failed. A delegation of Parisian diplomats arrived in Tours by train on February 5th to negotiate with Gambetta, and on February 6, 1871, Gambetta stepped down and surrendered control of the provincial armies to the Government of National Defence, which promptly ordered a ceasefire across France.

The Treaty of Frankfurt was signed 10 May 1871, marking the end of the Franco-Prussian War that in hindsight was the first Franco-German War, as the French aggression united the German states.

Aftermath

The Prussian Army held a brief victory parade in Paris on February 17, 1871 and Bismarck honoured the armistice by sending trainloads of food into Paris and withdrawing Prussian forces to the east of the city, which would be withdrawn as soon as France paid the agreed war indemnity. At the same time, Prussian forces were withdrawn from France and concentrated in the provinces of Alsace and Lorraine. A mass exodus occurred from Paris as some 200,000 people, predominantly middle-class, left the city for the countryside. Paris was quickly re-supplied with free food and fuel by the United Kingdom and several accounts recall life in the city settling back to normal. National elections returned an overwhelmingly conservative government, which, under President Adolphe Thiers, established itself in Versailles, fearing that the political climate of Paris was too dangerous to set up the capital in the city. The new government, formed mainly of conservative, middle-class rural politicians, passed a variety of laws which greatly angered the population of Paris, such as the controversial Law of Maturities, which decreed that all rents in Paris, which had been postponed since September 1870, and all public debts across France, which had been given a moratorium in November 1870, were to be paid in full, with interest, within 48 hours. Paris shouldered an unfairly high proportion of the indemnity payments made to the Prussians, and the population of the city quickly grew resentful of the Versailles government. With Paris under the protection of the revolutionary National Guard and few regular soldiers in the city, left-wing leaders established themselves in the Hôtel de Ville and established the Paris Commune.

Countries previously without a General Staff or a system of universal conscription soon adopted both, along with developments in logistics, military use of railways, and the telegraph system, all proven by the war to be indispensable. The creation of a unified German Empire destroyed the balance of power that had been created with the Congress of Vienna after the end of the Napoleonic Wars. Germany quickly established itself as the main power in Europe with one of the most powerful and professional armies in the world (although the United Kingdom remained the dominant world power, British involvement in European affairs during the late nineteenth century was very limited, allowing Germany to exercise great influence over the European mainland). In France, the defeat gave way to a feeling of revanchism that, by creating a permanent state of crisis between Germany and France, would be one of the contributing factors leading to World War I.

References

- Mitchner, E. Alyn, R. Joanne Tuffs. Century of Change. Canada: Reidmore Books Inc., 1997.
- Michael Howard: Franco-Prussian War 1870-1871, [6]
- Lexikon der deutschen Geschichte – Ploetz, Verlag Herder, Freiburg im Breisgau, Österreich 2001
- Der große Ploetz, Verlag Herder, Freiburg im Breisgau, Österreich 1998
- Dtv-Atlas Weltgeschichte, Deutscher Taschenbuch Verlag, München 2000
- Dennis E. Showalter: *Das Gesicht des modernen Krieges. Sedan, 1. und 2. September 1870*, in: *Schlachten der Weltgeschichte. Von Salamis bis Sinai*, hrsg. v. Stig Förster, Dierk Walter und Markus Pöhlmann, München ²2004. ISBN 3-423-34083-5
- Theodor Fontane: *Band 1 - Der Krieg gegen Frankreich 1870-1871*, Weißenburg - Wörth - Spicheren - Colombey -Vionville - Gravelotte - Sedan - Wilhelmshöhe - Straßburg - Toul - Metz, Verlag Rockstuhl, Bad Langensalza, Reprint 1873/2004, ISBN 3-937135-25-1
- Theodor Fontane: *Band 2 - Der Krieg gegen Frankreich 1870-1871*, Vor und in Paris vom 20. September bis 24. Dezember 1870 - Die großen Ausfallgefechte - Vor Paris im Dezember 1870 - Orleans, Verlag Rockstuhl, Bad Langensalza, Reprint 1876/2004, ISBN 3-937135-26-X
- Theodor Fontane: *Band 3 - Der Krieg gegen Frankreich 1870-1871*, Amiens - Dijon - Le Mans - Belfort -(Vor) Paris 25. Dezember 1870 bis 2. März 1871 - Bapaume = St. Quentin - Pontarlier, Verlag Rockstuhl, Bad Langensalza, Reprint 1876/2004, ISBN 3-937135-27-8
- Max Riemschneider: *Ein Erfurter im Deutsch-Französischen Krieg 1870/71*, Verlag Rockstuhl, Bad Langensalza, 2005, ISBN 3-937135-01-4
- Sigismund von Dobschütz: *„Wir sind dahin gekommen, ganze Dörfer niederzubrennen" — Briefe aus dem Deutsch-Französischen Krieg 1870/71 und der Okkupationszeit 1872/73 von Paul von Collas an seine Eltern.*, Ostdeutsche Familienkunde (OFK), Heft 1/2006, Seite 321f., Verlag Degener & Co., Neustadt (Aisch) 2006, ISSN 0472-190X. -- (*Paul von Collas war damals Generalstabsoffizier und Adjutant unter Karl Friedrich von Steinmetz und später unter General Edwin von Manteuffel, dessen Memoiren er schrieb.*)

Retrieved from "http://en.wikipedia.org/wiki/Franco-Prussian_War"

This page was last modified 04:53, 18 August 2006.

Francis Schaeffer Study Center

Mt. Juliet, Tennessee

Western Civilization, Year Four

From 1865 to 1990, Reconstruction to Modern Times

Rob Shearer, Tutor

Week Four Reading

The New Imperialism

New Imperialism

From Wikipedia, the free encyclopedia

Summary

The term **"New Imperialism"** refers to the policy and ideology of imperial colonial expansion adopted by Europe's powers and, later, Japan and the United States, during the late 19th and early 20th centuries; approximately from the Franco-Prussian War to World War I (c. 1871–1914). The period is distinguished by an unprecedented pursuit of what has been termed "empire for empire's sake," aggressive competition for overseas territorial acquisitions and the emergence in colonizing countries of doctrines of racial superiority which denied the fitness of subjugated peoples for self-government.

The term *imperialism* was used from the third quarter of the nineteenth century to describe various forms of political control by a greater power over less powerful territories or nationalities, although analytically the phenomena which it denotes may differ greatly from each other and from the "New" imperialism.

A later usage developed in the early 20th century among Marxists, who saw "imperialism" as the economic and political dominance of "monopolistic finance capital" in the most advanced countries and its acquisition — and enforcement through the state — of control of the means (and hence the returns) of production in less developed regions.

Elements of both conceptions are present in the "New imperialism" of the late 19th and early 20th centuries. But along with the adoption of ultra-nationalist and racial supremacist ideologies, the period saw a shift to pre-emptive colonial expansion, fueled by the imposition of tariff barriers aimed at excluding economic rivals from markets.

English writers have sometimes described elements of this period as the **"era of empire for empire's sake,"** **"the great adventure**,**"** and **"the scramble for Africa."** During this period, European nations added 20% of the Earth's land area (nearly 23,000,000 km^2) to their overseas colonial holdings (primarily occupying land in Africa). As it was mostly unoccupied by the Western powers as late as the 1880s, Africa became the primary target of the "new" imperialist expansion, although conquest took place also in other areas; notably Southeast Asia and the East Asian seaboard, where Japan, and the United States, joined the European powers' scramble for territory.

Contents

- 1 Rise of the New Imperialism
    - 1.1 The breakdown of Pax Britannica
    - 1.2 Britain and the New Imperialism
    - 1.3 France and the New Imperialism
    - 1.4 The New Imperialism and the newly-industrializing countries
    - 1.5 Social implications of the New Imperialism
- 2 Imperialism in Asia
- 3 The scramble for Africa
- 4 Imperial rivalry
- 5 Theories of the New Imperialism
- 6 See also
    - 6.1 Important concepts often associated with this era
    - 6.2 Biographies that may help shed more light on this era
- 7 External links

Rise of the New Imperialism

The breakdown of *Pax Britannica*

The expansions of the New Imperialism took place against a background of increasing competition (over resources, strategic power, and prestige) between the industrialized nations. This activity followed the erosion of *Pax Britannica*, during which British industrial and naval supremacy underpinned an informal empire of free trade and commercial hegemony.

During this period, between the 1815 Congress of Vienna (after the defeat of Napoleonic France) and the end of the Franco-Prussian War (1871), Britain reaped the benefits of being the world's sole modern, industrial power. As the "workshop of the world," Britain could produce finished goods so efficiently and cheaply that they could usually undersell comparable, locally manufactured goods in foreign markets.

The erosion of British hegemony after the Franco-Prussian War was occasioned by changes in the European and world economies and in the continental balance of power following the breakdown of the Concert of Europe, the balance of power established by the Congress of Vienna. The establishment of nation-states in Germany and Italy resolved territorial issues, which had kept potential rivals embroiled in internal affairs at the heart of Europe (to Britain's advantage).

Economically, adding to the commercial competition of old rivals like France were now the newly industrializing powers, such as Germany and the United States. All sought ways of challenging what they saw as Britain's undue dominance in world markets – the consequence of her early industrialization and maritime supremacy.

This competition was sharpened by the Long Depression of 1873-1896, a prolonged period of price deflation punctuated by severe business downturns, which added to pressure on governments to promote home industry, leading to the widespread abandonment of free trade among Europe's powers (in Germany from 1879 and in France from 1881).

The resulting limitation of both domestic markets and export opportunities led government and business leaders in Europe, and later the U.S., to see the solution in sheltered overseas markets united to the home country behind imperial tariff barriers: new overseas colonies would provide export markets free of foreign competition, while supplying cheap raw materials.

The revival of working-class militancy and emergence of socialist parties during the Depression decades led conservative governments to view colonialism as a force for national cohesion in support of the domestic *status quo*. Also, in Italy, and to a lesser extent in Germany and Britain, tropical empire was seen as an outlet, for what was deemed, a surplus home population.

Britain and the New Imperialism

Queen Victoria and Prime Minister Disraeli

In Britain, the latter half of the 19th century has been seen as the period of displacement of industrial capitalism by finance capitalism. As the country's relative commercial and industrial lag encouraged the creation of larger corporations and combines, close association of industry and banks added to the influence of financiers over the British economy and politics.

The unprecedented control of industry on the part of London financial houses by the 1870s aided their pursuit of British government "protection" of overseas investments — particularly those in the securities of foreign governments and in foreign-government-backed development activities, such as railroads.

Britain's lag in other fields deepened her reliance on invisible exports (such as banking, insurance and shipping services) to offset a merchandise trade deficit dating from the beginning of commercial liberalization in 1813, and thereby keep her "out of the red."

Although it had been official British policy for years to support such investments, the large expansion of these investments after about 1860 and economic and political instability in many areas of high investment, (such as Egypt), brought increased pressure for their systematic protection.

Britain's entry into the new imperial age is often dated to 1875, when the government of Benjamin Disraeli bought the indebted Egyptian ruler Ismail's shareholding in the Suez Canal to secure control of this strategic waterway, since its opening six years earlier as a channel for shipping between Britain and India. Joint Anglo-French financial control over Egypt ended in outright British occupation in 1882.

Fear of Russia's centuries-old southward expansion was a further factor in British policy: in 1878, Britain took control of Cyprus as a base for action against a Russian attack on the Ottoman Empire, and invaded Afghanistan to forestall an increase in Russian influence there. The Great Game in Inner Asia ended with a bloody and wholly unnecessary British expedition against Tibet in 1903-1904.

At the same time, some powerful industrial lobbies and government leaders in Britain, exemplified by Joseph Chamberlain, came to view formal empire as necessary to arrest Britain's relative decline in world markets. During the 1890s, Britain adopted the new policy wholeheartedly, quickly emerging as the front-runner in the scramble for tropical African territories.

Britain's adoption of the New Imperialism may be seen as a quest for captive markets or fields for investment of surplus capital, or as a primarily strategic or pre-emptive attempt to protect existing trade links and to prevent the absorption of overseas markets into the increasingly closed imperial trading blocs of rival powers. The failure in the 1900s of Chamberlain's campaign for Imperial tariffs illustrates the strength of free trade feeling even in the face of loss of international market share.

France and the New Imperialism

Government leaders, such as Jules Ferry of France, concluded that sheltered overseas markets would solve the problems of low prices and over-accumulation of surplus capital caused by shrinking continental markets.

The expansion of the French colonial empire was also seen as a method of 'rejuvenating' the country after its humiliating defeat in the Franco-Prussian War of 1870; the military actions needed to secure empire were seen by colonial enthusiasts as 'the first, faltering steps of convalescence'. This plan, however, did meet with some popular resistance in the 1870s and 1880s, wherein people protested that the first priority of France should be with the lost provinces of Alsace-Lorraine. Indeed public opinion in France was often highly erratic with regards to colonialism, and Ferry himself was removed from office twice over colonial disputes.

The New Imperialism and the newly-industrializing countries

Just as the U.S. emerged as one of the world's leading industrial, military and political powers after the Civil War, so would Germany following its own unification in 1871. Both countries undertook ambitious naval expansion in the 1890s. And just as Germany reacted to depression with the adoption of tariff protection in 1879 and colonial expansion in 1884-85, so would the U.S., following the landslide election (1896) of William McKinley, be associated with the high McKinley Tariff of 1890.

United States expansionism had its roots in domestic concerns and economic conditions, as in other newly industrializing nations where government sought to accelerate internal development. Advocates of empire also drew upon a tradition of westward expansion over the course of the previous century.

Economic depression led some U.S. businessmen and politicians from the mid-1880s to come to the same conclusion as their European counterparts — that industry and capital had exceeded the capacity of existing markets and needed new outlets. The "closing of the Frontier" identified by the 1890 Census report and publicized by historian Frederick Jackson Turner in his 1893 paper *The Significance of the Frontier in American History*, contributed to fears of constrained natural resource.

Like the Long Depression in Europe, the main features of the U.S. depression included deflation, rural decline, and unemployment, which aggravated the bitter social protests of the "Gilded Age" — the Populist movement, the free-silver crusade, and violent labor disputes such as the Pullman and Homestead strikes.

The Panic of 1893 contributed to the growing mood for expansionism. Influential politicians such as Henry Cabot Lodge, William McKinley, and Theodore Roosevelt advocated a more aggressive foreign policy to pull the United States out of the depression. However, opposition to expansionism was strong and vocal in the United States. The U.S. became involved in the War with Spain only after Cubans convinced the U.S. government that Spain was brutalizing them. Whatever the causes, the result of the war was that the U.S. came into the possession of Cuba, Puerto Rico and the Philippines. It was, however, only the Philippines that remained, for three decades, as a colonial possession.

Although U.S. capital investments within the Philippines and Puerto Rico were relatively small (figures that would seemingly detract from the broader economic implications on first glance), "imperialism" for the United States, formalized in 1904 by the Roosevelt Corollary to the Monroe Doctrine, would also spur on her displacement of Britain as the predominant investor in Latin America — a process largely completed by the end of the Great War.

In Germany, Imperial Chancellor Otto von Bismarck revised his initial dislike of colonies (which he had seen as burdensome and useless), partly under pressure for colonial expansion to match that of the other European states, but also under the mistaken notion that Germany's entry into the colonial scramble could press Britain into conceding to broader German strategic ambitions.

Japan's development after the Meiji Restoration of 1868 followed the Western lead in industrialization and militarism, enabling her to gain control of Korea in 1894 and a sphere of influence in Manchuria (1905), following her defeat of Russia in the Russo-Japanese War. Japan was responding in part to the actions of more established powers, and her expansionism drew on the harnessing of traditional Japanese values to more modern aspirations for great-power status: not until the 1930s was Japan to become a net exporter of capital.

Social implications of the New Imperialism

The New Imperialism gave rise to new social views of colonialism. Rudyard Kipling, for instance, urged the United States to "Take up the White Man's burden" of bringing the European version of civilization to the other peoples of the world, regardless of whether they wanted this form of civilization. While Social Darwinism became current throughout western Europe and the United States, the paternalistic French-style "civilizing mission" (In French: *mission civilisatrice*) appealed to many European statesmen.

Observing the rise of trade unionism, socialism, and other protest movements during an era of mass society in both Europe and later North America, elites sought to use imperial jingoism to co-opt the support of part of the industrial working class. The new mass media promoted jingoism in the Spanish-American War (1898), the Second Boer War (1899-1902), and the Boxer Rebellion (1900).

Many of Europe's major elites also found advantages in formal, overseas expansion: large financial and industrial monopolies wanted imperial support to protect their overseas investments against competition and domestic political tensions abroad; bureaucrats wanted and sought government offices; military officers desired promotion; and the traditional but waning landed gentries sought increased profits for their investments, formal titles, and high office.

The notion of rule over tropical lands commanded widespread acceptance among metropolitan populations: even among those who associated imperial colonization with oppression and exploitation. For example, the 1904 Congress of the Socialist International concluded that the colonial peoples should be taken in hand by future European socialist governments and led by them to eventual independence.

Imperialism in Asia

The transition to formal imperialism in India was effectively accomplished with the transfer of administrative functions from the chartered British East India Company to the British government in 1858, following the Indian Mutiny of the previous year. Acts in 1773 and 1784 had already empowered the government to control Company policies and to appoint the Governor-General, the highest Company official in India.

The new administrative arrangement, crowned with Queen Victoria's proclamation as Empress of India in 1876, replaced the rule of a monopolistic enterprise with that of a trained civil service headed by graduates of Britain's top universities. India's princely states (with about a quarter of the country's population) retained their quasi-autonomous status, subject to British overlordship and official "advice."

In South-East Asia, the 1880s saw the completion of Britain's conquest of Burma and France's takeover of Vietnam and Cambodia; during the following decade France completed her Indochinese empire with the annexation of Laos, leaving the kingdom of Siam (now Thailand) with an uneasy independence as a neutral buffer between British and French-ruled lands.

Imperialist ambitions and rivalries in East Asia inevitably came to focus on the vast empire of China, with more than a quarter of the world's population. China survived as a more-or-less independent state due to the resilience of her social and administrative structures, but can also be seen as a reflection of the limitations to which imperialist governments were willing to press their ambitions in the face of similar competing claims.

On the one hand, it is suggested that rather than being a backward country unable to secure the prerequisite stability and security for western-style commerce, China's institutions and level of economic development rendered her capable of providing a secure market in the absence of direct rule by the developed powers, despite her past unwillingness to admit western commerce (which had often taken the form of drug-pushing).

This may explain the West's contentment with informal "spheres of influence". Western powers did intervene militarily to quell domestic chaos, such as the epic Taiping Rebellion of 1850-1864, against which General Gordon (later the imperialist 'martyr' in the Sudan) is often credited with having saved the Qing Dynasty.

But China's size and cohesion compared to pre-colonial societies of Africa also made formal subjugation too difficult for any but the broadest coalition of colonialist powers, whose own rivalries would preclude such an outcome. When such a coalition did materialize in 1900, its objective was limited to suppression of the anti-imperialist Boxer Rebellion because of the irreconcilability of Anglo-American and Russo-German aims.

The scramble for Africa

In 1875, the two most important European holdings in Africa were French Algeria and the British Cape Colony. By 1914, only Ethiopia and the republic of Liberia remained outside formal European control. The transition from an "informal empire" of control through economic dominance to direct control took the form of a "scramble" for territory in areas previously regarded as open to British trade and influence.

David Livingstone's explorations, continued from the 1870s by H.M. Stanley, opened tropical Africa's interior to European penetration. In 1876, King Léopold II of Belgium organized the International African Association, which, by 1882, obtained over 900,000 square miles (2,300,000 sq km) of territory in the Congo basin through treaties with African chiefs.

France and Germany quickly followed, sending political agents and military expeditions to establish their own claims to sovereignty. The Berlin Conference of 1884-1885 sought to regulate the competition between the powers by defining "effective occupation" as the criterion for international recognition of territorial claims.

Léopold was allocated, the misnamed, "Congo Free State," where the activities of his agents and European concessionary companies led to international scandal (1903-1904) over atrocities committed by Léopold's agents and concession-holders, forcing him to submit the territory to formal Belgian colonial rule (1907-08).

The codification of the imposition of direct rule in terms of "effective occupation" necessitated routine recourse to armed force against indigenous states and peoples. Uprisings against imperial rule were put down ruthlessly, most spectacularly in German South-West Africa and German East Africa in the years 1904-1907.

Britain's 1882 formal occupation of Egypt (itself triggered by concern over the Suez Canal) contributed to a preoccupation over securing control of Nile valley, leading to the conquest of the neighboring Sudan in 1896-1898 and confrontation with a French military expedition at Fashoda (September 1898).

In 1899, Britain set out to complete her takeover of South Africa, begun with the annexation (1795) of the Cape, by invading the Afrikaner republics of the gold-rich Transvaal and the neighboring Orange Free State. The chartered British South Africa Company had already seized the land to the north, renamed Rhodesia after its head, the Cape tycoon Cecil Rhodes.

British gains in southern and East Africa prompted Rhodes and Alfred Milner, Britain's High Commissioner in South Africa, to urge a "Cape to Cairo" empire linking by rail the strategically important Canal to the mineral-rich South, though German occupation of German East Africa prevented such an outcome until the end of World War I.

Paradoxically Britain, the staunch advocate of free trade, emerged in 1914 with, not only the largest overseas empire, thanks to her long-standing presence in India, but also the greatest gains in the "scramble for Africa," reflecting her advantageous position at its inception. Between 1885 and 1914, Britain took nearly 30% of Africa's population under her control, to 15% for France, 9% for Germany, 7% for Belgium and only 1% for Italy: Nigeria alone contributed 15 million subjects to Britain, more than in the whole of French West Africa or the entire German colonial empire.

Imperial rivalry

The extension of European control over Africa and Asia added a further dimension to the rivalry and mutual suspicion which characterized international diplomacy in the decades preceding World War I. France's seizure of Tunisia (1881) initiated fifteen years of tension with Italy, which had hoped to take the country and which retaliated by allying with Germany and waging a decade-long tariff war with France. Britain's takeover of Egypt a year later caused a marked cooling of her relations with France.

The most striking conflicts of the era were the Spanish American War of 1898 and the Russo-Japanese War of 1904-05, each signaling the advent of a new imperial great power, the United States and Japan, respectively. The Fashoda incident of 1898 represented the worst Anglo-French crisis in decades, but France's climbdown in the face of British demands foreshadowed improved relations as the two countries set about resolving their overseas claims.

British policy in South Africa and German actions in the Far East contributed to the dramatic policy shift, which in the 1900s, aligned hitherto isolationist Britain first with Japan as an ally, and then with France and Russia in the looser Entente. German efforts to break the Entente by challenging French hegemony in Morocco resulted in the Tangier Crisis of 1905 and the Agadir Crisis of 1911, adding to tension in the years preceding World War I.

It may be debated whether the New Imperialism itself contributed in large measure to the subsequent global conflict, except to the extent that it broadened the geographical area of military operations. Both the European divisions of the 1870s onward and the accelerated colonial drive of the period can be said to derive from the same causes: strategic conditions, aggressive competing nationalisms and the economic and political imperatives of the new mass society.

Theories of the New Imperialism

The **accumulation theory** adopted by J.A. Hobson and later Lenin centered on the accumulation of surplus capital during and after the Industrial Revolution: restricted opportunities at home, the argument goes, drove financial interests to seek more profitable investments in less-developed lands with lower labor costs, unexploited raw materials and little competition.

Some have criticized Hobson's analysis, arguing that it fails to explain colonial expansion on the part of less industrialized nations with little surplus capital, such as Italy, or the great powers of the next century — the United States and Russia — which were in fact net borrowers of foreign capital.

Opponents of Hobson's accumulation theory often point to frequent cases when military and bureaucratic costs of occupation exceeded financial returns. In Africa (exclusive of what would become the Union of South Africa in 1909) the amount of capital investment by Europeans was relatively small before and after the 1880s, and the companies involved in tropical African commerce exerted limited political influence.

The **World-Systems theory** approach of Immanuel Wallerstein sees imperialism as part of a general, gradual extension of capital investment from the "core" of the industrial countries to a less developed "periphery." Protectionism and formal empire were the major tools of "semi-peripheral," newly industrialized states, such as Germany, seeking to usurp Britain's position at the "core" of the global capitalist system.

Echoing Wallerstein's global perspective to an extent, imperial historian Bernard Porter views Britain's adoption of formal imperialism as a symptom and an effect of her relative decline in the world, and not of strength: "Stuck with outmoded physical plants and outmoded forms of business organization, [Britain] now felt the less favorable effects of being the first to modernize."

Recent imperial historians Porter, P.J. Cain and A.G Hopkins contest Hobson's conspiratorial overtones and "reductionisms," but do not reject the influence of "the City's" financial interests.

Important concepts often associated with this era

- British Empire
- History of the United Kingdom
- Imperialism in Asia
- "The White Man's Burden"
- Commonwealth of Nations (successor to the British Empire)
- Dollar Diplomacy

Biographies that may help shed more light on this era

- Léopold II of Belgium
- Meiji Emperor of Japan
- Napoléon III of France
- Wilhelm II of Germany
- Chamberlain
- Disraeli
- Ferry
- Kipling
- McKinley
- Rhodes
- Queen Victoria

Retrieved from "http://en.wikipedia.org/wiki/New_Imperialism"

This page was last modified 00:16, 29 June 2006.

Francis Schaeffer Study Center
Mt. Juliet, Tennessee

Western Civilization, Year Four
From 1865 to 1990, Reconstruction to Modern Times

Rob Shearer, Tutor

Week Five Reading
Anarchism

Proudhon
The Propaganda of the Deed
Leon Czolgosz

Pierre-Joseph Proudhon

From Wikipedia, the free encyclopedia

Pierre Joseph Proudhon

Pierre-Joseph Proudhon (15 January 1809 – 19 January 1865) was a French economist and socialist philosopher who was the first individual to call himself an "anarchist" and is considered among the first anarchist thinkers. He was a workingman, a printer, who taught himself to read Latin so as to print books in that language well. Proudhon is most famous for his assertion of "Property is theft!", in his missive *What is Property? Or, an Inquiry into the Principle of Right and Government* with the original title: *Qu'est-ce que la propriété? Recherche sur le principe du droit et du gouvernement*, which was his first major work, published in 1840.

The publication of "*What is Property?*" attracted the attention of the French authorities, and also of Karl Marx who started up a correspondence with Proudhon. The two men influenced each other; they met in Paris when Marx was exiled there. Their friendship ended completely when Marx wrote a response to Proudhon's *The Philosophy of Poverty* entitled *The Poverty of Philosophy*. Their dispute was one of the origins to the split between the anarchists and the Marxists in the International Working Men's Association. There was also a split between the anarchists of Mikhail Bakunin and Proudhon. Proudhon believed that collective ownership was undesirable and that social revolution could be achieved in a peaceful manner.

In his book *The Confessions of a Revolutionary*, Proudhon wrote among other things, the well known phrase, *anarchy is order*. He attempted to create a national bank that gave out interest-free loans, similar in some respects to credit unions, which had been in place in England long before his birth.

- Contents 1 **Biography**
    - 1.1 Early Years
    - 1.2 Interest in politics
    - 1.3 Proudhon and the 1848 Revolution
- 2 Political philosophy
- 3 Criticisms
- 4 Quotes
- 5 Bibliography
- 6 Writers influenced
- 7 See also
- 8 Notes

Biography

Early Years

Proudhon and his children, by Gustave Courbet, 1865

Proudhon was born in Besançon, his father being a brewers cooper. As a boy, he herded cows and followed other simple pursuits of a like nature. But he was not entirely self-educated; at sixteen Proudhon entered the college of his native place, though his family was so poor that he could not procure the necessary books, and had to borrow them from his fellow students in order to copy the lessons. At nineteen he became a working compositor; afterwards he rose to be a corrector for the press, proofreading ecclesiastical works, and thereby acquiring a very competent knowledge of theology. In this way also he came to learn Hebrew, and to compare it with Greek, Latin and French; and it was the first proof of his intellectual audacity that on the strength of this he wrote an *Essai de grammaire génerale*. As Proudhon knew nothing whatever of the true principles of philology, his treatise was of no value. In 1838 he obtained the pension Suard, a bursary of 1500 francs a year for three years, for the encouragement of young men of promise, which was in the gift of the Academy of Besançon.

Interest in politics

In 1839 he wrote a treatise *L'Utilité de la célébration du dimanche*, which contained the germs of his revolutionary ideas. About this time he went to Paris, where he lived a poor, ascetic and studious life - making acquaintance, however, with the socialistic ideas which were then fomenting in the capital. In 1840 he published his first work *Qu'est-ce que la propriété*. His famous answer to this question, *La propriété, c'est le vol (property is theft)*, naturally did not please the academy of Besançon, and there was some talk of withdrawing his pension; but he held it for the regular period. For his third memoir on property, which took the shape of a letter to the Fourierist, M. Considérant, he was tried at Besançon but was acquitted. In 1846 he published his greatest work, the *Système des contradictions économiques ou Philosophie de la misère*. For some time Proudhon carried on a small printing establishment at Besançon, but without success; afterwards he became connected as a kind of manager with a commercial firm at Lyon. In 1847 he left this employment, and finally settled in Paris, where he was now becoming celebrated as a leader of innovation. In this year he also became a Freemason.

Proudhon and the 1848 Revolution

Proudhon was surprised by the revolt in Paris in February 1848. He participated in the February uprising and the composition of what he termed "the first republican proclamation" of the new republic. But he had misgivings about the new government because it was pursuing political reform at the expense of the socio-economic reform, which Proudhon considered basic.

Proudhon published his own perspective for reform, *Solution du problème social*, in which he laid out a program of mutual financial cooperation among workers. He believed this would transfer control of economic relations from capitalists and financiers to workers. The central part of his plan was the establishment of a bank to provide credit at a very low rate of interest and the issuing "exchange notes" that would circulate instead of money based on gold.

During the Second French Republic Proudhon made his biggest impact on the public through his journalism. He was involved with four different newspapers: *La Représentant du Peuple* (February 1848 - August 1848); *Le Peuple* (September 1848 - June 1849); *La Voix du Peuple* (September 1849 - May 1850); *Le Peuple de 1850* (June 1850 - October 1850). His polemical writing style, combined with his self-perception of himself as a political outsider, produced a cynical, combative journalism appealed to many French workers, although it alienated others. he repeatedly criticised the policies of the government and promoted reformation of credit and exchange. To this end, he attempted to establish a popular bank (Banque du peuple) early in 1849, but despite over 13,000 people signing up (mostly workers), receipts were limited falling short of 18,000FF and the whole enterprise was essentially stillborn.

Proudhon stood for the constituent assembly in April 1848, but failed to get elected, although his name appeared on the ballots in Paris, Lyon, Besançon, and Lille. However he was later successful, in the complementary elections held on June 4, and served as a deputy during the debates over the National Workshops. Proudhon was never enthusiastic about such workshops, perceiving them to be essentially charitable institutions that did not resolve the problems of the economic system. Still, he was against their elimination unless an alternative could be found for the workers who relied on the workshops for subsistence.

He was shocked by the violence of the June Days. Visiting the barricades personally he later reflected that his presence at the Bastille at this time was "one of the most honorable acts of my life." But in general during the tumultuous events of 1848, Proudhon opposed insurrection preaching peaceful conciliation, a stance that was in accord with his lifelong stance against violence. He disapproved of the revolts and demonstrations of February, May, and June, 1848, though sympathetic to the social and psychological injustices that the insurrectionaries had been forced to endure.

Political philosophy

Proudhon is the first known theorist to refer to himself as an "anarchist." He says, in *The Federal Principle* that the "notion of *anarchy* in politics is just as rational and positive as any other. It means that once industrial functions have taken over from political functions, then business transactions alone produce the social order."

In his earliest works, Proudhon analyzed the nature and problems of the capitalist economy. While deeply critical of capitalism, he also objected to contemporary socialists who idolized association. In series of commentaries, from What is Property? (1840) through the posthumously-published *Théorie de la propriété* (*Theory of Property*, 1863-64), he first declared that "property is theft", "property is impossible", "property is despotism" and "property is freedom". When he said property is theft, he was referring to the idle landowner who he believed *stole* the profits from laborers . In *Theory of Property*, he said that "property is the only power that can act as a counterweight to the State." Hence, "Proudhon could retain the idea of property as theft, and at the same time offer a new definition of it as liberty. There is the constant possibility of abuse, exploitation, which spells theft. At the same time property is a spontaneous creation of society and a bulwark against the ever-encroaching power of the State."[1]

In asserting that property is freedom, he was referring not only to the product of an individual's labor, but to the peasant or artisans home and tools of his trade and the income he received by selling his goods . For Proudhon, the only legitimate source of property is labor. What one produces is his property and anything beyond that is not. He can be considered a libertarian socialist, since he advocated worker self-management and argued against capitalist ownership of the means of production. However, he rejected the ownership of the products of labor by society, arguing that while "property in product [...] does not carry with it property in production [...] The right to product is exclusive [...] the right to means is common" and applied this to the land ("the land is [...] a common thing") and workplaces ("all accumulated capital being social property, no one can be its exclusive proprietor"). Proudhon had many arguments against entitlement to land and capital, including reasons based on morality, economics, politics, and individual liberty. One such argument was that it enabled profit, which in turn led to social instability and war by creating cycles of debt that eventually overcame the capacity of labor to pay them off. Another was that it produced "despotism" and turned workers into wage workers subject to the authority of a boss.

In *What Is Property?*, Proudhon wrote:

> Property, acting by exclusion and encroachment, while population was increasing, has been the life-principle and definitive cause of all revolutions. Religious wars, and wars of conquest, when they have stopped short of the extermination of races, have been only accidental disturbances, soon repaired by the mathematical progression of the life of

nations. The downfall and death of societies are due to the power of accumulation possessed by property.

Proudhon opposed both individual and collective property, however, he later abandoned his advocacy of "possession" over "property": in *Theory of Property* he maintains: "Now in 1840, I catagorically rejected the notion of property...for both the group and the individual," but then states his new theory of property: "property is the greatest revolutionary force which exists, with an unequaled capacity for setting itself against authority..." and the "principal function of private property within the political system will be to act as a counterweight to the power of the State, and by so doing to insure the liberty of the individual." (*Theory of Property* in *Selected Writings of Pierre-Joseph Proudhon* p. 136). However, though he now supported property in land (including a right of inheritance), he still believed that that "property" should be more equally distributed and limited in size to that actually used by individuals, families and workers associations. (*Theory of Property* in *Selected Writings of Pierre-Joseph Proudhon* p. 129, p. 133, p. 135) He supported the right of inheritance, and defended "as one of the foundations of the family and society." (Steward Edwards, Introduction to *Selected Writings of P.J. Proudhon*) However, he refused to extend this beyond personal possessions arguing that *"[u]nder the law of association, transmission of wealth does not apply to the instruments of labour."* (in Daniel Guerin (ed.), *No Gods, No Masters*, vol. 1, p. 62).

As a consequence of his opposition to profit, wage labour, worker exploitation, ownership of land and capital, as well as to state property, Proudhon rejected both capitalism and communism. He adopted the term mutualism for his brand of anarchism, which involved control of the means of production by the workers. In his vision, self-employed artisans, peasants, and cooperatives would trade their products on the market. For Proudhon, factories and other large workplaces would be run by 'labor associations' operating on directly democratic principles. The state would be abolished; instead, society would be organized by a federation of "free communes" (a commune is a local municipality in French). In 1863 Proudhon said: "All my economic ideas as developed over twenty-five years can be summed up in the words: agricultural-industrial federation. All my political ideas boil down to a similar formula: political federation or decentralization."

Proudhon opposed the charging of interest and rent, but did not seek to abolish them by law: "I protest that when I criticized... the complex of institutions of which property is the foundation stone, I never meant to... forbid or suppress, by sovereign decree, ground rent and interest on capital. I believe that all these forms of human activity should remain free and optional for all." (*Solution of the Social Problem*, 1848-49) He considered that once workers had organised credit and labour and replaced property by possession, such forms of exploitation would disappear along with the state.

Proundhon was a revolutionary, but his revolution did not mean violent upheaval or civil war, but rather the transformation of society. This transformation was essentially moral in nature and demanded the highest ethics from those who sought change. It was monetary reform, combined with organising a credit bank and workers associations, that Proudhon proposed to use as a lever to bring about the organization of society along new lines. He did not suggest how the monetary institutions would cope with the problem of inflation and with the need for the efficient allocation of scarce resources.

He made few public criticisms of Marx or Marxism, because in his lifetime Marx was a relatively minor thinker; it was only after Proudhon's death that Marxism became a large movement. He did, however, criticize authoritarian socialists of his time period. This included the state socialist Louis Blanc, of which

Proudhon said, "Let me say to M. Blanc: you desire neither Catholicism nor monarchy nor nobility, but you must have a God, a religion, a dictatorship, a censorship, a hierarchy, distinctions, and ranks. For my part, I deny your God, your authority, your sovereignty, your judicial State, and all your representative mystifications." It was Proudhon's book *What is Property?* that convinced the young Karl Marx that private property should be abolished.

In one of his first works, *The Holy Family*, Marx said, "Not only does Proudhon write in the interest of the proletarians, he is himself a proletarian, an ouvrier. His work is a scientific manifesto of the French proletariat." Marx, however, disagreed with Proudhon's anarchism and later published vicious criticisms of Proudhon. Marx wrote *The Poverty of Philosophy* as a refutation of Proudhon's *The Philosophy of Poverty*. In his socialism, Proudhon was followed by Mikhail Bakunin. After Bakunin's death, his libertarian socialism diverged into anarchist communism and collectivist anarchism, with notable proponents such as Peter Kropotkin and Joseph Déjacque.

Criticisms

David Leopold, editor of a recent academic edition of Stirner's "The Ego and Its Own", stated "Proudhon played an anti-democratic and counter-revolutionary role in the 1848 French Revolution, accepted slavery in the American South, supported violent strike-breaking, made detailed plans to suppress dissent among his supporters and was a vicious anti-semite."

Stewart Edwards, the editor of the Selected Writings Of Pierre-Joseph Proudhon, remarks: "Proudhon's diaries (Garnets, ed. P. Haubtmann, Marcel Rivière, Paris 1960 to date) reveal that he had almost paranoid feelings of hatred against the Jews, common in Europe at the time. In 1847 he considered publishing...an article against the Jewish race, which he said he 'hated.' The proposed article would have 'Called for the expulsion of the Jews from France... The Jew is the enemy of the human race. This race must be sent back to Asia, or exterminated. H. Heine, A. Weil, and others are simply secret spies. Rothschild, Crémieux, Marx, Fould, evil choleric, envious, bitter men etc., etc., who hate us' (Garnets, vol. 2, p. 337: No VI, 178)".

Zeev Sternhell states in his famous work, The Birth Of Fascist Ideology, that "the Action Française...from its inception regarded the author of *La philosophie de la misère* as one of its masters. He was given a place of honour in the weekly section of the journal of the movement entitled, precisely, 'Our Masters.' Proudhon owed this place in L'Action française to what the Maurrassians saw as his antirepublicanism, his anti-Semitism, his loathing of Rousseau, his disdain for the French Revolution, democracy, and parliamentarianism: and his championship of the nation, the family, tradition, and the monarchy."

Quotes

Proudhon's essay on *What Is Government?* is quite well known:

To be GOVERNED is to be watched, inspected, spied upon, directed, law-driven, numbered, regulated, enrolled, indoctrinated, preached at, controlled, checked, estimated, valued, censured, commanded, by creatures who have neither the right nor the wisdom nor the virtue to do so. To be GOVERNED is to be at every operation, at every transaction noted, registered, counted, taxed, stamped, measured, numbered, assessed, licensed, authorized, admonished, prevented, forbidden, reformed, corrected, punished. It is, under pretext of public utility, and in the name of the general interest, to be place[d] under contribution, drilled, fleeced, exploited, monopolized, extorted from, squeezed, hoaxed, robbed; then, at the slightest resistance, the first word of complaint, to be repressed, fined, vilified, harassed, hunted down, abused, clubbed, disarmed, bound, choked, imprisoned, judged, condemned, shot, deported, sacrificed, sold, betrayed; and to crown all, mocked, ridiculed, derided, outraged, dishonored. That is government; that is its justice; that is its morality. (P.-J. Proudhon, *General Idea of the Revolution in the Nineteenth Century*, translated by John Beverly Robinson (London: Freedom Press, 1923), pp. 293-294.)

Another famous quote was his "dialogue with a Philistine" in *What is Property?*:

"Why, how can you ask such a question? You are a republican."
"A republican! Yes; but that word specifies nothing. Res publica; that is, the public thing. Now, whoever is interested in public affairs -- no matter under what form of government -- may call himself a republican. Even kings are republicans."
"Well! You are a democrat?"
"No."
"What! "you would have a monarchy?"
"No."
" A Constitutionalist?"
"God forbid."
"Then you are an aristocrat?"
"Not at all!"
"You want a mixed form of government?"
"Even less."
"Then what are you?"
"I am an anarchist."
"Oh! I understand you; you speak satirically. This is a hit at the government."
"By no means. I have just given you my serious and well-considered profession of faith. Although a firm friend of order, I am (in the full force of the term) an anarchist. Listen to me."

Bibliography

- 1840 *Qu'est ce que la propriété?* (What is Property?)
- 1842 *Warning to Proprietors*
- 1846 *Système des contradictions économiques ou Philosophie de la misère* (The System of Economic Contradictions or the Philosophy of Misery)
- 1851 *General Idea of the Revolution in the 19th Century*
- 1853 *Le manuel du spéculateur à la bourse* (The Manual of the Stock Exchange Speculator)
- 1858 *De la justice dans la révolution et dans l'Eglise* (Of justice in the Revolution and the Church)
- 1861 *La Guerre et la Paix* (War and Peace)
- 1863 *Du principe Fédératif* (Principle of Federation)
- 1865 *De la capacité politique des classes ouvrières* (Of the Political Capacity of the Working Class)
- 1866 *Théorie de la propriété* (Theory of Property)
- 1870 *Théorie du mouvement constitutionnel* (Theory of the constitutionalist movement)
- 1875 *Du principe de l'art* (The priciple of art)
- 1875 *Correspondances* (Correspondances)

Writers influenced

- Peter Kropotkin
- Benjamin Tucker

See also

- Anarchism
- Co-operative
- Federalism
- Individualist anarchism
- Mutualism (economic theory)
- Property
- Self management
- Socialist economics

Notes

1. ^ Copleston, Frederick. *Social Philosophy in France*, A History of Philosophy, Volume IX, Image/Doubleday, 1994, p. 67

Retrieved from "http://en.wikipedia.org/wiki/Pierre-Joseph_Proudhon"

- This page was last modified 18:33, 15 July 2006.
- All text is available under the terms of the GNU Free Documentation License. (See **Copyrights** for details.)
Wikipedia® is a registered trademark of the Wikimedia Foundation, Inc.

Propaganda of the deed

From Wikipedia, the free encyclopedia

Propaganda of the deed (or *propaganda by the deed*, from the French *propagande par le fait*) is a concept of anarchist origin, which appeared slightly towards the end of the 19th century, that promotes the decisive action of individuals to inspire further action by others.

There is no single definition of propaganda of the deed. Propaganda by the deed shares some similarities with the Marxist conception of *praxis*. Propaganda of the deed may take many forms. The only common definition is that any true propaganda of the deed must take the form of direct action. Although it may involve political violence, that is not necessarily the case, and many anarchists both coherently uphold pacifism and propaganda of the deed [1].

Although the anarchist movement has often been arbitrarily caricatured as a violent and even "terrorist" movement, due in particular to its conception of "propaganda of the deed" and several bombings and assassinations at the end of the 19th century, much direct action does not involve violence, although it may involve illegal activity (such as stealing and other forms of expropriation). In its most simple expression, propaganda of the deed advocates exemplary forms of direct action over wishful thinking and empty theories. As the anarchist communist Peter Kropotkin put it, a single "act may, in a few days, make more propaganda than thousands of pamphlets." [2]

Contents

- 1 Anarchist origins
    - 1.1 Various definitions of propaganda of the deed
    - 1.2 Theorization of propaganda of the deed as a way to accelerate the coming of revolution
- 2 Regicides and other assassinations
    - 2.1 List of assassinated important figures and other propaganda by the deed acts
- 3 Later developments
    - 3.1 The abandonment of bombings, and new forms of propaganda of the deed
    - 3.2 Urban guerrilla groups of the 1970s and the autonomist movement
    - 3.3 Context of 1970s urban guerrilla groups
    - 3.4 Brief timeline of modern propaganda of the deed acts
- 4 Justifications for the political use of violence and "illegalism"
- 5 References
- 6 Bibliography
- 7 See also

Anarchist origins

Various definitions of propaganda of the deed

An early proponent of propaganda by the deed was the Italian revolutionary, Carlo Pisacane (1818-1857), who wrote in his "Political Testament" (1857) that "ideas spring from deeds and not the other way around." Mikhail Bakunin (1814-1876), in his "Letters to a Frenchman on the Present Crisis" (1870) stated that "we must spread our principles, not with words but with deeds, for this is the most popular, the most potent, and the most irresistible form of propaganda." [3]

The phrase "propaganda by the deed" was popularized by the French anarchist, Paul Brousse (1844-1912). In his article of that name, published in the August 1877 *Bulletin of the Jura Federation*, he cited the 1871 Paris Commune, a workers' demonstration in Berne provocatively using the socialist red flag, and the Benevento uprising in Italy as examples of "propaganda by the deed." [4]

Some anarchists, such as Johann Most, advocated publicizing violent acts of retaliation against counter-revolutionaries because "we preach not only action in and for itself, but also action as propaganda." [5] Most was an early influence on American anarchists Emma Goldman and Alexander Berkman. Berkman attempted propaganda by the deed when he tried in 1892 to kill industrialist Henry Clay Frick following the shooting deaths of several striking workers. [6]

By the 1880s, the slogan "propaganda of the deed" had begun to be used both within and outside of the anarchist movement to refer to individual bombings, regicides and tyrannicides. However, as soon as 1887, important figures in the anarchist movement distanced themselves from such individual acts. Peter Kropotkin thus wrote that year in *Le Révolté* that "it is an illusion to believe that a few kilos of dynamite will be enough to win against the coalition of exploiters" [7]. A variety of anarchists advocated the abandonment of these sorts of tactics in favor of collective revolutionary action, for example through the trade union movement. The anarcho-syndicalist, Fernand Pelloutier, argued in 1895 for renewed anarchist involvement in the labor movement on the basis that anarchism could do very well without "the individual dynamiter."[2]

State repression (including the infamous 1894 French *lois scélérates*) of the anarchist and labor movements following the few successful bombings and assassinations may have contributed to the abandonment of these kinds of tactics, although reciprocally state repression, in the first place, may have played a role in these isolated acts. The destructuration of the French socialist movement, divided into many groups, and, following the suppression of the 1871 Paris Commune, the execution and exile of many *communards* to penal colonies, favored individualist political expression and acts. [8]

Other theorists advocating propaganda of the deed included the Italian anarchists Luigi Galleani and Errico Malatesta, although Malatesta was clear that by "propaganda by the deed" he did not mean terrorism, which he rejected as authoritarian, but rather communal insurrections that were meant to ignite a general uprising [9]. For the German anarchist Gustav Landauer "propaganda of the deed" meant the creation of libertarian social forms and communities that would inspire others to transform society [10]. In "Weak Statesmen, Weaker People," he wrote that the state is not something "that one can smash in order to destroy. The state is a relationship between human beings... one destroys it by entering into other relationships" [11]

In 1886, French anarchist Clément Duval achieved a form of propaganda of the deed stealing 15 000 francs from the mansion of a Parisian socialite, before accidentally setting the house on fire. Caught two weeks later, he was dragged from the court crying "Long live anarchy!", and condemned to death. His sentence was later commuted to hard labor on Devil's Island, French Guiana. In the anarchist paper *Révolte*, Duval famously declared that, "Theft exists only through the exploitation of man by man... when Society refuses you the right to exist, you must take it... the policeman arrested me in the name of the Law, I struck him in the name of Liberty".

Theorization of propaganda of the deed as a way to accelerate the coming of revolution

Propaganda of the deed thus included stealing (in particular bank robberies - named "expropriations" or "revolutionary expropriations" to finance the organization), rioting and general strikes which aimed at creating the conditions of an insurrection or even a revolution. Direct actions, including violent ones, were justified as the necessary counterpart to state repression. As sociologist Max Weber had shown, the state has the "monopoly on the legitimate use of physical force", or, in Karl Marx's words, the state was only the repressive apparatus of the bourgeois class. Propaganda by the deed, including assassinations (sometimes involving bombs, named in French "*machines infernales*" - "hellish machines", usually made with bombs, sometimes only several guns assembled together), were thus legitimized by part of the anarchist movement and the First International as a valid means to be used in class struggle. The predictable state repressive responses to such direct actions were supposed to display to the people the inherently repressive nature of the bourgeois state. This would in turn bolster the revolutionary spirit of the people, leading to the overthrow of the state. This is the basic formula of the cycle protests-repression-protests, which in specific conditions may lead to an effective state of insurrection.

This cycle has been observed during the 1905 Russian Revolution or in Paris in May 1968. However, it failed to achieve its revolutionary objective on the vast majority of occasions, thus leading to the abandonment by the vast majority of the anarchist movement of such bombings. However, the state never failed in its repressive response, enforcing various *lois scélérates* which usually involved tough clampdowns on the whole of the labor movement. These harsh laws, sometimes accompanied by the proclamation of the state of exception, progressively led to increased criticism among the anarchist movement of assassinations. The role of several *agent provocateurs* and the use of deliberate strategies of tension by governments, using false flags terrorist actions, achieve to discredibilize this violent tactic to the eyes of most socialist libertarians.

Regicides and other assassinations

Numerous heads of state were assassinated between 1881 and 1914 by members of the libertarian socialist movement. Regicides were for obvious reasons celebrated as popular victory over counter-revolutionary forces, which remained strong a century after the 1789 French Revolution. The first assassinations were carried out by Russian anarchists, which would lead to the creation of the term of "nihilism". For example, U.S. President McKinley's assassin Leon Czolgosz claimed to have been influenced by anarchist and feminist Emma Goldman. This was in spite of Goldman's disavowal of any association with him, his registered membership in the Republican, and never having belonged to an anarchist organization. Bombings were associated in the media with anarchists because international terrorism arose during this time period with the widespread distribution of dynamite. This image remains to this day. Private media are typically hostile to anarchism. As a result, depictions in the press and popular fiction helped create a lasting public impression that anarchists are violent terrorists. This perception was enhanced by events such as the 1886 Haymarket Riot, where anarchists were blamed for throwing a bomb at police who came to break up a public meeting in Chicago, Illinois.

List of assassinated important figures and other *propaganda by the deed* acts:

- **April 4, 1866.** A bullet shot at Alexander II by Dmitry Karakozov misses narrowly. It is the first of many such assassination attempts by revolutionaries. He fails and is hanged, with four others, on September 3.
- **January 1878.** Vera Zasulich shot and wounded General Theodore Trepov, military governor of St. Petersburg, after he had ordered the flogging of political prisoner Arkhip Bogoliubov (real name: Alexander Emelianov). At her trial a sympathetic jury found her not guilty.
- **May 11, 1878.** Failed assassination attempt of Max Hödel against Kaiser Wilhelm I.
- **June 2, 1878.** Failed assassination attempt of Karl Nobiling against the Kaiser.
- **August 1878.** Sergey Kravchinsky stabs to death General Nikolai Mezentsov, head of the Tsar's secret police, in response of the execution of Ivan Kovalsky.
- **February 1879.** Grigori Goldenberg shoots to death the Governor of Kharkov, Prince Dmitri Kropotkin.
- **April 1879.** Alexander Soloviev shoots at Alexander II. This second attempt on the royal's life also fails.
- **November 1879.** Lev Bronstein attempts, without success, to blow up the Imperial railway carriage. His more famous nephew of the same name goes on to become a founding father of the Soviet Union.
- **1880.** Stepan Khalturin's successfully blows up part of the Imperial Palace—8 dead, 45 wounded. Referring to the 1862 invention of dynamite, historian Benedict Anderson observes that "Nobel's invention had now arrived politically." [12]
- **March 1 (Julian calendar) 1881.** Tsar Alexander II is killed in a bomb-blast by Narodnaya Volya.
- **December 9, 1893.** Auguste Vaillant throws a nail bomb in the French National Assembly, killing nobody and injuring one. He is then sentenced to death and executed by the guillotine on February 4, 1894, shouting "Death to bourgeois society and long life anarchy!" (*A mort la société bourgeoise et vive l'anarchie!*). During his trial, Auguste Vaillant declared that he hadn't intended to kill anybody, but only to injure several deputies in retaliation against the execution of Ravachol, who had engaged himself in four bombings.
- **December 11 and 18, 1893.** Vote of the French *lois scélérates*.
- **February 12, 1894.** Emile Henry set a bomb in *Café Terminus*, killing one and injuring twenty. During his trial, he declares: "There is no innocent bourgeois". This act is one of the rare exceptions to the rule that propaganda of the deed targets only specific powerful individuals.
- **June 24, 1894.** Italian anarchist Caserio stabs to death French president Sadi Carnot to avenge Auguste Vaillant and Emile Henry. Caserio is then executed by guillotine on August 15.

- **August 8, 1897.** Michele Angiolillo assassinates Spanish Prime minister Castillo, who had been a key figure in the 1874 overthrow of the Republic, helping the Bourbon monarchy back to the throne.
- **September 10, 1898.** Luigi Lucheni stabs to death with a needle file Elisabeth of Bavaria, Empress consort of Austria and Queen consort of Hungary due to her marriage to Emperor Franz Joseph.
- **July 29, 1900.** Gaetano Bresci shoots dead Umberto I of Italy, avenging the Bava Beccaris massacre in Milan.
- **September 6, 1901.** Leon Czolgosz shoots at point-blank range on U.S. president William McKinley, killing him. He is then killed by electrocution on October 29(Czolgosz' anarchist status is a matter of debate. He attended anarchist meetings and read anarchist texts yet was a registered republican).
- **October 1902.** Gennaro Rubino attempts to execute Leopold II of Belgium.
- **1904.** Yegor Sozonov throws a bomb in Russian minister of Interior von Plehve's carriage, killing him. Sozonov was a member of the Socialist-Revolutionary Combat Group, which was headed by agent provocateur Evno Azef.
- **1905.** Socialist-Revolutionary Ivan Kalyayev kills by a bomb Duke Sergei Alexandrovich, fifth son of tsar Alexander II.
- **February 1, 1908.** Two Portuguese Republicans shoots on King Carlos I and his son Luis Filipe, whom both die. Manuel, the other son who had been injured in the assassination attempt, succeeded to Carlos I.
- **September 14, 1911.** Dmitri Bogrov shoots to death prime minister Pyotr Stolypin.
- **18 March 1913.** Aleksander Schinas assassinates king George I of Greece.
- **1922.** Gustave Bouvet attempts to kill French president Alexandre Millerand.
- **1926.** Sholom Schwartzbard assassinates Symon Petlura, head of the government-in-exile Ukrainian's People Republic, in Paris. After an eight-days trial, he is acquitted by the jury, who has been convinced of Schwartzbard's just cause: the core of his defence was that he was avenging the deaths of victims of pogroms organized by Symon Petlura.

Later developments

The abandonment of bombings, and new forms of propaganda of the deed

Propaganda of the deed, as a violent form of direct action involving bombings and targeted assassinations, was abandoned by the vast majority of the anarchist movement after World War I (1914-18) and the 1917 October Revolution. There are various causes for this, but important factors include state repression (including the use of agent provocateurs and of what would later be called a "strategy of tension"), the level of organization of the labour movement (in particular the new importance of anarcho-syndicalism in European Latin countries such as France, Italy and Spain) and, of course, the influence of the October Revolution on revolutionary theory and means of organization. Although the Leninist thesis of an *avant-garde* party composed of professional revolutionaries didn't break that much with the Socialist-Revolutionary organization, it did make completely individual acts of propaganda of the deed less relevant. Despite this abandonment, the concept of propaganda of the deed remained popular in the anarchist movement, and thus influenced various social and cultural movements, including the Underground, during the 20th century.

For example, the concept of direct action itself continued to be central in the socialist libertarian movement, in particular in the anarcho-syndicalism movement through the concept of the "revolutionary strike" inspired by French theorist Georges Sorel's *Reflections on Violence* (1908). In the 1950s, the Situationist International's conception of creating "situations" may be related quite easily to propaganda of the deed (which is not surprising, given the influence of council communism on Guy Debord). The autonomist movement and urban guerrilla group then took on the concept in the 1970s (*See next section*). It is also during this period that the concept of culture jamming, spass guerrilla, guerrilla communication and other kinds of non-violent and sometimes simultaneously artistic and political acts become popular as a new form of direct action.

The importance of riots and rebellions in the creation of the conditions of an insurrection has never been abandoned, going through anarcho-syndicalism to autonomism and today's anti-globalization mediatic Black blocs.

Urban guerrilla groups of the 1970s and the autonomist movement

The concept of "propaganda of the deed" received renewed attention in the 1970s-1980s, especially among "urban guerrilleros" and the Italian autonomist movement, which had a large part in the creation of the squatting and Social Center movement.

Since some of the most radical autonomist or other far-left activists engaged not only in direct action (stealing, squatting, bank robberies - called expropriations - etc.) but also in assassination and bombing, "propaganda of the deed" again became synonymous (especially in the mainstream media) with terrorism. However, if "terrorism" is defined as the spreading terror among the civilian population in order to influence state policies, in particular through indiscriminate bombings, such bombings would not be classed as terrorist, since they targeted specific important individuals (heads of state - monarchs or presidents - , government officials, military commanders or major business figures). For example, the German Red Army Faction (RAF) kidnapped and murdered Hanns Martin Schleyer, who was president of the German Employer's Association and a former high-ranking SS member during the Third Reich, and targeted NATO centers. In contrast, right-wing Italian terrorist groups such as *Ordine Nuovo* and *Avanguardia Nazionale* engaged in indiscriminate bombings against civilians.

Many of Italy's bombings during the *years of lead* were false flag attacks that were at first attributed to far-left militant groups such as the Red Brigades. Especially after Italian prime minister Giulio Andreotti's October 24, 1990 public revelation of the existence of the Gladio "stay-behind" secret army, it was incrasingly accepted that terrorist attacks such as the May 1972 Peteano attack (carried out by far-right activist Vincenzo Vinciguerra), the December 1969 Piazza Fontana bombing and the 1980 Bologna massacre had actually been carried out not by far-left groups, but by members of *Ordine Nuovo* or *Avanguardia Nazionale*, protected by elements within the Italian secret services, who also cooperated with Propaganda Due masonic lodge, the mafia and the CIA in Operation Gladio [13]. It might be argued that this "strategy of tension", starting with the 1969 Piazza Fontana bombing, achieved its aim of terrorizing the civilian population (even though no state of emergency was declared, defeating the plans of Vincenzo Vinciguerra and other neofascists).

Context of 1970s urban guerrilla groups

The appearance in developed countries during the 1970s of leftist militant groups - such as the Red Brigades, the RAF or the less important French *Action Directe* - which (although they did not claim to be specifically anarchist) did engage in propaganda of the deed, carrying out selective assassinations, must be understood in context. Firstly, these groups were part of a larger social movement, including the autonomist movement in Italy, which practiced various types of direct action other than assassinations (in Italy, shootings in the legs was more often used). Secondly, these groups explicitly theorized their actions from a global point of view, in order to link them with world struggles, whether with the Vietnam War (1965-75) or with South American struggles against military *juntas* (see for example the RAF's actions against NATO and its ideological relations with Uruguayan Tupamaros). Thirdly, at least in Italy, the general context of a "strategy of tension" (*strategia della tensione*) can not be ignored. Figures such as Italian right-wing terrorist Stefano Delle Chiaie, involved in Gladio's strategy of tension, didn't mind occasionnally helping South American dictators. Delle Chiaie was in contact with the Chilean DINA and prepared Christian-Democrat Bernardo Leighton's 1975 failed assassination in Rome, and participated (along with Nazi war criminal Klaus Barbie) in Luis García Meza Tejada's *cocaine coup* in Bolivia; in 1995. Italian attorney general Giovanni Salvi even accused the Italian secret services of having concealed proofs of DINA's involvement in the terrorist attack on Bernardo Leighton.

Brief timeline of modern propaganda of the deed acts:

- **April 20, 1963**. Gabriel Hudon, member of the *Front de libération du Québec* (FLB - National Liberation Front of Quebec) kills a night watchman in a bombing.
- **May 1968**. Riots in Paris. The New-York based group "Black Mask" becomes Up Against the Wall Motherfuckers and carry out propaganda of the deed, excluding assassinations and bombings.
- **October 8, 1969**. The U.S. group Weatherman's first event is to blow up a statue in Chicago, Illinois, dedicated to police casualties in the 1886 Haymarket Riot. The "Days of Rage" riots then occur in Chicago during four days. 287 Weatherman members are arrested, and one of them killed.
- **December 6, 1969**. Several Chicago Police cars parked in a Precinct parking lot at 3600 North Halsted Street, Chicago, are bombed. The Weather Underground Organization (WUO) later stated in their book *Prairie Fire* that they had perpetrated the explosion to protest the shooting deaths of the Illinois Black Panther Party leaders Fred Hampton and Mark Clark two days earlier by police officers.
- **December 12, 1969**. Piazza Fontana bombing (carried out by neofascists), beginning of Italy's *lead of years*. In 1998, David Carrett, officer of the U.S. Navy, was put under investigations on charge of political and military espionage and his participation to the Piazza Fontana bombing, among other events. Judge Guido Salvini also opened up a case against Sergio Minetto, Italian official for the US-NATO intelligence network, and *pentito* Carlo Digilio, who was suspected as a CIA informant. *La Repubblica* newspaper underlined that Carlo Rocchi, CIA's man at Milan, was surprised in 1995 searching for information concerning Operation Gladio, thus demonstrating that all was not over [14].
- **1970-1972**. The British Angry Brigade group carries out at least 25 bombings (police numbers). Almost all property damage, although one person was slightly injured.
- **September 12, 1970**. The WUO helps Dr. Timothy Leary, LSD scientist, break out and escape from the California Men's Colony prison.
- **October 8, 1970**. Bombing of Marin County Courthouse (US) in retaliation for the killing of Black activists Jonathan Jackson, William Christmas, and James McClain.
- **October 10, 1970**. The Queens Courthouse is bombed to express support for the New York prison riots.
- **October 14, 1970**. The Harvard Center for International Affairs is bombed to protest the war in Vietnam.

- **May 1972**. Peteano attack. Although the Italian Red Brigades were accused of it, it would be later discovered that neofascist Vincenzo Vinciguerra was the true responsible of it.
- **September 28, 1973**. The ITT headquarters in New York and Rome, Italy are bombed in response to ITT's role in the September 11, 1973 Chilean coup.
- **November 6, 1973**. The U.S. group Symbionese Liberation Army (SLA) assassinates Oakland, California superintendent of schools Dr. Marcus Foster and badly wound his deputy Robert Blackburn.
- **September 11, 1974**. Bombing of Anaconda Corporation (part of the Rockefeller Corporation) in retribution for Anaconda's involvement in Pinochet's coup exactly a year before.
- **1975**. The German group Movement 2 June kidnaps Peter Lorenz, CDU candidate for mayor in Berlin, who is exchanged against four emprisonned comrades.
- **January 28, 1975**. Bombing of the U.S. State Department in response to escalation in Vietnam.
- **April 21, 1975**. The remaining members of the SLA rob the Crocker National Bank in Carmichael, California and kill Myrna Opsahl, a bank customer, in the process.
- **September 1975**. Bombing of the Kennecott Corporation in retribution for Kennecott's involvement in the Chilean coup two years prior.
- **1977**. Hanns-Martin Schleyer, president of the German Employer's Association and a former high-ranking SS member, is executed by the Red Army Faction (RAF).
- **May 1978**. Italian prime minister Aldo Moro and leader of the Christian Democracy was murdered by the Second Red Brigades, led by Mario Moretti, in obscure circumstances, involving a specific context of strategy of tension deliberately followed by Gladio, NATO's secret paramilitary "stay-behind" organization.
- **May 1, 1979**. French group *Action Directe* carries out a machine gun attack on the employers' federation headquarters.
- **1980**. Bologna massacre. Licio Gelli, head-master of Propaganda Due masonic lodge, would eventually be convicted of a sentence for investigation diversion, while Italian intelligence agents are also involved. Two neofascists are found directly responsible of the bombing (more than 80 killed).
- **May 30, 1982**. The Canadian group Direct Action (aka "Squamish Five") set off a large bomb at an electricity transmission project. Four transformers were wrecked beyond repair, but no one was injured.
- **1984-1993**. Bomb-attacks of the Dutch terrorist organisation RaRa (Radical Anti-Racist Action). 1984: Van Heutsz monument (Van Heutzsch was the Dutch commander during the Aceh War); 1985-1987: several bomb-atacks on the Makro, which was active in South Africa; 1991: the house of state secretary of justice Aad Kosto was blown up; 1993: bomb-attack on the Dutch ministry of social affairs and employment.
- **1985**. *Action Directe* assassinates René Audran, in charge of the state's arms-dealing.
- **July 10, 1985**. The French DGSE secret service sinks the Greenpeace Rainbow Warrior flagship to prevent her from interfering in a nuclear test in Mururoa. Fernando Pereira, a photographer, dies.
- **1986**. Georges Besse, CEO of Renault but before leader of Eurodif nuclear consortium (in which Iran had a 10% stake), is allegedly assassinated by *Action Directe* (although this thesis would be questionned, in particular by investigative journalist Dominique Lorentz).
- **November 30, 1999**. Black blocs destroy the storefronts of The Gap, Starbucks, Old Navy, and other multi-nationals with retail locations in downtown Seattle during the anti-WTO demonstrations.
- **2000**. An Italian parliamentary report from the Olive center-left coalition concluded that the strategy of tension had been supported by the United States to "stop the PCI [Italian Communist Party], and to a certain degree also the PSI [Italian Socialist Party], from reaching executive power in the country". It also stated that "Those massacres, those bombs, those military actions had been organized or promoted or supported by men inside Italian state

institutions and, as has been discovered more recently, by men linked to the structures of United States intelligence." [15]
- **2001**. After the July Genoa G8 summit, the Publixtheatre Caravan, part of the No Border network, is accused of being part of a "criminal organization" called "Black blocs", although such "Black blocs" are not organized and only form themselves on a spontaneous manner during demonstrations, as in the older autonomist movement.
- **May 6, 2002**. Dutch politician Pim Fortuyn, who got millions of Dutch followers by stating that muslims are backward, that the anti-discrimination laws should be terminated and who was in favour of fur, was killed by veganist and left-wing activist Volkert van der Graaf.

Justifications for the political use of violence and "illegalism"

Anarchists and similar radicals often distinguish between their use of political violence and terrorism, arguing that there is a fundamental distinction between indiscriminate bombings carried out against a civilian population, and targeted assassinations carried out against people in positions of political, military or economic power. They emphasize that many scholars define terrorism as the attempt to spread terror in the population through indiscriminate bombings, thus excluding anarchist propaganda of the deed from the definiton of terrorism.

However, even though propaganda of the deed may be distinguished from terrorism, it still often takes the form of violent and illegal actions, which have been theorized as "illegalism". This political use of violence is understood by its proponents in the frame of a general conception of the state as the control apparatus of the bourgeoisie, and of class struggle as a form of effective civil war. The historic conditions of the Cold War and the strategy of tension are also taken into account. Thus, as anarchists often put it, "peace without justice isn't peace", but war between exploited and exploiters. In their eyes, this "social war" morally legitimizes the use of violence against broader "social violence." This view, of course, is not shared by pacifist libertarians. Rioting is thus justified as a means to enhance class consciousness and prepare the objective conditions for a popular uprising. This view of rioting may be one of the most permanent aspect of propaganda of the deed, which runs like a thread from the end of the 19th century and Georges Sorel's theory of the "revolutionary strike" through anarcho-syndicalism and even through surrealist and situationists' provocations, the autonomist and the anti-globalization Black Blocs.

A heated controversy concerning the use of violence continues to take place inside the anarchist movement. Even those who are not opposed to the political use of violence for theoretical reasons (as pacifist anarchists are) may consider it unnecessary and even dangerous strategically speaking, in certain conditions. Many note that the events of 1970s showed clearly how terrorism may be used to influence politics in the frame of the "strategy of tension" by a state and its secret services, through agents provocateurs and false flag terrorist attacks. In Italy and other countries, the *years of lead* led to reinforced anti-terrorism legislation, criticized by social activists as a new form of *lois scélérates* which were used to repress the whole of the socialist movement, not just militant groups. Many also note that the rare cases in which terrorism has achieved its revolutionary aims are mostly in the context of national liberation struggles, while the urban guerrilla movements have all failed.

References

1. ^ It should be noted, however, that most anarchists are not strictly speaking pacifists but rather antimilitarists. This is easily explained by the conception, shared by Marxists, of the state has a repressive bourgeois apparatus and of political domination as a form of violence. See also Pierre Bourdieu's analysis of "symbolic violence" for more discussions about various types of violence.
2. ^ "Spirit of Revolt" by Kropotkin
3. ^ "Letter to a Frenchman on the Present Crisis" (1870) by Mikhail Bakunin
4. ^ Anarchism: A Documentary History of Libertarian Ideas
5. ^ "Action as Propaganda" by Johann Most, July 25, 1885
6. ^ *Prison Memoirs of an Anarchist* (1912) by Alexander Berkman
7. ^ Dynamite had been invented in 1862 by Nobel, who gave his name to the eponymous prize and... to the Nobel peace prize.
8. ^ Historian Benedict Anderson thus writes:

   "In March 1871 the Commune took power in the abandoned city and held it for two months. Then Versailles seized the moment to attack and, in one horrifying week, executed roughly 20,000 Communards or suspected sympathizers, a number higher than those killed in the recent war or during Robespierre's 'Terror' of 1793–94. More than 7,500 were jailed or deported to places like New Caledonia. Thousands of others fled to Belgium, England, Italy, Spain and the United States. In 1872, stringent laws were passed that ruled out all possibilities of organizing on the left. Not till 1880 was there a general amnesty for exiled and imprisoned Communards. Meantime, the Third Republic found itself strong enough to renew and reinforce Louis Napoleon's imperialist expansion—in Indochina, Africa, and Oceania. Many of France's leading intellectuals and artists had participated in the Commune (Courbet was its quasi-minister of culture, Rimbaud and Pissarro were active propagandists) or were sympathetic to it. The ferocious repression of 1871 and after was probably the key factor in alienating these milieux from the Third Republic and stirring their sympathy for its victims at home and abroad." (in Benedict Anderson. "In the World-Shadow of Bismarck and Nobel", *New Left Review*, July-August 2004.)

   According to some analysts, in post-war Germany, the prohibition of the Communist Party (KDP) and thus of institutional far-left political organization may also, in the same manner, have played a role in the creation of the Red Army Faction.

9. ^ "Violence as a Social Factor," (1895) by Malatesta
10. ^ Gustav Landauer, "Anarchism in Germany," 1895[1]
11. ^ *Der Sozialist, 1910)*
12. ^ Benedict Anderson. "In the World-Shadow of Bismarck and Nobel", *New Left Review*, July-August 2004.
13. ^ See Vincenzo Vinciguerra's testimony about the help received from Italian secret services; See also Daniele Ganser, "Terrorism in Western Europe: An Approach to NATO's Secret Stay-Behind Armies" in Winter/Spring 2005 *Whitehead Journal of Diplomacy and International Relations* , and Operation Gladio for more information
14. ^ (Italian) "Strage di Piazza Fontana spunta un agente USA", *La Repubblica*, February 11, 1998. ("A U.S. agent appears in the Piazza Fontana bombing")
15. ^ "*Sennato della Repubblica. Commissione parlamentare d'inchiesta sul terrorismo in Italia e sulle cause della mancata individuazione dei responsabiliy delle stragi: Stragi e terrorismo in Italia dal dopoguerra al 1974.*" Relazione del Gruppo Democratici di Sinistra l'Ulivo, Roma, June 2000. Quoted by Daniele Ganser in NATO's Secret Armies - Operation Gladio and Terrorism in Western Europe, 2005, Frank Cass, London. ISBN 0714685003. See Operation Gladio *for more details*

Bibliography

- Cockburn, Alexander. "Torture, Terrorism and the Rise of the Spanish Anarchists; 'There Are No Innocents'", *Counterpunch*, October 9/10, 2004.
- Hansen, Ann, *Direct Action: Memoirs Of An Urban Guerrilla*, AK Press, 2001
- Christie, Stuart, *Granny Made me an Anarchist: General Franco, The Angry Brigade and Me*, 2002
- Turgenev, Ivan, *Fathers and Sons*, 1862, paints the portrait of Russian nihilists.

See also

- Autonomism movement
- Black blocks in the anti-globalization movement
- Bonnot gang (French group involved in illegalism during the *Belle Epoque*)
- Civil disobedience
- Direct Action
- Draft dodging and military desertions may also be considered forms of propaganda of the deed
- Endorsement terrorism
- Expropriation
- False flag actions
- First International (International Workers Association)
- Greenpeace and the Wild Greens have engaged themselves in direct actions
- Hakim Bey's poetic terrorism
- The Living Theater, a U.S. group in the 1970s which theorized direct action in art
- State Monopoly on the legitimate use of physical force
- Russian Nihilist movement
- Performance, an art concept which may be related to propaganda of the deed under some aspects
- Regicide and tyrannicide
- Strategy of tension
- Urban guerrilla warfare

Retrieved from "http://en.wikipedia.org/wiki/Propaganda_of_the_deed"

This page was last modified 13:35, 10 August 2006.

Leon Czolgosz

From Wikipedia, the free encyclopedia

Leon Frank Czolgosz (May 1873 – October 29, 1901) (also used his mother's maiden name "Nieman" and variations thereof[1]) was the assassin of U.S. President William McKinley. In the last few years of his life, he was heavily influenced by anarchists like Emma Goldman and Alexander Berkman.

Leon Frank Czolgosz

Photo from 1900, found among effects

Early life

Paul Czolgosz, Leon's father

Jacob Czolgosz, Leon's brother

One of seven children of Polish immigrants,[2] Czolgosz was born in Alpena, Michigan[1] in 1873. His family moved to Detroit when he was five years old, and at the age of sixteen he was sent to work in a glass factory in Natrona, Pennsylvania for two years before moving back home.[1]

He left his family farm in Warrensville, Ohio, at the age of ten to work at the American Steel and Wire Company with two of his brothers. At the height of his employment, he was making $4 a day, a high wage at the time.

After the workers of his factory went on strike, he and his brothers were fired. Czolgosz then returned to the family farm in Warrensville.

Interest in anarchism

In 1898, after witnessing a series of similar strikes (many ending in violence), Czolgosz again returned home, where he was constantly at odds with his stepmother and with his family's Roman Catholic beliefs. It was later recounted that through his life he had never shown any interest in friendship or romantic relationships, and was bullied throughout his childhood by peers. [1] He became a recluse and spent much of his time alone reading socialist and anarchist newspapers. He was impressed after hearing a speech by the political radical Emma Goldman, whom he met for the first time during one of her lectures in Cleveland in 1901. After the lecture, Czolgosz approached the speakers' platform and asked for reading recommendations. A few days later, he visited her home in Chicago and introduced himself as *Nieman* (Low German for *new man*), but Goldman was on her way to the train station. He only had enough time to explain to her about his disappointment in Cleveland's socialists, and for Goldman to introduce him to her anarchist friends who were at the train station.[3] She later wrote a piece in defense of Czolgosz.[4]

Czolgosz was never known to be accepted into any anarchist group. Indeed, his fanaticism and comments about violence aroused anarchists' suspicions; some even thought he might have been a covert government agent. Furthermore, Czolgosz was known to have been a Republican (the same party as President McKinley), and had voted in the Republican primaries in Cleveland.[5]

The radical *Free Society* newspaper issued a warning pertaining to Czolgosz reading:

> *"The attention of the comrades is called to another spy. He is well dressed, of medium height, rather narrow shouldered, blond, and about 25 years of age. Up to the present he has made his appearance in Chicago and Cleveland. In the former place he remained a short time, while in Cleveland he disappeared when the comrades had confirmed themselves of his identity and were on the point interested in the cause, asking for names, or soliciting aid for acts of contemplated violence. If this individual makes his appearance elsewhere, the comrades are warned in advance and can act accordingly."*

Czolgosz's experiences had convinced him there was a great injustice in American society, an inequality which allowed the wealthy to enrich themselves by exploiting the poor. He concluded that the reason for this was the structure of government itself. Then on July 29, 1900, King Umberto I of Italy was assassinated by anarchist Gaetano Bresci. Bresci told the press he had to take matters into his own hands for the sake of the common man. The assassination sent shockwaves through the American anarchist movement. In Bresci, Czolgosz found his hero: a man who had the courage to sacrifice himself for the cause. The assassination inspired Czolgosz enough that he went to the trouble to duplicate the event as much as possible, buying the same type Iver Johnson revolver Bresci had used. When he was later arrested, police found a folded newspaper clipping about Bresci in Czolgosz's pocket.

Assassination of President McKinley

A sketch of Czolgosz shooting McKinley.

On August 31, 1901, Czolgosz moved to Buffalo, New York and rented a room near the site of the Pan-American Exposition.

On September 6 he went to the exposition with a .32 caliber Iver-Johnson "Safety Automatic" revolver (serial #463344) he had purchased on September 2 for $4.50.[6] With the gun wrapped in a handkerchief in his pocket, Czolgosz approached McKinley's procession, the President having been standing in a receiving line outside of the Temple of Music greeting the public for ten minutes. At 4:07 p.m., Czolgosz reached the front of the line. The President thrust out his hand; Czolgosz slapped it aside and shot McKinley twice at point blank range.

Members of the crowd immediately subdued Czolgosz, before the 4th Bridgade, National Guard Signal Corps[1] and police intervened. He had been beaten so severely it was initially thought he might not live to stand trial.[7]

Trial and execution

Police mug shot of Leon Czolgosz.

On September 13, the day before McKinley succumbed to his wounds, Czolgosz was transferred from the police headquarters, which were undergoing repairs, to the Erie County Women's Penitentiary until the 16th, after which he was taken to the Erie County Jail before being arraigned before County Judge Emery. After the

Year Four Sourcebook, page 85

arraignment, he was transferred to Auburn State Prison.[1]

A grand jury indicted Czolgosz, who spoke freely with his guards, yet refused all interaction with Robert C. Titus and Lorin L. Lewis, the prominent judge-turned-attorneys assigned to defend him, and with the expert sent to test his sanity.[8]

The district attorney at trial was Thomas Penny and his assistant Mr. Haller, who made a "flawless" performance.[9] Although Czolgosz answered that he was pleading "Guilty", the presiding Judge overruled and entered a "Not Guilty" plea on his behalf.[10]

First photograph of Czolgosz in jail.

He was convicted and sentenced to death on September 23, in a brief trial that lasted eight and a half hours from jury selection to verdict. Upon returning to Auburn Prison, he asked the Warden if this meant he would be transferred to Sing Sing to be electrocuted, and seemed surprised to learn that Auburn had its own electric chair.[1]

So, unlike Lincoln and Garfield's assassins, Czolgosz was tried and executed under state authority, not federal.

He was executed by electrocution, by three jolts at 1700 volts each, on October 29, 1901, in Auburn Prison in Auburn, New York. His brother Waldek and his brother-in-law Frank Bandowski were in attendance, though when Waldek asked the Warden for his brother's body to be taken for proper burial, he was informed that he "would never be able to take it away" and that crowds of people would mob him, so the body had to be buried on prison grounds.[1]

Czolgosz' prisoner card at Auburn.

His last words were "I killed the President because he was the enemy of the good people — the good working people. I am not sorry for my crime." As the prison guards strapped him into the chair, however, he did say through clenched teeth, "I am sorry I could not see my father." Sulfuric acid was thrown into his coffin so that his body would be completely disfigured, resulting in its decomposition within twelve hours.[11] His letters and clothes were burned.

Emma Goldman was arrested on suspicion of being involved in the assassination, but was released because there was no evidence to support this suspicion.

The scene of the crime, the Temple of Music, was torn down in November 1901. A stone marker in the middle of Fordham Drive, a residential street in Buffalo today marks the approximate spot where the event occurred. Czolgosz's revolver is on display at the Pan-American Exposition exhibit of the Erie County Historical Society in Buffalo.

Czolgosz in Film and Pop Culture

The McKinley Monument in front of Buffalo's City Hall

Czolgosz's story was the fictionalized theme of the play *Americans*, by Eric Schlosser.

Czolgosz's story, along with those of 8 other presidential assassins and would-be assassins, was the basis of Sondheim's and Weidman's Broadway musical *Assassins*. His story is told in the song *The Ballad of Czolgosz*.

Czolgosz's activities on the day of the assassination are depicted in Brian Josepher's fictionalized chronicle of the 20th century, *What the Psychic Saw*.

Czolgosz's execution by electrocution was recreated on film by Thomas Edison[12], who also helped invent the Electric Chair.

See also

   Anarchism and violence
   Propaganda of the deed

References

1. ^ <u>a</u> <u>b</u> <u>c</u> <u>d</u> <u>e</u> <u>f</u> <u>g</u> <u>h</u> <u>i</u> Briggs, L. Vernon. "The Manner of Man That Kills", 1921
2. ^ Eric Rauchway, Murdering McKinley: The Making of Theodore Roosevelt's America. New York: Hill and Wang, 2003.
3. ^ Emma Goldman. *Living My Life*. New York: Alfred A. Knopf, 1931. p. 289 and 290
4. ^ American Experience | Emma Goldman | Transcript | PBS
5. ^ Kick, Russ. *You Are Being Lied To*. New York: The Disinformation Company, 2001. p.77 ISBN
6. ^ Leon Czolgosz and the Trial - "Lights out in the City of Light" Anarchy and Assassination at the Pan-American Exposition
7. ^ The Trial and Execution of Leon Czolgosz
8. ^ Andrews, E. Benjamin (1912). *History of the United States*. New York: Charles Scribner's Sons.
9. ^ Dr. McDonald's description of the trial
10. ^ Hamilton, Dr. Allan McLane. "Autobiography". Pre-1921
11. ^ The Execution of Leon Czolgosz - "Lights Out in the City of Light" - Anarchy and Assassination at the Pan-American Exposition
12. ^ Execution of Czolgosz, with panorama of Auburn Prison / Thomas A. Edison, Inc.

This page was last modified on 22 June 2008, at 22:42.

All text is available under the terms of the GNU Free Documentation License.

Francis Schaeffer Study Center
Mt. Juliet, Tennessee

Western Civilization, Year Four
From 1865 to 1990, Reconstruction to Modern Times
Rob Shearer, Tutor

Week Six Reading

The Spanish American War

Spanish-American War

From Wikipedia, the free encyclopedia

Spanish-American War

Charge of the Rough Riders at San Juan Hill
by Frederic Remington

Date:	April 25 – August 12, 1898
Location:	Caribbean and Pacific
Result:	Treaty of Paris: Cuba gains its independence (1902), Spain cedes the Philippines, Guam, and Puerto Rico to the United States for $20 million. Start of the Philippine-American War.
***Casus belli*:**	Cuban rebellion; Sinking of the USS Maine

Combatants

United States Republic of Cuba Philippine Revolutionaries	Spain

Casualties

379 U.S. dead; considerably higher though undetermined Cuban and Filipino casualties	Unknown[1]

The Spanish-American War took place in **1898**, and resulted in the United States gaining control over the former colonies of Spain in the Caribbean and Pacific. The US lost 379 troops in combat and over 5,000 to disease. As a result of the war, Cuba would be declared independent in 1902.

Contents
1 Background
      1.1 Sinking of the USS Maine
2 Declaration of war
3 Theaters of operation
      3.1 The Philippines
      3.2 Cuba
            3.2.1 Colonel Theodore Roosevelt and his "Rough Riders"
            3.2.2 Naval operations in Cuba
            3.2.3 Ground operations in Cuba
            3.2.4 Battle of El Caney and San Juan Hill
            3.2.5 Subsequent operations
      3.3 Puerto Rico
4 Peace treaty
5 Aftermath
      5.1 Effects of the Puerto Rican annexation
6 Propaganda in the War
7 Military decorations
8 Further reading
9 Diplomacy and Causes of the War
10 The War
      10.1 Historiography
11 References
12 Notes
13 External links

Background

By the late nineteenth century Spain was left with only a few scattered possessions in the Pacific, Africa, and the West Indies. Much of the empire had gained its independence and a number of the areas still under Spanish control were clamoring to do so. Guerrilla forces were operating in the Philippines (see Philippine revolution, Philippine revolts against Spain, and Juan Alonso Zayas), and had been present in Cuba since before the 1868-1878 Ten Years' War decades. The Spanish government did not have the financial resources or the personnel to deal with these revolts and resorted to forcibly emptying the countryside and the filling of the cities with concentration camps (in Cuba) to separate the rebels from their rural base of support. Many hundreds of thousands of Cubans died of starvation and disease in these circumstances, 200,000 alone in the more peaceful western Cuba [5]. The Spaniards also carried out many executions of suspected rebels and harshly treated suspected sympathizers. The war saw both Cuban rebels and Spanish troops burning and destroying infrastructure, crops, tools, livestock, and anything else that might aid the enemy. Nevertheless, by 1897 the rebels had mostly defeated the Spanish. They were firmly in control of the eastern countryside and the Spanish could only leave urban centers in columns of considerable strength.

William Randolph Hearst's newspaper in New York documented the atrocities committed in Cuba. The civilian death toll was very high, and a real rebellion was being fought against Spanish rule[6]. Public opinion in Cuba favored American intervention. Joseph Pulitzer was also a key in publicizing the war in New York City. His newspapers, along with Hearst's, practiced yellow journalism in which atrocities in Cuba were exaggerated.

Fueled by the reports of inhumanity of the Spanish, a majority of Americans became convinced that an "intervention" was becoming necessary. Hearst was famously (though probably erroneously) [7] quoted, in a response to a request by his illustrator Frederic Remington to return home from an uneventful and docile stay in Havana, as writing: "Please remain. You furnish the pictures and I'll furnish the war."

Sinking of the USS Maine

On February 15, 1898, an explosion sank the American battleship USS Maine in Havana harbor with a loss of 266 men. Evidence as to the cause of the explosion was inconclusive and contradictory. It might have been an accident, or a Spanish or Cuban mine. Although several newspapers practiced Yellow Journalism in their reporting, most remained cautious. Americans remained unsure of the cause; most blamed the Spanish for not controlling their harbor.

There were, however, very real pressures pushing toward war within Cuba. Faced with defeat, a lack of money, and resources to continue fighting Spanish occupation, Cuban revolutionary and future president Tomás Estrada Palma, then Head of the Cuban Revolutionary Junta, offered $150 million dollars to purchase Cuba's independence, but Spain refused. He then deftly negotiated and propagandized his cause in the U.S. Congress.

Humanitarian interests dominated American opinion. President McKinley and House Speaker Reed worked hard to calm the mood, as did many Republicans, but the pressure from Democrats across the country, steadily increased.

Spain could not back down without creating a crisis at home. Spain was on the verge of civil war and surrender to American demands would be politically dangerous. Much more acceptable to the Spanish was fighting a war (even though they expected to lose). That way the albatross of Cuba could be shed without civil war at home. The U.S. government had considered purchase of Cuba over the years but had always decided against making an offer. No one thought Cuba could be assimilated into the American political system, even if its location was so close. Much of the island's export business and high technology was already in American hands, and most of Cuba's trade was with the U.S. Thus there was no economic need for acquisition of the island, and no major business interests proposed acquisition. Most businessmen opposed war and supported McKinley.

Senator John M. Thurston of Nebraska: "War with Spain would increase the business and earnings of every American railroad, it would increase the output of every American factory, it would stimulate every branch of industry and domestic commerce."

The United States Navy had recently grown considerably and been reorganized, but it was still untested, and Navy leaders hoped war would help it prove itself. To this end, the U.S. Navy drew up contingency plans for attacking the Spanish in the Philippines over a year before hostilities broke out.

Year Four Sourcebook, page 92

1 Spanish infantary uniforms

In Spain, the government was not entirely averse to war. The U.S. was an unproven power, while the Spanish Navy, however decrepit, had a glorious history, and it was thought it could be a match for the U.S. The DeLome Letter was an example of the doubts of Spain as to whether the U.S. was powerful enough to defeat them. There was also a widely held notion among Spain's aristocratic leaders that the United States' ethnically mixed army and navy could never survive under severe pressure.

Declaration of war

2 Wreckage of USS Maine, 1898

U.S. President William McKinley was not inclined towards war, and had long held out against intervention, but the *Maine* explosion so forcefully shaped public opinion that he had to agree. Spanish minister Práxedes Mateo Sagasta did much to try to prevent this, including withdrawing the officials in Cuba against whom complaints had been made, and offering the Cubans autonomy. This was well short of full independence for Cuba, however, and would have done little to change the status quo.

Thus, on April 11, McKinley went before Congress to ask for authority to send American troops to Cuba for the purpose of ending the civil war there. On April 19, Congress passed joint resolutions proclaiming Cuba "free and independent" and disclaiming any intentions in Cuba, demanded Spanish withdrawal, and authorized the President to use as much military force as he thought necessary to help Cuban patriots gain freedom from Spain. (This was adopted by Congress from Senator Henry Teller of Colorado as the Teller Amendment, which passed unanimously.) In response, Spain broke off diplomatic relations with the United States. On April 25, Congress declared that a state of war between the United States and Spain had existed since April 21st (Congress later passed a resolution backdating the declaration of war to April 20th).

Theaters of operation

The Philippines

The first battle was in the Philippines where, on May 1, 1898, Commodore George Dewey, commanding the United States Pacific fleet, in a matter of hours, defeated the Spanish squadron, under Admiral Patricio Montojo y Pasarón, without sustaining a casualty at sea, at the Battle of Manila Bay. The success of the Pacific Fleet was due to the Spanish Navy being trapped in the bay. This naval battle became a textbook example for future Naval commanders.

Meanwhile, Dewey allowed Emilio Aguinaldo to return to the Philippines. Aguinaldo's forces attacked the Spanish on land, successfully defeating them and capturing much of the country, with the exception of Manila which was encircled by the Filipinos. The last significant action on the Philippines ended with the Battle of Manila (July 25 1898 - August 13, 1898) where the Spanish surrendered Manila to the U.S. Army.

3 Staff of the 1st US Volunteer Regiment, the "Rough Riders" in Tampa - LtCol Roosevelt on right.

4 from Charge of the 24th and 25th Colored Infantry and Rescue of Rough Riders at San Juan Hill, July 2nd 1898 depicting the Battle of San Juan Hill. Lithograph by Chicago

Cuba

Colonel Theodore Roosevelt and his "Rough Riders"

Theodore Roosevelt had actively encouraged intervention in Cuba and, while assistant secretary of the Navy, placed the Navy on a war-time footing. He ordered Dewey and the Pacific fleet to the Philippines and he worked with Leonard Wood in convincing the Army to raise an all-volunteer regiment, the 1st U.S. Volunteer Cavalry. Wood was given command of the regiment that became quickly known as the "Rough Riders" because they could not take horses with them to Cuba.

Naval operations in Cuba

The first action in Cuba was the establishing of a base at Guantánamo Bay on 10 June by U.S. Marines (see 1898 invasion of Guantánamo Bay)

Spanish Admiral Cervera, who had arrived from Spain, held up his naval forces in Santiago harbor where they would be protected from sea attack. Assistant Naval Constructor Richmond Pearson Hobson was soon ordered by Admiral Sampson to sink the collier *Merrimac* in the harbor to bottle up the fleet. Hobson modified a broken down collier and gathered a small crew of eight volunteers, and rigged the vessel with explosives. The plan was to sink the *Merrimac* in the narrow entry of Santiago Harbor, trapping the Spanish fleet within the harbor. The mission was a failure. Hobson and his crew were captured. They were exchanged on July 6, and Hobson became a national hero.

Ground operations in Cuba

The Americans planned to capture the city of Santiago in order to destroy Cervera's fleet. The Americans forces would be aided in Cuba by the pro-independence rebels led by General Calixto García.

On June 22 and June 24, the US V Corps under General William R. Shafter landed at Daiquiri and Siboney East of Santiago and established the American base of operations, unopposed by the Spaniards who had retreated under assault by Cuban land forces. An advance guard of U.S. forces under former Confederate General Joseph Wheeler ignored Cuban scouting parties and orders to proceed with caution. They caught up with, and were ambushed by, the Spanish rear guard in the Battle of Las Guasimas. Here, U.S. forces were checked momentarily although the Spanish continued the retreat.

Battle of El Caney and San Juan Hill

On July 1 a combined force of about 20,000 American regular, all-colored Cavalry (as they were known at the time), volunteer regiments, including Roosevelt and his "Rough Riders," and rebel Cuban forces attacked 1,700 entrenched Spaniards in dangerous frontal assaults at the Battle of El Caney and Battle of San Juan Hill outside of Santiago. These assaults were the bloodiest battle in the war with 1,600 American and 593 Spanish casualties. Supporting fire by Gatling guns was critical to the success of the assault [8][9]. It was then that Cervera decided to escape Santiago two days later.

The Spanish forces at Guantánamo were so isolated by Marines and Cuban forces that they did not know that Santiago was under siege, and their forces in the northern part of the province could not break through Cuban lines. This was not true of the Escario relief column from Manzanillo [10] which fought its way past determined Cuban resistance, but arrived too late to participate in the siege.

Subsequent operations

After the battles of San Juan Hill and El Caney, the action was slowed by the successful defenses at and around Fort Canosa [11]. The campaign turned into a bloody strangling siege (Daley, 2000). During the nights, Cuban troops were used to dig successive series of progressively advancing "trenches," which were actually raised parapets. Once completed, these parapets were occupied by US troops and a new set of parapets constructed. The US troops, while suffering some losses from Spanish fire, suffered far more casualties from heat exhaustion and mosquito borne disease (McCook, 1899). At the western approaches to the city Cuban General Calixto Garcia began to encroach on the city, causing much panic and fear of reprisals among the Spanish forces.

The Americans defeated Spanish Admiral Cervera as his fleet left the safety of the port of Santiago in the Battle of Santiago de Cuba and gained control of the waterways around Cuba. This prevented re-supply of the Spanish forces and also allowed the U.S. to land considerable reserve forces unopposed. Within a month most of the island was in US or Cuban hands. Soon the Spanish abandoned Havana under US protection and Cuban harassing fire.

Puerto Rico

5 U.S. 1st Kentucky Volunteers in "Puerto Rico", 1898

During May 1898, Lt. Henry H. Whitney of the United States Fourth Artillery was sent to Puerto Rico on a reconnaissance mission, sponsored by the Army's Bureau of Military Intelligence. He provided maps and information on the Spanish military forces to the U.S. government prior to the invasion. On May 10, 1898, U.S. Navy ships were sighted off the coast of Puerto Rico. Spanish gunners stationed at Fort San Cristóbal, under the orders of Capt. Angel Rivero Mendez, fired the first shot (a 15-cm breech loaded Ordóñez rifle round), missing the USS Yale, an auxiliary ship under the command of Capt. William Clinton Wise. Two days later on May 12, a squadron of 12 U.S. ships commanded by Rear Adm. William T. Sampson bombarded San Juan, Puerto Rico. During the bombardment, many buildings were shelled, terrifying the population of San Juan. On June 25, the Yosemite blocked San Juan harbor.

On July 18, General Nelson A. Miles, commander of the invading forces, received orders to sail for Puerto Rico to land his troops. On July 21, a convoy of 3,300 soldiers and nine transports escorted by the USS Massachusetts sailed for Puerto Rico from Guantánamo, Cuba. On July 25, U.S. troops landed at Guánica, Puerto Rico and took over the island with little resistance.

Peace treaty

With both fleets incapacitated, Spain realized its forces in the Pacific and Caribbean could not be supplied or reinforced, so Spain sued for peace.

Hostilities were halted on August 12. The formal peace treaty, the Treaty of Paris, was signed in Paris on December 10, 1898 and was ratified by the United States Senate on

February 6, 1899. It came into force on April 11, 1899. Cubans participated only as observers.

The United States gained almost all of Spain's colonies, including the Philippines, Guam, and Puerto Rico. Cuba was granted independence, but the United States imposed various restrictions on the new government, including prohibiting alliances with other countries.

On August 14, 1898, 11,000 ground troops were sent to occupy the Philippines. When U.S. troops began to take the place of the Spanish in control of the country, warfare broke out between U.S. forces and the Filipinos. The resulting Philippine-American War was long, bloody, incurring thousands of military and civilian casualties during its fourteen-year span.

Aftermath

6 With the end of the war, Colonel Roosevelt musters out of the US Army at Montauk, Long Island, in 1898

A war that was in part fueled by the American public's ambition to end the abuse of Cuban natives would in the end result in three territorial conquests for the U.S., tens of thousands of Spaniards and Cubans killed, and the deaths of perhaps a quarter of a million Filipinos [12].

The Spanish-American War is significant in American history, as it saw the young nation emerge as an imperial power, though with domains far smaller than Britain or France. The war marked American entry into world affairs; over the course of the next century, the United States had a large hand in various conflicts around the world. The Panic of 1893 was over by this point, and the United States entered a lengthy and prosperous period of high economic growth, population growth, and technological innovation which would last through the 1920s.

The Spanish-American war marked the end of Spain as a colonial power. The defeat paradoxically postponed the civil war that seemed imminent in 1898 and created a renaissance known as the Generation of 1898. The Spanish eventually had a civil war in the 1930s.

Congress had passed the Teller Amendment prior to the war, promising Cuban independence. However, the Senate passed the Platt Amendment as a rider to an Army appropriations bill, forcing a peace treaty on Cuba which severely curtailed its freedom of action in foreign affairs and allowed the United States considerable freedom to intervene in Cuban affairs. It also provided for the establishment of a permanent American naval base in Cuba, which would lead to the base still in use today at Guantánamo Bay. The Cuban peace treaty of 1903 would govern Cuban-American relations until 1934.

The United States annexed the former Spanish colonies of Puerto Rico, the Philippines, and Guam. The idea of the United States as an imperial power with foreign colonies was hotly debated domestically, with President McKinley and the Pro-Imperialists winning their way over vocal opposition. The American public largely supported the possession of colonies, but there were many outspoken critics such as Mark Twain, who wrote The War Prayer in protest.

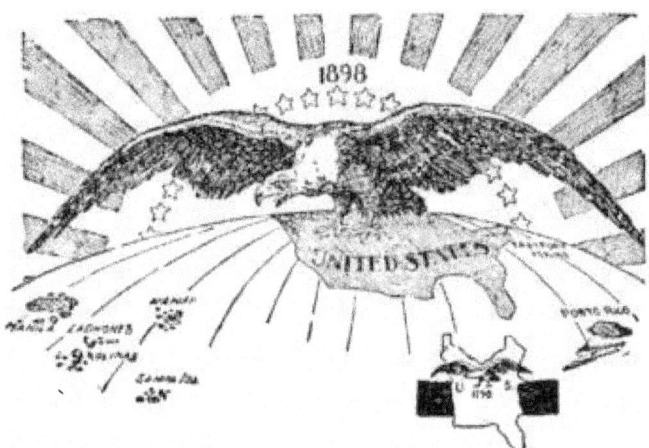

7 1898 political cartoon: "Ten Thousand Miles From Tip to Tip" meaning the extension of U.S. domination (symbolized by a bald eagle) from Puerto Rico to the Philippines. The cartoon contrasts this with a map of the smaller United States 100 years earlier

Mark Twain's writings attacked U.S. Army General Frederick Funston with particular ferocity. However, Funston, who was in the Philippines because, after fighting with Cuban rebel forces [13] [14] he had given his parole [not to again fight in Cuba], is notable for his adroit capture of Emilio Aguinaldo which much decreased the Philippine-American War's intensity, and other deeds which earned him the Medal of Honor [15] and promotion by Lieutenant General Arthur MacArthur, Jr., father of Douglas McArthur

William Randolph Hearst emerged as a national institution: the first media tycoon in American history. The Hearst papers became so extremely successful at agitating public sentiment in favor of war, that he eventually became an archetypal figure in his own right. He had become more influential than even many politicians, and, at various levels, would be sought after for that influence. Decades later, a young filmmaker named Orson Welles would immortalize the Hearst archetype with Citizen Kane, a portrayal which William Hearst, in later life, would find quite displeasing, though he reportedly never saw the film himself.

Another interesting, but little-noted effect of this short war, was that it served to further cement relations between the American North and South. The war gave both sides a common enemy for the first time since the end of the American Civil War in 1865, and many friendships would have been formed between soldiers of both Northern and Southern states during their tour of duty. This was an important development as many soldiers in this war were the children of Civil War Veterans on both sides, and many would have been raised to have opinions of their Northern or Southern neighbors which would steer more towards the negative rather than positive.

8 Segregation in the US Military, 1898

The 1890s were a period of reconciliation between the former Yankees and Confederates, marked by "Blue-Gray" Reunions and increased political harmony between Northern and Southern politicians. The "Lost Cause" view took hold in the popular imagination and many former Confederate leaders were held in general high esteem nationally. The 1890s also saw resurgent racism in the North and the passage of Jim Crow laws that increased segregation of blacks from whites, culminating in the Plessy v. Ferguson decision by the Supreme Court in 1896 that codified the "separate but equal" doctrine into law. The Spanish-American War provoked widespread feelings of jingoistic American nationalism that fused often-divergent Northern and Southern public opinion.

Union and Confederate Veterans had organizations such as the Grand Army of the Republic and the United Confederate Veterans. In 1904, the United Spanish War Veterans was created from smaller groups of the veterans of the Spanish American War. Today, that organization is defunct, but it left an heir in the form of the Sons of Spanish American War Veterans, created in 1937 at the 39th National Encampment of the United Spanish War Veterans.

According to data from the United States Department of Veterans Affairs, the last surviving U.S. veteran of the conflict, Nathan E. Cook, died on September 10, 1992 at the age of 106. (Thus, if the data is to be believed, Cook, born October 10, 1885, would have been a mere 12 years of age when he served in the war.)

Effects of the Puerto Rican annexation

Over 100 years have passed since the Guánica landing, yet the annexation of Puerto Rico continues to be an intensely debated issue today.

"The voice of Puerto Rico has not been heard. Not even by way of formality were its inhabitants consulted as to whether they wanted to ask for, object to, or suggest any conditions bearing on their present or future political status...The island and all its people were simply transferred from one sovereign power to another, just as a farm with all its equipment, houses, and animals is passed from one landlord to another." This statement was part of a pamphlet titled, "The Case of Puerto Rico", written by Dr. Julio J. Henna and Roberto H. Todd, leaders of the delegation that had previously advised President William McKinley on the prospective invasion of Puerto Rico, as part of the War against Spain.

The Spanish-American War was an unexpected twist in the Antillean revolution, a legacy which had seen prominent figures such as José Martí and Ramon Emeterio Betances not only inspire legions to revolt against Spanish rule in the Caribbean, but to form a federation of the Major Antilles, independent of Spain and the United States.

"I do not want us to be a colony, neither a colony of Spain nor a colony of the United States," wrote Betances.

The people of Puerto Rico have thrice voted to remain a commonwealth of the United States, rejecting measures both for independence and for full statehood within the union. As residents of a United States commonwealth, Puerto Ricans are entitled to some of the benefits of statehood. Since they are not allowed to vote for the President they are exempt from Federal income tax. All commerce also is controlled by the U.S. and undergoes extensive Federal regulation and taxation. Puerto Rico has one representative in the U.S. Congress who does not vote except in committee. Puerto Rico's congressman is elected as the Resident-Commissioner of Puerto Rico. Any Puerto Rican law can be repealed by the U.S. at anytime for any reason.

Propaganda in the War

It is said one of the most important aspects of the Spanish-American War is the propaganda. In the 1890s, while competing over readership of their newspapers, William Randolph Hearst and Joseph Pulitzer's yellow journalism are said to sway public opinion and contribute significantly to America's decision to join the Spanish-American War. Yellow journalism, the story goes, the use of sensationalized reporting to form public opinion, was utilized by Pulitzer's New York World and Hearst's New York Journal American. This view proposes, that by reporting graphic stories of embellished, or sometimes falsified, atrocities committed by the Spanish soldiers against the Cuban citizens, Hearst and Pulitzer created public outrage that not only greatly bolstered the sales of their newspapers, but eventually led America into the Spanish-American War. Ultimately, Hearst would defeat Pulitzer in newspaper sales, before going on to pursue political ambitions. [16].

Yellow Journalism is a form of propaganda, according to the idea outlined by Ronald F. Reid. By appealing to the territoriality and ethnocentrism of readers, Hearst and Pulitzer had great influence over American opinion of the Spanish. The Spanish soldiers, portrayed as cruel and bloodthirsty, were accused of countless illegal and immoral acts. Allegations were made that innocent women were strip searched by callous troops, or taken prisoner and thrown into Cuban jails full of violent criminals. These images and stories invoked the public outcry that led to war.

One of the most effective ways to rouse emotion was to portray the victimization of women, the most prominent being Evangelina Betancourt Cisneros. The articles do not only mention Evangelina, but also describe her as an affluent, innocent, and young woman. She was intentionally described this way to invoke a sympathetic response. The response the authors wanted was support for the Cubans. Evangelina Cisneros was, in fact, the daughter of a rebel leader who had been imprisoned. In order to get her father moved to a better prison, Evangelina offered to stay in prison with him. After an incident with a Spanish Colonel, the nature of which is unclear, Evangelina was moved to a much harsher prison.

The Spanish American War also saw the very first use of film in propaganda. A short ninety second film, called *Tearing Down the Spanish Flag*, produced in 1898, was a simple moving image designed to inspire patriotism and hatred for the Spanish in America. This film, as the title suggests, depicts the removal of the Spanish national flag and its replacement by the Stars and Stripes of America. This film was very effective in rousing its audience.

For Further Reading:

Diplomacy and Causes of the War

James C. Bradford , ed., *Crucible of Empire: The Spanish-American War and Its Aftermath* (1993), essays on diplomacy, naval and military operations, and historiography.

Lewis L. Gould, *The Spanish-American War and President McKinley* (1982)

Hendrickson, Kenneth E., Jr. *The Spanish-American War* Greenwood, 2003. short summary

Ernest R. May, *Imperial Demoracy: The Emergence of America as a Great Power* (1961)

Walter Millis, *The Martial Spirit: A Study of Our War with Spain* (1931)

H. Wayne Morgan, *America's Road to Empire: The War with Spain and Overseas Expansion* (1965)

John L. Offner, *An Unwanted War: The Diplomacy of the United States and Spain over Cuba, 1895-1898* (1992).

Offner, John L. "McKinley and the Spanish-American War" *Presidential Studies Quarterly* 2004 34(1): 50-61. Issn: 0360-4918

Pratt, Julius W. *The Expansionists of 1898* (1936)

Schoonover, Thomas. *Uncle Sam's War of 1898 and the Origins of Globalization.* 2003

Tone, John Lawrence. *War and Genocide in Cuba, 1895-1898* (2006)

The War

Benjamin R. Beede, ed. *The War of 1898 and U.S. Interventions, 1898-1934* (1994). an encyclopedia

Donald Barr Chidsey, The SpanishAmerican War (New York, 1971)

Cirillo, Vincent J. *Bullets and Bacilli: The Spanish-American War and Military Medicine* 2004.

Graham A. Cosmas, *An Army for Empire: The United States Army and the Spanish-American War* (1971)

Frank Freidel, *The Splendid Little War* (1958), well illustrated narrative by scholar

Allan Keller, *The Spanish-American War: A Compact History* 1969

Gerald F. Linderman, *The Mirror of War: American Society and the Spanish-American War* (1974), domestic aspects

G. J. A. O'Toole, *The Spanish War: An American Epic--1898* (1984).

John Tebbel, *America's Great Patriotic War with Spain* (1996)

David F. Trask, *The War with Spain in 1898* (1981)

Historiography

Duvon C. Corbitt, "Cuban Revisionist Interpretations of Cuba's Struggle for Independence," *Hispanic American Historical Review* 32 (August 1963): 395-404.

Edward P. Crapol, "Coming to Terms with Empire: The Historiography of Late-Nineteenth-Century American Foreign Relations," *Diplomatic History* 16 (Fall 1992): 573-97;

Hugh DeSantis, "The Imperialist Impulse and American Innocence, 1865-1900," in Gerald K. Haines and J. Samuel Walker, eds., *American Foreign Relations: A Historiographical Review* (1981), pp. 65-90

James A. Field Jr., "American Imperialism: The Worst Chapter' in Almost Any Book," *American Historical Review* 83 (June 1978): 644-68, past of the "AHR Forum," with responses

Joseph A. Fry, "William McKinley and the Coming of the Spanish American War: A Study of the Besmirching and Redemption of an Historical Image," *Diplomatic History* 3 (Winter 1979): 77-97

Joseph A. Fry, "From Open Door to World Systems: Economic Interpretations of Late-Nineteenth-Century American Foreign Relations," *Pacific Historical Review* 65 (May 1996): 277-303

Thomas G. Paterson, "United States Intervention in Cuba, 1898: Interpretations of the Spanish-American-Cuban-Filipino War," *History Teacher* 29 (May 1996): 341-61;

Louis A. Pérez Jr.; *The War of 1898: The United States and Cuba in History and Historiography* University of North Carolina Press, 1998

Ephraim K. Smith, "William McKinley's Enduring Legacy: The Historiographical Debate on the Taking of the Philippine Islands," in James C. Bradford, ed., *Crucible of Empire: The Spanish-American War and Its Aftermath* (1993), pp. 205-49

References

Books

Bryson, G. E. New York Journal. Weyler throws nuns into prison. 17 January 1897.

Cross, W. American Heritage Magazine. The perils of Evangelina. Feb. 1968.

Cull, N. J., Culbert, D., Welch, D. Propaganda and Mass Persuasion: A Historical Encyclopedia, 1500 to the Present. Spanish-American War. Denver: ABC-CLIO. 2003. 378-379.

Daley, L. El Fortin Canosa en la Cuba del 1898. in Los Ultimos Dias del Comienzo. Ensayos sobre la Guerra Hispano-Cubana-Estadounidense. B. E.Aguirre and E. Espina eds. RiL Editores, Santiago de Chile 2000.pp. 161-171.

Davis, R. H. New York Journal. Does our flag shield women? 13 February 1897.

Duval, C. New York Journal. Evengelina Cisneros rescued by The Journal. 10 October 1897.

Everett, Marshall History of the Philippines and the life and achievements of Admiral George Dewey: Also containing the life and exploits of Brig.-Gen. Fred Funston, and ... and the history of American expansion. J.S. Ziegler 1899 ASIN: B00087QNNS

Funston, Frederick. Memoirs of Two Wars, Cuba and Philippine Experiences. New York: Charles Schribner's Sons, 1911

Kendrick M. New York Journal. Better she died then reach Ceuta. 18 August 1897.

Kendrick, M. New York Journal. The Cuban girl martyr. 17 February 1897.

Kendrick, M. New York Journal. Spanish auction off Cuban girls. 12 February 1897.

McCook, Henry C. The Martial Graves of Our Fallen Heroes in Santiago de Cuba. Philadelphia: Jacobs, 1899.

Muller y Tejeiro, Jose. Combates y Capitulacion de Santiago de Cuba. Marques, Madrid:1898. 208 p. English traslation by US Navy Dept.

Rubens, Horatio S. Liberty. The Story of Cuba. AMS Press New York, 1970 reprint of 1932 edition. SBN 404-00633-7

Wheeler, Joseph. The Santiago Campaign, 1898.Lamson, Wolffe, Boston 1898.

U.S. War Dept. Military Notes on Cuba. 2 vols. Washington, DC: GPO, 1898.

Notes

1. ^ McCook (1899 pp. 417-442) who examined each known grave lists each of about 938 dead in his "Index of the Fallen" and mentions 1,415 treated at Siboney Hospital after the battle of San Juan Hill, which would include the numbers killed in the action around fort Canosa (Daley 2000). McCook mentions very few died of wounds (these are included in the Index) once they reached this hospital. This differs from more official US figures: 385 killed in action 1,662 wounded and 2,061 dead from other causes [1]. Patrick McSherry lists for all theaters 332 combat deaths, 1,641 wounded, other causes of death 2,957, for a total of 3,549 US deaths [2]. Although these figures differ in proportions, the sum of US battle casualties in Cuba are congruent at about 2,200. McSherry lists 21 US Military killed in Philippines and Puerto Rico is about the same approximately 2,000 plus 260 sailors dead in the Maine explosion. The number of Spanish dead in and around Cuba including sailors is hard to estimate: "One century after the war experts still do not a clear idea about the Spanish casualties in the Spanish American War". McSherry estimates 5,000–6,000 thousand battle losses between 1895 and 1898 in campaigns against Cuban insurgents. Cuban forces, especially Supreme Cuban commander Máximo Gòmez deliberately lured the Spanish into known fever areas. In addition it is widely reported that it was financially advantageous for the Spanish military field leadership to underreport casualties. Estimates of Spanish losses to the insurgents in the Philippines were not found; however the war is described as bloody [3], such as in "The Siege of Baler"[4]. See individual battle articles for precise losses for each engagement.

This page was last modified 21:29, 14 July 2006.

All text is available under the terms of the GNU Free Documentation License. (See **Copyrights** for details.)

Wikipedia® is a registered trademark of the Wikimedia Foundation, Inc.

Francis Schaeffer Study Center
Mt. Juliet, Tennessee

Western Civilization, Year Four
From 1865 to 1990, Reconstruction to Modern Times
Rob Shearer, Tutor

Week Seven Reading

The Boxer Rebellion

The Boxer Rebellion

From Wikipedia, the free encyclopedia

Boxer Rebellion

Boxer forces (1900 photograph).

Date:	November 1899 - September 7, 1901
Location:	China
Result:	Alliance victory
Casus belli:	Unequal Treaties
Combatants	
Eight-Nation Alliance	Righteous Harmony Society
Commanders	
Edward Seymour Alfred Gaselee	Ci Xi
Strength	
20,000	Over 100,000
Casualties	
230 foreigners, thousands of civilians	Unknown

Summary

The **Boxer Uprising** (Traditional Chinese: 義和團起義; Simplified Chinese: 和 起 ; pinyin: Yìhétuán Qǐyì; literally "The Righteous and Harmonious Fists") or **Boxer Rebellion** (義和團之亂 or 義和團匪亂) was a Chinese rebellion against foreign influence in areas such as trade, politics, religion and technology that occurred in China during the final years of the Qing Dynasty from November 1899 to September 7, 1901[1]. By August 1900, over 230 foreigners, tens of thousands of Chinese Christians, an unknown number of rebels, their sympathizers and other innocent bystanders were killed in the ensuing chaos. The brutal uprising crumbled on August 4, 1900 when 20,000 foreign troops entered the Chinese capital, Peking (Beijing).(pg 232. The search for Modern China, Spence)

Contents

1 Anti-Foreign movement
2 The Rebellion
3 Eight-Nation Alliance
3.1 First intervention
3.2 Second intervention
3.3 Aftermath
4 Results
5 Controversy in modern China
6 In fiction
9 References

Anti-Foreign movement

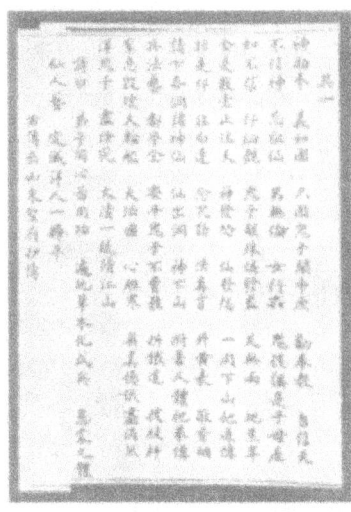

1 Anti-Foreign pamphlet, circa 1899

In 1839, the First Opium War broke out, and China was defeated by Britain. In view of the weakness of the Qing government, Britain and other nations such as France, Russia and Japan started to exert influence over China. Due to their inferior army and navy, the Qing Dynasty was forced to sign many agreements which became known as the "Unequal Treaties". These include the Treaty of Nanking (1842), the Treaty of Aigun (1858), the Treaty of Tientsin (1858), the Convention of Peking (1860), the Treaty of Shimonoseki (1895), and the Second Convention of Peking (1898).

Such treaties were regarded as grossly unfair by many Chinese. They had always considered themselves to be superior to foreigners, but their prestige was sorely damaged by the treaties, as foreigners were perceived to receive special treatment compared to Chinese.

Rumours circulated of foreigners committing crimes as a result of agreements between foreign and the Chinese governments over how foreigners in China should be prosecuted. In Guizhou, local officials were reportedly shocked to see a cardinal using a sedan chair decorated in the same manner as one reserved for the governor. The Catholic Church's prohibition on some Chinese rituals and traditions were another issue of contention.

Thus in the late 19th century such feelings increasingly resulted in civil disobedience and violence towards both foreigners and Chinese Christians.

The rebellion was initiated by a society known as the **Righteous Harmony Society** (義和拳) or in contemporary English parlance, "Boxers", a group which initially opposed, but later reconciled itself, to China's ruling Manchu Qing Dynasty. The Boxer rebellion was concentrated in northern China where the European powers had begun to demand territorial, rail and mining concessions. Imperial Germany responded to the killing of two missionaries in Shandong province in November 1897 by seizing the port of Qingdao. A month later, a Russian naval squadron took possession of Lushun, in southern Liaoning. Britain and France followed, taking possession of Weihai and Zhanjiang respectively.

The Rebellion

2 Boxer forces in Tianjin

Boxer activity developed in Shandong province in March 1898, in response to both foreign influence in the region and the failure of the Imperial court's "self-strengthening" strategy of officially-directed development, whose shortcomings had been shown graphically by China's defeat in the Sino-Japanese War (1894-1895). One of the first signs of unrest appeared in a small village in Shandong province, where there had been a long dispute over the property rights of a temple between locals and the Catholic authorities. The Catholics claimed that the temple was originally a church abandoned decades previously after the Kangxi Emperor banned Christianity in China. The local court ruled in a favor of the Church, angering the villagers who claimed they needed the temple for various rituals and had traditionally used it to practice martial arts. After the local authorities seized the temple and gave it to the Catholics, villagers attacked the church under the leadership of the Boxers.

The early months of the movement's growth coincided with the Hundred Days' Reform (June 11–September 21, 1898), during which the Guangxu Emperor of China sought to improve the central administration, before the process was reversed at the behest of his powerful aunt, the Empress Dowager Cixi. After a mauling at the hands of loyal Imperial troops in October 1898, the Boxers dropped their anti-government slogans, turning their attention to foreign missionaries (such as Hudson Taylor) and their converts, whom they saw as agents of foreign imperialist influence. The Empress Dowager Cixi, who credited the Boxers' claim of magical imperviousness to both blade and bullet, decided to use the Boxers to remove the foreign powers from China. The Imperial Court, now under Cixi's firm control, issued edicts in defence of the Boxers, drawing heated complaints from foreign diplomats in January, 1900.

3 A Boxer Rebel

The conflict came to a head in June, 1900, when the Boxers, now joined by elements of the Imperial army, attacked foreign compounds within the cities of Tianjin and Peking. The legations of the United Kingdom, France, Belgium, the Netherlands, the United States, Russia and Japan were all located on the same city block close to the Forbidden City, built there so that Chinese officials could keep an eye on the ministers - the legations themselves were strong structures surrounded by walls. The legations were hurriedly linked into a fortified compound and became a refuge for foreign citizens in Peking. However the Spanish, Belgian, and German legations were not in the same compound. Although the Spanish and Belgian legations were only a few streets away and their staff were able to arrive safely at the compound, the German legation was on the other side of the city and was stormed before the staff could escape. When the Envoy for the German Empire, Klemens Freiherr von Ketteler, was kidnapped and killed on June 20, the foreign powers declared open war against China. The Chinese Court in turn proclaimed hostilities against those nations, who began to prepare military forces to relieve the besieged embassies. In Peking, the fortified legation compound remained under siege from Boxer forces from June 20 to August 14. Under the command of the British minister to China, Claude Maxwell MacDonald, the legation staff and security personnel defended the compound with one old muzzle-loaded cannon (it was nicknamed the "International Gun" because the barrel was British, the carriage was Italian, the shells were Russian, and the crew was American) and small arms.

Stories appeared in the foreign media describing the fighting going on in Peking. Some were mere rumor or exaggerated the nature of the conflict, but others more accurately described the torture and murder of captured foreigners. Chinese Christians suffered even more greatly, as there were more of them and most were not able to seek refuge in the legations, having to seek shelter elsewhere. Those that were caught were raped as well as tortured and murdered. As a result of these reports, a great deal of anti-Chinese sentiment was generated in Europe, America, and Japan.

Despite their efforts, the Boxer rebels were unable to break into the compound, which was relieved by the international army of the Eight-Nation Alliance in July.

Eight-Nation Alliance

Military of the Powers during the Boxer Rebellion, with their naval flags,
from left to right: Italy, United States, France, Austria-Hungary, Japan, Germany, United Kingdom, Russia.
Japanese print, 1900.

First intervention

Foreign navies started to build up their presence along the northern China coast from the end of April 1900. Upon the request of foreign embassies in Beijing 750 troops, from five countries, were dispatched to the capital on May 31.

←Contingent of Japanese marines who served under the British commander Seymour.

As the situation worsened, a second International force of 2,000 marines under the command of the British Vice Admiral Edward Seymour, the largest contingent being British, was dispatched from Tianjin to Beijing on June 10th. They met however with stiff resistance from Chinese governmental troops. They were finally rescued by allied troops from Tianjin, where they retreated back on June 26, with the loss of 350 men.

Second intervention

With a difficult military situation in Tianjin, and a total breakdown of communications between Tianjin and Beijing, the allied nations took steps to reinforce their military presence dramatically. On June 17th, they took the Taku Forts commanding the approaches to Tianjin, and from there brought more and more troops on shore.

The international force, with British Lt-General Alfred Gaselee acting as the commanding officer, called the Eight-Nation Alliance, eventually numbered 54,000, with the main contingent being composed of Japanese soldiers: Japanese (20,840), Russian (13,150), British (12,020), French (3,520), American (3,420), German (900), Italian (80), Austro-Hungarian (75), and anti-Boxer Chinese troops.

The international force finally captured Tianjin on July 14 under the command of the Japanese colonel Kuriya, after one day of fighting.

Forces of the Eight-Nation Alliance (1900 Boxer Rebellion)			
Countries	Warships (units)	Marines (men)	Army (men)
Japan	18	540	20,300
Russia	10	750	12,400
Great Britain	8	2,020	10,000
France	5	390	3,130
United States	2	295	3,125
Germany	5	600	300
Italy	2	80	
Austria	1	75	
Total	51	4,750	49,255

The capture of the southern gate of Tianjin.
British troops were positioned on the left,
Japanese troops at the center, French troops on the right.

Notable exploits during the campaign were the seizure of the Taku Forts commanding the approaches to Tianjin, and the boarding and capture of four Chinese destroyers by Roger Keyes.

In general, the march, about 120 km, from Tianjin to Beijing by the allies, on August 4, was not particularly harsh despite approximately 70,000 Imperial troops and anywhere from 50,000 to 100,000 Boxers along the way. They only encountered minor resistance and a battle was engaged in Yangcun, about 30 km outside Tianjin, where the 14th Infantry Regiment of the U.S. and British troops led the assault. However, the weather was a major obstacle, extremely humid with temperatures sometimes reaching 110 degrees Fahrenheit (43 Celsius).

4 American troops in China during the Boxer Rebellion

The International force reached and occupied Beijing on August 14.

The United States was able to play a secondary, but significant, role in suppressing the Boxer Rebellion because of the large number of

American ships and troops deployed in the Philippines as a result of the U.S. conquest of the islands during the Spanish American War (1898) and the subsequent Philippine-American War. In the United States military, the suppression of the Boxer Rebellion was known as the China Relief Expedition.

Aftermath

Troops from most nations (bar American and Japanese troops) engaged in plunder, looting and rape. German troops in particular were criticized for their enthusiasm in carrying out Kaiser Wilhelm II of Germany's July 27 order to "make the name German remembered in China for a thousand years so that no Chinaman will ever again dare to even squint at a German". This speech, in which Wilhelm invoked the memory of the 5th century Huns, gave rise to the British derogatory name "Hun" for their German enemy during World War I.

5 Russian troops in Beijing during the Boxer rebellion

On September 7, 1901, the Qing court was compelled to sign the "Boxer Protocol", also known as Peace Agreement between the Eight-Nation Alliance and China, undertaking to execute ten officials linked to the outbreak and to pay war reparations of $333 million. Much of it was later earmarked by both Britain and the U.S. for the education of Chinese students at overseas institutions, subsequently forming the basis of Tsinghua University. The British signatory of the Protocol was Sir Ernest Satow.

The court's humiliating failure to defend China against the foreign powers contributed to the growth of republican feeling, which was to culminate a decade later in the dynasty's overthrow and the establishment of the Republic of China.

The foreign privileges which had angered Chinese people were largely cancelled in the 1930s and 1940s.

Russia had meanwhile been busy (October 1900) with occupying much of the north-eastern province of Manchuria, a move which threatened Anglo-American hopes of maintaining what remained of China's territorial integrity and openness to commerce (the "Open Door Policy") to all comers, but paid the concept only lip service. This behavior led ultimately to a disastrous Russian defeat (conflict) at the hands of an increasingly confident Japan (1904-1905), as they maintained garrisons and improved fortifications between Port Arthur and Harbin along the southern spur line of the Manchurian Railway constructed on their leased lands.

Results

During the incident, 48 Catholic missionaries and 18,000 members were killed, along with 182 Protestant missionaries and 500 Chinese Christians.

The effect on China was a weakening of the dynasty, although it was temporarily sustained by the Europeans who were under the impression that the Boxer Rebellion was anti-Qing. China was also forced to pay almost $333 million in reparations. China's defenses were weakened, and the aunt (Dowager Cixi) of the reigning Guangxu Emperor, who was the actual person in command of the country at that time, realized that in order to survive, China would have to reform, despite her previous opposition. Among the Imperial powers, Japan gained prestige due to its military aid in suppressing the Boxer Rebellion and was first seen as a power. Its clash with Russia over the Liaodong and other provinces in eastern Manchurian, long considered by the Japanese as part of their sphere of influence led to the Russo-Japanese War when two years of negotiations broke down in February 1904. Germany, as mentioned above, earned itself the nickname "Hun" and occupied Qingdao bay, consequently fortifying to serve as Germany's primary naval base in East Asia. The Russian Lease of the Liaodong (1898) was confirmed. The American U.S. 9th Infantry Regiment earned the nickname "Manchus" for its actions during this campaign. Current members of the regiment (stationed in Camp Casey, South Korea) still do a commemorative 25-mile (40 km) footmarch every quarter in remembrance of the brutal fighting. Soldiers who complete this march are authorized to wear a special belt buckle that features a Chinese imperial dragon on their uniforms.

Controversy in modern China

Though the reaction of the Boxers against foreign imperialism in China is regarded by some as patriotic, the violence that they caused in committing acts of murder, robbery, vandalism and arson cannot be considered much different from the events of other rebellions in China, if not worse. Some people in China consider this movement as a rebellion (亂; disorder; Mandarin Pinyin: luàn), a negative term in Chinese language, when described by commentators during the years of the Qing dynasty and Republic of China. However, Chinese Communists have shifted the perception of the rebellion by referring to it as an uprising (起義; being upright; qǐyì), a more positive term in the Chinese language. It is frequently referred to as a "patriotic movement" in the People's Republic of China by Communist politicians.

In January 2006, Freezing Point, a weekly supplement to the China Youth Daily newspaper, was closed partly due to its running of an essay by Yuan Weishi (History professor at Zhongshan University) that criticised the way in which the Boxer Rebellion and 19th century history about foreign interaction with China was portrayed in Chinese textbooks and taught at school. [1]

Nevertheless, Chinese people used to be very sensitive towards the history of foreign imperialism in the late 19th and the early 20th century. The kind of anti-foreignism still persists under the surface. It may be due to this, together with the view imposed by the Chinese Government, that many Chinese people do not regard this as a rebellion.

In fiction

6 Lobby Card for 55 Days at Peking

The events were made into the 1963 film, 55 Days at Peking. The film, which was shot in Spain, needed thousands of Chinese extras, and the company sent scouts throughout Spain to hire as many as they could find. The result was that many Chinese restaurants in Spain closed for the duration of the filming because the restaurant staff--often the restaurant's owners--were hired away by the film company. The company hired so many that for several months there was scarcely a Chinese restaurant to be found open in the entire country.[2]

In 1975, Hong Kong's Shaw Brothers studio made a movie, titled *Pa kuo lien chun*, of the events, giving director Chang Cheh one of the highest budgets up to that time to tell a sweeping story of disillusionment and revenge. [2] It depicts followers of the Boxer clan being duped into believing they were impervious to attacks by firearms. The fight sequences were choreographed by Liu Chia-Liang (Lau Kar Leung) and it starred Alexander Fu Sheng as well as Wang Lung-Wei.

In the 1995 postcyberpunk novel, *The Diamond Age*, by Neal Stephenson, the Boxer Rebellion is vaguely retold in a 2100s Shanghai setting.

In the television series, *Buffy the Vampire Slayer*, it was during the Boxer rebellion that the vampire Spike killed his first slayer - a young Chinese woman named Xin Rong.

The popular film series, *Once Upon a Time in China*, starring Jet Li as the legendary martial artist/Chinese doctor Wong Fei Hung, conveys the ambiance and tumult of this time period with many historic events woven into the plotlines.

In the movie, *Shanghai Knights*, the Boxers, led by Wu Chow and backed by British Lord Nelson Rathbone, killed Chon Wang and Chon Lin's father, attempt to assassinate Queen Victoria, unite the Emperor's enemies and storm the Forbidden City in order for their leaders to become King of the United Kingdom and Emperor of China, but they fail.

The novel, *Moment In Peking*, by Lin Yutang, opens during the Boxer Rebellion, and provides a child's-eye view of the turmoil through the eyes of the protagonist.

The novel, *Los Impostores* (The Impostors), by Colombian fiction author Santiago Gamboa, deals with a modern day Boxer sect and its members' efforts to recover a sacred Boxer text held by Catholic priests in China.

References

- *The Boxer Rebellion* by Diana Preston, Berkley Books, New York, 2000 ISBN 0-425-18084-0
- *Dragon Lady: The Life and Legend of the Last Empress of China* by Sterling Seagrave, Vintage Books, New York, 1992 ISBN 0-679-73369-8 This book challenges the notion that the Empress-Dowager used the Boxers. She is portrayed sympathetically.
- *The dragon empress : life and times of Tz'u-hsi 1835-1908 : empress dowager of China* by Marina Warner, Vintage, UK, US 1993, ISBN 0099165910

This page was last modified 16:34, 14 July 2006.

Francis Schaeffer Study Center
Mt. Juliet, Tennessee

Western Civilization, Year Four
From 1865 to 1990, Reconstruction to Modern Times

Rob Shearer, Tutor

Week Eight Reading
Theodore Roosevelt

Theodore Roosevelt

From Wikipedia, the free encyclopedia

Theodore Roosevelt

26th President of the United States
In office
September 14, 1901 – March 3, 1909

Vice President(s)	*None* (1901-1905) Charles Warren Fairbanks (1905-1909)
Preceded by	William McKinley
Succeeded by	William Howard Taft
Born	October 27, 1858 New York City, New York, in Gramercy, Manhattan
Died	January 6, 1919 Oyster Bay, New York
Political party	Republican Party
Spouse	1st: Alice Hathaway Lee Roosevelt; 2nd: Edith Carow Roosevelt
Religion	Dutch Reformed
Signature	*Theodore Roosevelt*

25th Vice President of the United States
In office
March 4, 1901 – September 14, 1901

President	William McKinley
Preceded by	Garret Hobart
Succeeded by	Charles W. Fairbanks

Theodore Roosevelt, Jr. (October 27, 1858 – January 6, 1919), also known as **T.R.** and to the public as **Teddy**, was the 26th President of the United States (1901–1909). He was the 25th Vice President before becoming President upon the assassination of President William McKinley. At age 42, he was the youngest President. Within the Republican Party he was a Progressive reformer who sought to bring his party's conservative ideals into the 20th century. He broke with his friend and appointed successor William Howard Taft and ran as a third-party candidate in 1912 on the Progressive Party ticket.

Before 1901, Roosevelt served as a New York State assemblyman, Police Commissioner of New York City, U.S. Civil Service Commissioner, and Assistant Secretary of the U.S. Navy. He organized and helped command the First U.S. Volunteer Cavalry Regiment, the "Rough Riders", during the Spanish-American War. As a war hero he was elected Republican governor of New York in 1898. He was a professional historian, naturalist and explorer of the Amazon Basin; his 35 books, listed online [1], include works on outdoor life, natural history, U.S. Western and political history, and his autobiography.

Roosevelt understood the strategic significance of the Panama Canal, and negotiated for the U.S. to take control of its construction in 1904. It was completed in 1914, after he left office. He felt that the Canal's completion was his most important and historically significant international achievement. He was the first American to be awarded the Nobel Prize, winning its Peace Prize in 1906 for his successful mediation of the Russo-Japanese War. He was posthumously awarded the Medal of Honor in January 2001. He preached and lived the "strenuous life," ridiculing the sedentary life of luxury and attempting the most strenuous and dangerous feats--which finally cost him his life. [Dalton 2002] Historian Thomas Bailey once concluded, "Roosevelt was a great personality, a great activist, a great preacher of the moralities, a great controversialist, a great showman. He dominated his era as he dominated conversations....the masses loved him; he proved to be a great popular idol and a great vote getter." [1] His image stands alongside George Washington, Thomas Jefferson and Abraham Lincoln on the Mount Rushmore monument. Surveys of scholars have consistently ranked him from #3 to #7 on the list of greatest American presidents. On June 26, 2006, Roosevelt, once again, made the cover of Time Magazine with the lead story, "The Making of Modern America - The 20th Century Express": "At home and abroad, Theodore Roosevelt was the locomotive President, the man who drew his flourishing nation into the future." [2]

Contents

- 1 Childhood and education
- 2 Early life
    - 2.1 Early public life
    - 2.2 First marriage
    - 2.3 Life in Badlands and second marriage
- 3 Return to public life
- 4 Assistant Secretary of the Navy
    - 4.1 War in Cuba
    - 4.2 Vice presidency
- 5 Presidency 1901-1909
    - 5.1 Anthracite coal strike of 1902
    - 5.2 Square Deal
    - 5.3 Regulation of industry
    - 5.4 Conservationist
    - 5.5 Foreign policy
        - 5.5.1 Panama Canal
        - 5.5.2 The Great White Fleet
    - 5.6 Life in White House
    - 5.7 Presidential firsts
    - 5.8 Administration and Cabinet
    - 5.9 Supreme Court appointments
    - 5.10 States admitted to the Union
- 6 Post-presidency
    - 6.1 African safari
    - 6.2 Republican Party rift
    - 6.3 Election of 1912
    - 6.4 South American expedition
    - 6.5 Writer
    - 6.6 First World War
- 7 Last years
- 8 Personal life
- 9 Legacy
    - 9.1 Popular culture
- 10 Media
- 11 See also
- 12 References
    - 12.1 Primary sources
    - 12.2 Secondary sources
- 13 External links
    - 13.1 Notes

Childhood and education

Roosevelt was born at 28 East 20th Street in the modern-day Gramercy section of New York City on October 27, 1858, the second of four children of Theodore Roosevelt, Sr. (1831–1878) and Martha Bulloch (1834–1884). He had an elder sister Anna, nicknamed "Bamie" as a child and "Bye," as an adult for being always on the go; and two younger siblings—his brother Elliott (the father of Eleanor Roosevelt), and his sister Corinne. The Roosevelts had been in New York since the mid 17th century and had grown with the emerging New York commerce class after the American Revolution. Until the birth of the Republican Party, just before the Civil War, the family was strongly Democratic in its political outlook. By the 18th Century, the family had grown in wealth, power and influence from the profits of several businesses including hardware and plate-glass importing. Theodore's father, known in the family as "Thee," was a New York City philanthropist, merchant, and partner in the family glass-importing firm Roosevelt and Son. Martha Bulloch was a Southern belle from a slave-owning family in Georgia and had Confederate sympathies. On his mother's side, Theodore's uncle, James Dunwoody Bulloch, "Uncle Jimmy," was a 14 year U.S. Navy officer turned secret Confederate naval procurement agent in England. James' brother Irvine Bulloch was the youngest officer on the Confederate raider, CSS Alabama and both had been exiled to Liverpool, England after the war. During the Civil War, Martha supported her southern relatives' struggles and quietly mailed packages south.

Sickly and asthmatic as a youngster, Roosevelt had to sleep propped up in bed or slouching in a chair during much of his early childhood, and had frequent ailments. Despite his illnesses, he was a hyperactive and often mischievous young man. His lifelong interest in zoology was formed at age seven upon seeing a dead seal at a local market. After obtaining the seal's head, the young Roosevelt and two of his cousins formed what they called the "Roosevelt Museum of Natural History". Learning the rudiments of taxidermy, he filled his makeshift museum with many animals that he caught, studied, and prepared for display. At age nine, he codified his observation of insects with a paper titled "The Natural History of Insects." [3]

To combat his poor physical condition, his father compelled the young Roosevelt to take up exercise. To deal with bullies, Roosevelt started boxing lessons. [4]

Two trips abroad had a permanent impact: family tours of Europe in 1869 and 1870, and of the Middle East 1872 to 1873.

The *pater familias* of the Roosevelts, Theodore Sr., who was also known to friends and family as "Great Heart," was more than an ordinary father to Roosevelt. He had a tremendous influence on young Theodore and was a life-long source of inspiration. Of him Roosevelt wrote, "My father, Theodore Roosevelt, was the best man I ever knew. He combined strength and courage with gentleness, tenderness, and great unselfishness. He would not tolerate in us children selfishness or cruelty, idleness, cowardice, or untruthfulness." [5] Some Roosevelt biographers have argued that the senior Roosevelt's influence served as a check on negative aspects of his son's adult personality. From childhood on, Roosevelt wanted to live up to the ideals instilled in him by his father. Roosevelt's sister later wrote, "He told me frequently that he never took any serious step or made any vital decision for his country without thinking first what position his father would have taken."[6]

Young "Teedie," as he was nicknamed as a child [7], was mostly homeschooled by tutors and his parents. A leading biographer says: "The most obvious drawback to the home schooling Roosevelt received was uneven coverage of the various areas of human knowledge." He was solid in geography (thanks to his careful observations on all his travels) and very well read in history, strong in biology, French and German, but deficient in mathematics, Latin and Greek. [8]. He matriculated at Harvard College in 1876. His father's death in 1878 was a tremendous blow, but Roosevelt redoubled his activities. He did well in science, philosophy and rhetoric courses but fared poorly in Latin and Greek. He studied biology with great interest and indeed was already an accomplished naturalist and published ornithologist. He had a photographic memory and developed a life-long habit of devouring books, memorizing every detail[9]. He was an unusually eloquent conversationalist who, throughout his life, sought out the company of the smartest men and women. He could multitask in extraordinary fashion, dictating letters to one secretary and memoranda to another, while browsing through a new book. As an adult, a visitor would get a not so subtle hint that he was losing interest in the conversation at when he would pick up a book and begin looking at it now and then as the conversation continued.

While at Harvard, Roosevelt was active in numerous clubs, including Delta Kappa Epsilon and Alpha Delta Phi fraternities. He also edited a student magazine. He was runner-up in the Harvard boxing championship, losing to C.S. Hanks. The sportsmanship Roosevelt showed in that fight was long remembered. [10]

He graduated Phi Beta Kappa and *magna cum laude* (22nd of 177) from Harvard in 1880 [11], and entered Columbia Law School. Finding law boring, however, he researched and wrote his first major book, "The Naval War of 1812", in 1882, which still is considered the only comprehensive history on the subject. [12] Presented with an opportunity to run for New York Assemblyman in 1881, he dropped out of law school to pursue his new goal of entering public life. [13]

Early life

Roosevelt as NY State Assemblyman 1883, photo

Early public life

Roosevelt was a Republican activist during his years in the Assembly, writing more bills than any other New York state legislator. Already a major player in state politics, he attended the Republican National Convention in 1884 and fought alongside the Mugwump reformers who opposed the Stalwarts; they lost to the conservative faction that nominated James G. Blaine. Refusing to join other Mugwumps in supporting Grover Cleveland, the Democratic nominee, he stayed loyal to the party and supported Blaine.[14]

First marriage

At the age of 22, Roosevelt married his first wife, 19-year-old Alice Hathaway Lee, on October 27, 1880, at the Unitarian Church in Brookline, Massachusetts. Alice was the daughter of the prominent banker George Cabot Lee and Caroline Haskell Lee. The couple first met in 1878. He proposed in June 1879. However, Alice waited another six months before accepting the proposal. They announced their engagement on Valentine's Day 1880. Alice Roosevelt died exactly four years later, only two days after the birth of their first child, also named Alice. In a tragic coincidence, Roosevelt's mother died of typhoid fever on the same day at the Roosevelt family home in Manhattan.

Diary Entry Feb 14, 1884

[15] Roosevelt was beyond consolation. After drawing a large "X" in his diary, he wrote, "The light has gone out of my life."

Although he noted her loss in his diary and made several references to her in the subsequent months, from the next year on Roosevelt refused to speak his first wife's name again (even omitting her name from his autobiography) and did not allow others to speak of her in his presence. He came to despise his popular nickname "Teddy", both because he thought it undignified and because it was the lover's name used by his first wife.

Later that year, Roosevelt left the General Assembly and his infant daughter Alice, whom he had left in the long-term care of his older sister, Bamie. He moved to his ranch in the Badlands of the Dakota Territory to live a more simple life as a rancher and lawman.

This practice put an early strain on his relationship with his daughter who was given his late wife's name. However, as she grew into adulthood and better understood her father's deep moral convictions, the bond between them became strong. Alice continued to support her father's ideas after his death in 1919.

Life in Badlands and second marriage

Theodore Roosevelt as Badlands hunter in 1885. New York studio photo. Note the engraved knife and rifle courtesy of Tiffany and Co.

Living near the boomtown of Medora, North Dakota, Roosevelt learned to ride and rope, occasionally getting involved in fistfights, and spent his time in the rough-and-tumble world of the final days of the American Old West. On one occasion, as a deputy sheriff, he hunted down three outlaws taking a stolen boat down the Little Missouri River, successfully taking them back overland for trial.

While working on a tough project aimed at hunting down a group of relentless horse thieves, Roosevelt came across the famous Deadwood Sheriff Seth Bullock. The two would remain friends for life. (Morris, Rise of, 241-245, 247-250)

After the 1886-1887 winter wiped out his herd of cattle and

his $60,000 investment (together with those of his competitors), he returned to the East, where in 1885, he had purchased *Sagamore Hill* in Oyster Bay, New York. It would be his home and estate until his death. Roosevelt ran as the Republican candidate for mayor of New York City in 1886, coming in a distant third.

Following the election, he went to London in 1886 and married his childhood sweetheart, Edith Kermit Carow. [16] They honeymooned in Europe, and Roosevelt climbed Mont Blanc, leading only the third expedition of record to reach the summit. They had five children: Theodore Jr., Kermit, Ethel Carow, Archibald Bulloch "Archie", and Quentin. Although Roosevelt's father was also named Theodore Roosevelt, he died while the future president was still childless and unmarried, so the future President Roosevelt took the suffix of Sr. and subsequently named his son Theodore Roosevelt, Jr. Because Roosevelt was still alive when his grandson and namesake was born, his grandson was named Theodore Roosevelt III, and the president's son retained the Jr. after his father's death.

Roosevelt is the only President to have become a widower and remarry before becoming President.

In the 1880s, he gained recognition as a serious historian. His *The Naval War of 1812* (1882) was the standard history for two generations, but his hasty biographies of Thomas Hart Benton (1887) and Gouverneur Morris (1888) were potboilers. His major achievement was a four-volume history of the frontier, *The Winning of the West* (1889-1896), which had a notable impact on historiography as it presented a highly original version of the frontier thesis elaborated upon in 1893 by his friend Frederick Jackson Turner. His many articles in upscale magazines provided a much-needed income, as well as cementing a reputation as a major national intellectual. He was later chosen president of the American Historical Association.

Return to public life

In the 1888 presidential election, Roosevelt campaigned for Benjamin Harrison in the Midwest. President Harrison appointed Roosevelt to the United States Civil Service Commission, where he served until 1895. [17] In his term, he vigorously fought the spoilsmen and demanded the enforcement of civil service laws. In spite of Roosevelt's support for Harrison's reelection bid in the presidential election of 1892, the eventual winner, Grover Cleveland (a Bourbon Democrat), reappointed him to the same post.

In 1895, he became president of the New York City Board of Police Commissioners. During the two years that he held this post, Roosevelt radically changed the way a police department was run. He required his officers to be registered with the Board and to pass a physical fitness test. He also had telephones installed in station houses. Always an energetic man, he made a habit of walking officers' beats late at night and early in the morning to make sure that they were on duty. He also engaged a pistol expert to teach officers how to shoot their firearms. While serving on the Board, he opened job opportunities in the department to women and Jews for the first time. [18]

Assistant Secretary of the Navy

Assistant Secretary of the Navy Roosevelt (front center) at the Naval War College, c. 1897

Roosevelt had always been fascinated by navies and their history. Urged by Roosevelt's close friend, Congressman Henry Cabot Lodge, President William McKinley appointed a delighted Roosevelt to the post of Assistant Secretary of the Navy in 1897. (Because of the poor health and inactivity of the Secretary of the Navy John D. Long at the time, this basically gave Roosevelt reign over the department.)

Roosevelt had grown up fascinated with stories of naval battles by his mother and his uncles in Liverpool. Roosevelt had persistently encouraged his uncle James Dunwoody Bulloch to tell his unique story of Confederate operations in Britain during the Civil War and the secret fitting-out of such ships as the CSS Alabama on which Bulloch's brother Irvine had served as its youngest officer. His uncle in turn had helped him develop his ideas that led to his War of 1812 naval history. In that book, Roosevelt explained how near criminal neglect of Naval issues and apathy toward British seapower had almost led to the destruction of the new country. It was only the nautical skills of the commanders and the training and ship handling skills of the crews that had saved the Navy and the country. The overwhelming seapower of Britain had shaped every aspect of the war and made the events on land, to Roosevelt, seem almost secondary until the Battle of New Orleans. The book was but the first link in the chain of Roosevelt's developing views of the importance of a strong Navy to the security of the United States.

Concurrently with Roosevelt's arrival in Washington, D.C., a contemporary and friend, Alfred Thayer Mahan, who had met Roosevelt in 1887, had organized his earlier Naval War College lectures into his seminal book, *The Influence of Sea Power upon History, 1660-1783*. Roosevelt read it in a single weekend during the summer of 1890 and immediately appreciated its importance. But the book, while revolutionary to many Americans, simply reinforced Roosevelt's own understanding of the role that Navies would play on the world stage. His view was that only a dramatic expansion of the Navy into a service with a global reach would put the United States on par with the growing naval might of European nations and Japan. When asked to speak to the Naval War College, the scope and force of Roosevelt arguments stunned both the Secretary of the Navy as well as the President, as they had not been approved by either man. But so persuasive was Roosevelt's speech, that neither man publicly repudiated him. Within days of becoming assistant secretary, Roosevelt was pushing for the modernization of the Navy and the reorganization of both the Department and its officer corps. He also fought for an increase in ship-building capability, warning that building modern steel ships would take years instead of the mere weeks of construction in the age of sail.

Roosevelt was instrumental in consciously preparing the Navy for what he saw as an unavoidable conflict with Spain. Events would prove him right. During the Spanish-American War, the U.S. Navy searched the world for ships to support world-wide operations.

War in Cuba

Roosevelt left his civilian Navy post to form the famous "Rough Riders" Regiment

Colonel Roosevelt and his "Rough Riders" after capturing San Juan Hill during the Spanish-American War

Upon the declaration of war in 1898 that would be known as the Spanish-American War, Roosevelt resigned from the Navy Department and, with the aid of U.S. Army Colonel Leonard Wood, organized the First U.S. Volunteer Cavalry Regiment out of a diverse crew that ranged from cowboys from the Western territories to Ivy League friends from New York. The newspapers called them the "Rough Riders." Originally Roosevelt held the rank of Lieutenant Colonel and served under Colonel Wood, but after Wood was promoted to Brigadier General of Volunteer Forces, Roosevelt was promoted to Colonel and given command of the Regiment. Under his leadership, the Rough Riders became famous for their dual charges up Kettle Hill and San Juan Hill in July 1898 (the battle was named after the latter hill). [19] Roosevelt was posthumously awarded the Medal of Honor in 2001 for his actions.

Upon his return from Cuba, Roosevelt re-entered New York state politics and was elected governor of New York in 1898. [20] He made such a concerted effort to root out corruption and "machine politics" that Republican boss Thomas Collier Platt forced him on McKinley as a running mate in the 1900 election to simplify their control of the state. [21]

Vice presidency

McKinley and Roosevelt won the presidential election of 1900, defeating William Jennings Bryan and Adlai E. Stevenson I. Roosevelt found the vice-presidency unfulfilling.

Chicago newspaper sees cowboy-TR campaigning for governor

Thinking that he had little future in politics, he considered returning to law school after leaving office. [22]

On September 2, 1901, Roosevelt first uttered a sentence that would become strongly associated with his presidency, urging Americans to "speak softly and carry a big stick" during a speech at the Minnesota State Fair. It has been claimed that the famous phrase was actually inspired by a discussion Roosevelt had with French diplomat Comte Édouard Sébastien de Malo when the latter visited the US in 1900. As France was just coming out of the traumatic Dreyfus affair, Roosevelt asked Comte de Malo what lesson could be learned from the episode. De Malo replied: "France may have been humbled by this event, but we still stand strong and proud. Although we speak softly, we are still carrying a big stick."

Presidency 1901-1909

John Singer Sargent, *Theodore Roosevelt*, 1903, oil on canvas, 58 1/2 × 40 1/2 in., Washington, DC: White House.

President McKinley was shot by an anarchist, Leon Czolgosz, on September 6, 1901. When it looked as if he would recover, Roosevelt decided to take a break and go hiking in the mountains. However, a messenger found him in the woods and told him that the President had taken a turn for the worse and that he should return immediately.

McKinley died on September 14, vaulting Roosevelt into the presidency. Roosevelt took the oath of office on September 14 in the Ansley Wilcox House at Buffalo, New York. He was the youngest person to assume the presidency, and he promised to continue McKinley's cabinet and his basic policies. Roosevelt did so, but after reelection in 1904, he moved to the political left, stretching his ties to the Republican Party's conservative leaders.

Anthracite coal strike of 1902

A national emergency was averted in 1902 when Roosevelt found a compromise to the anthracite coal strike by the United Mine Workers of America that threatened the heating supplies of most homes. Workers in eastern Pennsylvania were on strike for 163 days before it ended, and they were granted a 10% pay increase and a 9-hour day (from the previous 10 hours).

Square Deal

Roosevelt promised to continue McKinley's program, and at first he worked closely with McKinley's men, eventually winning them to his team or breaking with them. His 20,000-word address to the Congress in December 1901, asked Congress to curb the power of trusts "within reasonable limits." They did not act but Roosevelt did, issuing 44 lawsuits against major corporations; he was called the "trust-buster."

Mark Hanna was the rival power in the Republican party. Hanna died, and Roosevelt had an easy renomination and reelection in 1904. He won 336 of 476 electoral votes, and 56.4% of the total popular vote. He therefore became the first President who came into office due to the death of his predecessor to be elected in his own right.

Democrats attack Roosevelt as militarist and ineffective in this 1904 election cartoon

Building on McKinley's effective use of the press, Roosevelt made the White House the center of news every day, providing interviews and photo opportunities. His children were almost as popular as he was, and their pranks in the White House made headlines. His daughter, Alice Lee Roosevelt, became quite popular in Washington.

Regulation of industry

Roosevelt firmly believed, "The Government must in increasing degree supervise and regulate the workings of the railways engaged in interstate commerce." Inaction was a danger, he argued, "Such increased supervision is the only alternative to an increase of the present evils on the one hand or a still more radical policy on the other." (Annual Message Dec 1904) His biggest success was passage of the Hepburn Act of 1906, giving the Interstate Commerce Commission (ICC) the power to set maximum railroad rates; it also stopped free passes given to friends of the railroad. Everyone at the time assumed railroads would always be a vast and powerful force; no one dreamed they would be challenged by trucks and automobiles and struggle to survive under the provisions of the Hepburn Act designed to help merchants and consumers.

In response to public clamor, Roosevelt pushed Congress to pass the Pure Food and Drug Act of 1906, as well as the Meat Inspection Act of 1906. These laws provided for labeling of foods and drugs, inspection of livestock and mandated sanitary conditions at meatpacking plants. Congress replaced Roosevelt's proposals with a version supported by the major meatpackers who worried about the overseas markets, and did not want small unsanitary plants undercutting their domestic market. [Blum 1980 pp 43-44]

Conservationist

Roosevelt was the first American president to grasp the growing negative influence and long-term effects of human forces on the planet. This growing awareness was not accidental; Roosevelt had personally witnessed and commented on the extinction of the passenger pigeons that once blotted out the sun when migrating in flocks of tens of millions of birds. He had once described his brother Elliott nearly being trampled by a mile-wide bison herd in Texas. Now the "lordly buffalo," as he called them had plummeted to near extinction in only 20 years; to no herd larger than 100 and a total U.S. count of less than a thousand. Roosevelt had also seen the effects of uncontrolled and unregulated industrial growth on the environment. Assuming the conservationist role was a natural step for him, and he decided that it was overdue to put the issue high on the national agenda. He worked with all the major figures of the movement, especially his chief advisor on the matter Gifford Pinchot. Roosevelt set aside more land for national parks and nature preserves than all of his predecessors combined. The Theodore Roosevelt National Park in the Badlands commemorates his conservationist philosophy. In 1907, Roosevelt designated 16 million acres (65,000 km²) of new national forests just minutes before a deadline. In May 1908, he sponsored the Conference of Governors held in the White House, with a focus on natural resources and their most efficient use. In an age when the natural resources of the United States seemed almost unlimited, Roosevelt took much different approach, writing to the governors of all the states and territories as well as the 500 most influential men in the country and telling them, "It seems time for the country to take account of its natural resources and to enquire how long they are likely to last." Roosevelt delivered the opening address: "Conservation as a National Duty." On the subject of conservation, Roosevelt said, "There is an intimate relation between our streams and the development and conservation of all the other great permanent sources of wealth. In 1903, Roosevelt toured the Yosemite Valley with John Muir, who had a very different view of conservation and tried to minimize commercial use of water resources and forests. During his presidency, Roosevelt wrote several times about the growing conservation movement in essays for Outdoor Life magazine.

Foreign policy

Roosevelt's administration was marked by an active approach to foreign policy. Roosevelt saw it as the duty of more developed ("civilized") nations to help the underdeveloped ("uncivilized") world move forward. In Cuba, the Philippines, Puerto Rico, and the Panama Canal Zone, he used the Army's medical service, under Walter Reed and William C. Gorgas, to eliminate the yellow fever menace and install a new regime of public health. He used the army to build up the infrastructure of the new possessions, building railways, telegraph and telephone lines, and upgrading roads and port facilities.

Roosevelt dramatically increased the size of the navy, forming the Great White Fleet, which toured the world in 1907. Roosevelt also added the Roosevelt Corollary to the Monroe Doctrine, which stated that the United States could intervene in Caribbean affairs when corruption of governments made it necessary.

Roosevelt gained international praise for helping negotiate the end of the Russo-Japanese War, for which he was awarded the Nobel Peace Prize. Roosevelt later arbitrated a dispute between France and Germany over the division of Morocco. Some historians have argued these latter two actions helped in a small way to avert a world war. [23]

Panama Canal

Roosevelt's most famous foreign policy initiative, following the Hay-Pauncefote Treaty, was the construction of the Panama Canal, which upon its completion shortened the route of freighters between San Francisco, California and New York City by 8,000 miles (13,000 km).

Colombia first proposed the canal in their country as opposed to rival Nicaragua, and Colombia signed a treaty for an agreed-upon sum. At that time, Panama was a province of Colombia. According to the treaty, in 1902, the U.S. was to buy out the equipment and excavations from France, which had been attempting to build a canal since 1881. While the Colombian negotiating team had signed the treaty, ratification by the Colombian Senate became problematic.

The Colombian Senate balked at the price and asked for 10 million dollars over the original agreed upon price. When the U.S. refused to re-negotiate the price, the Colombian politicians proposed cutting the original French company that started the project out of the deal and giving that difference to Colombia. The original deal stipulated that the French company was to be reasonably compensated. Realizing that the Colombian Senate was no longer bargaining in good faith, Roosevelt tired of these last-minute attempts by the Colombians to cheat the French out of their entire investment.

Roosevelt ultimately decided, with the encouragement of Panamanian business interests, to help Panama declare independence from Colombia in 1903. A brief revolution, of only a few hours, followed the declaration, and Colombian soldiers were bribed $50 each to lay down their arms. On November 3, 1903, the nation of Panama was created, with its constitution written in advance by the United States. Shortly thereafter, a treaty was signed with Panama. The U.S. paid $10 million to secure rights to build on and control the Canal Zone. Construction began in 1904 and was completed in 1914.

The Great White Fleet

The USS Conneticut, BB-18 leads the Great White Fleet steaming in column

Roosevelt, (on the 12" gun turret at right), addresses the crew of USS Connecticut (BB18), in Hampton Roads, Virginia, upon her return

As Roosevelt's administration drew to a close, the president dispatched a fleet consisting of four US Navy battleship squadrons and their escorts, on a world-wide voyage of circumnavigation from December 16, 1907, to February 22, 1909. With their hulls painted white except for the beautiful gilded scrollwork with a red, white, and blue banner on their bows, these ships would come to be known as The Great White Fleet. Roosevelt wanted to demonstrate to his country and the world that the US Navy was capable of operating in a global theater, particularly in the Pacific. This was extraordinarily important at a time when tensions were slowly growing between the United States and Japan. The latter had recently shown its navy's competence in defeating the Russians in the Russo-Japanese War and the US Navy fleet to the west was relatively small. The Atlantic Fleet battleships only later came to be known as the "Great White Fleet." When the fleet sailed into Yokahama, Japan, the Japanese went to extraordinary lengths to show that their country desired peace with the US. Thousands of Japanese school children waving American flags greeted the Navy brass as they came ashore. In February 1909, Roosevelt was in Hampton Roads, Virginia to witness the triumphant return of the fleet and indicating that he saw the fleet's long voyage as a fitting finish for his administration. To the officers and men of the Fleet Roosevelt said, "Other nations may do what you have done, but they'll have to follow you." This parting act of Grand Strategy by Roosevelt greatly expanded the respect for as well as the role of the United States in the international arena.

Life in White House

Roosevelt relished the presidency and seemed to be everywhere at once. He took Cabinet members and friends on long, fast-paced hikes, boxed in the state rooms of the White House, romped with his children, and read voraciously. [24] In 1908, he was permanently blinded in his left eye during one of his boxing bouts, but this injury was kept from the public at the time. [25] His many enthusiastic interests and limitless energy led one ambassador to wryly explain, "You must always remember that the President is about six." [26]

Roosevelt shoots holes in the dictionary as the ghosts of Chaucer, Shakespeare and Dr Johnson moan

During his presidency, Roosevelt tried but failed to advance the cause of simplified spelling. He tried to force government to adopt the system, sending an order to the Public Printer to use the system in all public documents. The order was obeyed, and among the documents thus printed was the President's special message regarding the Panama Canal. The *New York World* translated the Thanksgiving Day proclamation:

When nerly three centuries ago, the first settlers kam to the kuntry which has bekom this great republik, tha confronted not only hardship and privashun, but terrible risk of thar lives.

. . . The kustum has now bekum nashnul and hallowed by immemorial usaj.

The reform annoyed the public, forcing him to rescind the order. Roosevelt's friend, literary critic Brander Matthews, one of the chief advocates of the reform, remonstrating with him for abandoning the effort. Roosevelt replied on December 16: "I could not by fighting have kept the new spelling in, and it was evidently worse than useless to go into an undignified contest when I was beaten. Do you know that the one word as to which I thought the new spelling was wrong — thru — was more responsible than anything else for our discomfiture?" Next summer Roosevelt was watching a naval review when a launch marked "Pres Bot" chugged ostentatiously by. The President waved and laughed with delight.[27]

Roosevelt's daughter, Alice, was a controversial character during Roosevelt's stay in the White House. When friends asked if he could rein in his elder daughter, Roosevelt said, "I can be President of the United States, or I can control Alice. I cannot possibly do both." [24] In turn, Alice said of him that he always wanted to be "the bride at every wedding and the corpse at every funeral." [28]

Roosevelt's influence on the White House is seen today in the famed West Wing, which he had built to replace the cramped office in the main body of the building which formerly housed the President. He and Edith also had the entire house refurbished and repaired, which it had desperately needed for years.

Year Four Sourcebook, page 130

Presidential firsts

Roosevelt's presidency saw a number of firsts. In the sphere of race relations, Booker T. Washington became the first Black man to dine at the White House in 1901. Oscar S. Straus became the first Jew appointed as a Cabinet Secretary, under Roosevelt. Roosevelt was the first President to wear a necktie for his official portrait, a tradition which all of his successors followed. Although four Vice Presidents before Roosevelt had succeeded to the presidency upon the death of their predecessor, in 1904, Roosevelt became the first to be elected in his own right or even win his party's nomination for reelection. After Roosevelt, three more Vice Presidents who succeeded to the Presidency would be elected to second terms (Calvin Coolidge, Harry Truman, and Lyndon Johnson).

In 1906, Roosevelt became the first American to be awarded a Nobel Prize, when he received the Nobel Peace Prize for his work towards ending the Russo-Japanese War. That same year, he made the first official trip by a President outside the United States, visiting Panama to inspect the construction progress of the Panama Canal on November 9.

Supreme Court appointments

Roosevelt appointed three Justices to the Supreme Court of the United States:

- Oliver Wendell Holmes, Jr. - 1902
- William Rufus Day - 1903
- William Henry Moody - 1906

Although Moody was a close associate of Roosevelt, Holmes, who would serve on the Supreme Court until 1932, gained his appointment by virtue of sharing a mutual acquaintance with Roosevelt, Henry Cabot Lodge. Moody was forced to resign due to ill health four years after his appointment, and after retiring, Roosevelt would clash with both Holmes and Day for not supporting reforms he backed.

States admitted to the Union

During Roosevelt's Presidency, one state, Oklahoma, was admitted to the Union. This new state included the former Indian Territory, which had attempted to gain admission on its own into the Union as the State of Sequoyah. (Formerly, the state of Oklahoma had been divided into the Oklahoma Territory and Indian Territory.) In 1906, a bill was introduced in Congress providing for the admission of the Oklahoma and Indian Territories as one state, and Arizona and New Mexico as another state. Although the bill passed on June 14 and was signed into law by Roosevelt, the people of Arizona and New Mexico rejected the offer of statehood.

Post-presidency

African safari

Roosevelt standing next to a dead elephant during a safari

In March 1910, shortly after the end of his second term, Roosevelt left New York for a safari in Africa. The trip was sponsored by the Smithsonian Institution and the National Geographic Society and received worldwide media attention. Despite his commitment to conservation, his party, which included scientists from the Smithsonian, killed or trapped over 11,397 animals, from insects and moles to hippopotamuses and elephants. 512 of the animals were big game animals, of which 262 were consumed by the expedition. This included six white rhinos. Tons of salted animals and their skins were shipped to Washington; the number of animals was so large, it took years to mount them. The Smithsonian was able to share many duplicate animals with other museums. Of the large number of animals taken, Roosevelt said, "I can be condemned only if the existence of the National Museum, the American Museum of Natural History, and all similar zoological institutions are to be condemned." [29]

Republican Party rift

Handing off responsibility to Taft in 1909

Roosevelt certified William Howard Taft to be a genuine "progressive" in 1908, when Roosevelt pushed through the nomination of his Secretary of War for the Presidency. Taft easily defeated three-time candidate William Jennings Bryan. Taft had a different progressivism, one that stressed the rule of law and preferred that judges rather than administrators or politicians make the basic decisions about fairness. Taft usually proved a less adroit politician than Roosevelt and lacked the energy and personal magnetism, not to mention the publicity devices, the dedicated supporters, and the broad base of public support that made Roosevelt so formidable. When Roosevelt realized that lowering the tariff would risk severe tensions inside the Republican Party—pitting producers (manufacturers and farmers) against merchants and consumers—he stopped talking about the issue. Taft ignored the risks and tackled the tariff boldly, on the one hand encouraging reformers to fight for lower rates, and then cutting deals with conservative leaders that kept overall rates high. The resulting Payne-Aldrich tariff of 1909 was too high for most reformers, but instead of blaming this on Senator Nelson Aldrich and big business, Taft took credit, calling it the best tariff ever. Again he had managed to alienate all sides. While the crisis was building inside the Party, Roosevelt was touring Africa and Europe, so as to allow Taft to be his own man. [30]

Unlike Roosevelt, Taft never attacked business or businessmen in his rhetoric. However, he was attentive to the law, so he launched 90 antitrust suits, including one against the largest corporation, U.S. Steel, for an acquisition that Roosevelt had personally approved. The upshot was that Taft lost the support of antitrust reformers (who disliked his conservative rhetoric), of big business (which disliked his actions), and of Roosevelt, who felt humiliated by his protégé. The left wing of the Republican Party began agitating against Taft. Senator Robert LaFollette of Wisconsin created the National Progressive Republican League to defeat the power of political bossism at the state level and to replace Taft at the national level. More trouble came when Taft fired Gifford Pinchot, a leading conservationist and close ally of Roosevelt. Pinchot alleged that Taft's Secretary of Interior Richard Ballinger was in league with big timber interests. Conservationists sided with Pinchot, and Taft alienated yet another vocal constituency.

Roosevelt, back from Europe, unexpectedly launched an attack on the federal courts, which deeply upset Taft. Not only had Roosevelt alienated big business, he was also attacking both the judiciary and the deep faith Republicans had in their judges (most of whom had been appointed by McKinley, Roosevelt or Taft.) In the 1910 Congressional elections, Democrats swept to power, and Taft's reelection in 1912 was increasingly in doubt. In 1911, Taft responded with a vigorous stumping tour that allowed him to sign up most of the party leaders long before Roosevelt announced. Taft thereby demonstrated that he was a better political operator than Roosevelt.

Election of 1912

The battle between Taft and Roosevelt bitterly split the Republican Party. Taft's people dominated the party until 1936.

Late in 1911, Roosevelt finally broke with Taft and LaFollette and announced himself as a candidate for the Republican nomination. Roosevelt had delayed too long, and Taft had already won the support of most party leaders in the country. Most of LaFollette's supporters went over to Roosevelt, leaving the Wisconsin Senator embittered. Roosevelt, stepping up his attack on judges, carried 9 of the states with preferential primaries, LaFollette took two, and Taft only one. Most professional Republican politicians were supporting Taft, and they proved difficult to upset in non-primary states.

Roosevelt, along with key allies such as Pinchot and Albert Beveridge created the Progressive Party, structuring it as a permanent organization that would field complete tickets at the presidential and state level. It was popularly known as the "Bull Moose Party," which got its name after Roosevelt told reporters, "I'm as tough as a bull moose." At his Chicago convention Roosevelt cried out, "We stand at Armageddon and we battle for the Lord." The crusading rhetoric resonated well with the delegates, many of them long-time reformers, crusaders, activists and opponents of politics as usual. Included in the ranks were Jane Addams and many other feminists and peace activists. The platform echoed Roosevelt's 1907-08 proposals, calling for vigorous government intervention to protect the people from the selfish interests. [31]

While campaigning in Milwaukee, Wisconsin, he was shot by saloonkeeper John Schrank in a failed assassination attempt on October 14, 1912. With the bullet lodged in his chest, Roosevelt delivered his scheduled speech. He was not seriously wounded (the bullet's progress was slowed by hitting a copy of the speech he was carrying in his jacket), although his doctors thought it too dangerous to attempt to remove the bullet; Roosevelt carried it with him until he died.

Roosevelt failed to move the political system in his direction. He did win 4.1 million votes (27%), compared to Taft's 3.5 million (23%). However, Wilson's 6.3 million votes (42%) were enough to garner 435 electoral votes. Roosevelt had only 88 electoral votes; Pennsylvania was his only Eastern state; in the Midwest he carried Michigan, Minnesota and South Dakota; in the West, California and Washington; in the South, he did not win any states.

South American expedition

The initial party. From left to right (seated): Father Zahm, Rondon, Kermit, Cherrie, Miller, four Brazilians, Roosevelt, Fiala. Only Roosevelt, Kermit Cherrie, Rondon and the Brazilians traveled up the River of Doubt.

Just as Roosevelt, after his first administration, had gone to Africa in search of adventure, so also, after his failed attempt at regaining the White House, he found himself on another adventure. On this trip, however, he would get far more drama than he had bargained for.

His popular book *Through the Brazilian Wilderness* describes his expedition into the Brazilian jungle in 1913 as a member of the Roosevelt-Rondon Scientific Expedition co-named after its leader, Brazilian explorer Cândido Rondon. Perhaps in the interest of the scientific aspects of the expedition, the book describes all of the scientific discovery, scenic tropical vistas and exotic flora, fauna and wild life experienced on the expedition. However, the book does not encapsulate the whole truth of an expedition that went awry and involved hardship, suffering, death and even murder.

A friend, Father John Augustine Zahm, had searched for new adventures and found them in the forests of South America. After a briefing of several of his own expeditions, he convinced Roosevelt to commit to such an expedition in 1912. To finance the expedition, Roosevelt received support from the American Museum of Natural History, promising to bring back many new animal specimens. Once in South America, a new far more ambitious goal was added: to find the headwaters of the Rio da Duvida, the River of Doubt, and trace it north to the Madiera and thence to the Amazon River. It was later renamed Rio Roosevelt in honor of the former President. Roosevelt's crew consisted of his 24-year-old son Kermit, Colonel Cândido Rondon, a naturalist sent by the American Museum of Natural History named George K. Cherrie, Brazilian Lieutenant Joao Lyra, team physician Dr. José Antonio Cajazeira, and sixteen highly skilled paddlers (called camaradas in Portuguese). The initial expedition started, probably unwisely, on December 9, 1913, at the height of the rainy season. The trip up the River of Doubt started on the February 27, 1914.

During the trip up the river, Roosevelt contracted malaria and a serious infection resulting from a minor leg wound. These illnesses so weakened Roosevelt that, by six weeks into the expedition, he had to be attended day and night by the expedition's physician, Dr. Cajazeira and his son, Kermit. By this time, Roosevelt considered his own condition a threat to the survival of the others. At one point, Kermit had to talk him out his wish to be left behind so as not to slow down the expedition, now with only a few weeks rations left. Roosevelt was having chest pains when he tried to walk, his temperature soared to 103 F (39 C), and at times he was delirious. By now he was so weakened that he could not even sit up in his dugout but had to lie almost on his back. When the expedition reached civilization, Roosevelt had to be carried off by stretcher. He had lost over fifty pounds (20 kg). Kermit and all the expedition's members' physical conditions had suffered as well. In the final analysis, without the constant support of Dr. Cajazeira, and Rondon's leadership, Roosevelt would have perished. Without Kermit's insistence on not abandoning the river for an overland trek that would have failed for lack of food if nothing else, without Kermit's rope and canoe-handling skills that preserved the dugouts from destruction, his unflinching courage, dogged determination—in short, the devotion and loving support of a dedicated son—it is unlikely that anyone would have survived the expedition.

Upon his return by ship to New York, friends and family were startled by Roosevelt's physical appearance, for he was no longer the vibrant man with a seemingly endless supply of energy that they had always known. Roosevelt wrote to a friend that the trip had cut his life short by ten years. He might not have really known just how accurate that analysis would prove to be, because the effects of the South America expedition had so greatly weakened him that they significantly contributed to his declining health. For the rest of his life, he would be plagued by flareups of malaria and leg inflammations so severe that they would require hospitalization. [24][32]

When Roosevelt had recovered enough of his strength, he found that he had a new battle on his hands. In professional circles, there was doubt about his claims of having discovered and navigated a completely uncharted river over 625 miles (1,000 km) long. Roosevelt would have to defend himself and win international recognition of the expedition's newly-named Rio Roosevelt. Toward this end, Roosevelt went to Washington, D.C., and spoke at a standing-room-only convention to defend his claims. His official report and its defense silenced the critics, and he was able to triumphantly return to his home in Oyster Bay.

Writer

Despite his weakened condition and slow recovery from his South America expedition, Roosevelt continued to write with great passion on subjects ranging from foreign policy to the importance of the national park system. As an editor of *Outlook* magazine, he had weekly access to a large, educated national audience. In all, Roosevelt wrote about 18 books (each in several editions), including his *Autobiography*, *Rough Riders* and *History of the Naval War of 1812*, ranching, explorations, and wildlife. His most important book was the 4 volume narrative *The Winning of the West*, which traced the origin of a new "race" of Americans to frontier conditions in the 18th century.

First World War

Roosevelt angrily complained about the foreign policy of President Wilson, calling it "weak". When World War I began in 1914, Roosevelt strongly supported Britain, France and the Allies of World War I because he admired their fight for civilization; he demanded a harsher policy against Germany, especially regarding submarine warfare. In 1916, he campaigned energetically for Hughes and repeatedly denounced those Irish-Americans and German-Americans whose pleas for neutrality Roosevelt said were unpatriotic because they put the interest of Ireland and Germany ahead of America's. He insisted that one had to be 100% American, not a "hyphenated-American" who juggled multiple loyalties. When the U.S. entered the war in 1917, Roosevelt sought to raise a volunteer division, but Wilson refused. [33] Roosevelt's attacks on Wilson helped the Republicans win control of Congress in the elections of 1918. Had Roosevelt remained alive and healthy, he might have contested the 1920 Republican nomination, but his health was broken by 1918 because of the lingering malaria. His son Quentin, a daring pilot with the American forces in France, was shot down behind German lines in 1918. Quentin was his youngest son and probably the most like him. It is said that the death of his son distressed him so much that Roosevelt never recovered from the mourning.

Last years

Despite the setbacks from South American diseases and the death of his son, Roosevelt remained popular and upbeat to the end of his life. He was an enthusiastic proponent of the Scouting movement. The Boy Scouts of America gave him the title of **Chief Scout Citizen**, the only person to hold such title. One early Scout leader said, "The two things that gave Scouting great impetus and made it very popular were the uniform and Teddy Roosevelt's jingoism." [34] After his death, Boy Scout leaders led annual pilgrimages to his gravesite for several years.

On January 6, 1919, at the age of 60, Roosevelt died in his sleep of a coronary embolism at Oyster Bay, and was buried in nearby Young's Memorial Cemetery. Upon receiving word of his death, his son, Archie, telegraphed his siblings simply, "The old lion is dead."

Personal life

Roosevelt Family in 1903 with Quentin on the left, TR, Ted, Jr., "Archie", Alice, Kermit, Edith, and Ethel

Roosevelt was baptized in the family's church, part of the Reformed Church in America; he attended the Madison Square Presbyterian Church until the age of 16. Later in life, when Roosevelt lived at Oyster Bay he attended an Episcopal church with his wife. While in Washington he attended services at Grace Reformed Church. [35] As President he firmly believed in the separation of church and state and thought it unwise to have In God We Trust on currency, because he thought it sacrilegious to put the name of the Deity on something so common as money. [36] He was also a Freemason, and regularly attended the Matinecock Lodge's meetings. He once said that "One of the things that so greatly attracted me to Masonry that I hailed the chance of becoming a Mason was that it really did act up to what we, as a government, are pledged to — namely to treat each man on his merit as a man." [37]

Roosevelt had a lifelong interest in pursuing what he called "the strenuous life." To this end, he exercised regularly and took up boxing, tennis, hiking, rowing, polo, and horseback riding. As governor of New York, he boxed with sparring partners several times a week, a practice he regularly continued as President until one blow detached his left retina, leaving him blind in that eye. Thereafter, he practiced jujutsu and continued his habit of skinny-dipping in the Potomac River during winter. [38] [39]

Sagamore Hill, Roosevelt's estate

He was an enthusiastic singlestick player and, according to Harper's Weekly, in 1905 showed up at a White House reception with his arm bandaged after a bout with General Leonard Wood. [40] Roosevelt was also an avid reader, reading tens of thousands of books, at a rate of several a day in multiple languages. Along with Thomas Jefferson Roosevelt is often considered the most well read of any American politician. [41]

Legacy

For his gallantry at San Juan Hill, Roosevelt's commanders recommended him for the Medal of Honor, but his subsequent telegrams to the War Department complaining about the delays in returning American troops from Cuba doomed his chances. In the late 1890s, Roosevelt's supporters again took up the flag on his behalf and overcame opposition from elements within the U.S. Army and the National Archives. On January 16, 2001, President Bill Clinton posthumously awarded Theodore Roosevelt the Medal of Honor for his charge up San Juan Hill, Cuba, during the Spanish-American War. Roosevelt's eldest son, Brigadier General Theodore Roosevelt, Jr., received the Medal of Honor for heroism at the Battle of Normandy in 1944. The Roosevelts thus became one of only two father-son pairs to receive this honor.

Roosevelt's legacy includes several other important commemorations. Roosevelt was included with George Washington, Thomas Jefferson and Abraham Lincoln at the Mount Rushmore Memorial. The United States Navy named two ships for Roosevelt: the first, a George Washington class submarine was in commission from 1961 to 1982; and the second, a Nimitz class aircraft carrier has been on active duty in the Atlantic Fleet since 1986.

The Roosevelt Memorial Association (later the Theodore Roosevelt Association) was founded in 1919 to preserve Roosevelt's legacy. The Association preserved TR's birthplace, "Sagamore Hill," home, papers, and video film. It later published the Roosevelt Cyclopedia, a topical collection of Roosevelt's key statements on many issues.

1910 cartoon shows Roosevelt's multiple roles to 1898

Roosevelt's multiple roles from 1899 to 1910

Overall, historians credit Roosevelt for changing the nation's political system by permanently placing the presidency at center stage and making character as important as the issues. His notable accomplishments include trust-busting and conservationism. However, he has been criticized for his interventionist and imperialist approach to nations he considered "uncivilized". Even so, history and legend have been kind to him. His friend, historian Henry Adams, proclaimed, "Roosevelt, more than any other living man ....showed the singular primitive quality that belongs to ultimate matter — the quality that mediaeval theology assigned to God — he was pure act." Historians typically rank Roosevelt among the top five presidents. [42][43]

Popular culture

As a charismatic President often considered larger than life, Roosevelt (or characters using his name loosely based on him) has appeared in numerous fiction books, television shows, films, and other media of popular culture.

Theodore Roosevelt as depicted in the Scrooge McDuck Universe.

In the Scrooge McDuck comics by Keno Don Rosa, Roosevelt appears several times, often as the mentor of an adolescent Scrooge, teaching him the values of self-confidence and self-reliance.

He is also a major character in Harry Turtledove's fictional Timeline-191 alternate history, along with Caleb Carr's novels The Alienist and The Angel of Darkness, and is the protagonist of Benito Cereno's *Tales From the Bully Pulpit* comic book. In the comic play and movie Arsenic and Old Lace part of the zany atmosphere is created by a character who holds the delusion that he is Theodore Roosevelt. The Sonic the Hedgehog villain Dr. Eggman was based on a design of Theodore Roosevelt wearing pajamas.

Roosevelt's lasting popular legacy is the stuffed toy bears (teddy bears), named after him following an incident on a hunting trip in 1902. Roosevelt famously refused to kill a captured black bear simply for the sake of making a kill. Bears and later bear cubs became closely associated with Roosevelt in political cartoons thereafter. [44]

References

Primary sources

- Brands, H.W. ed. *The Selected Letters of Theodore Roosevelt.* (2001)
- Harbaugh, William ed. *The Writings Of Theodore Roosevelt* (1967). A one-volume selection of Roosevelt's speeches and essays.
- Hart, Albert Bushnell and Herbert Ronald Ferleger, eds. *Theodore Roosevelt Cyclopedia* (1941), Roosevelt's opinions on many issues; online version at [2]
- Morison, Elting E., John Morton Blum, and Alfred D. Chandler, Jr., eds., *The Letters of Theodore Roosevelt*, 8 vols. (1951-1954). Very large, annotated edition of letters from TR.

- Roosevelt, Theodore (1999). *Theodore Roosevelt: An Autobiography*. online at Bartleby.com.
- Roosevelt, Theodore. *The Works of Theodore Roosevelt* (National edition, 20 vol. 1926); 18,000 pages containing most of TR's speeches, books and essays, but not his letters; a CD-ROM edition is available; some of TR's books are available online through Project Bartleby
- Theodore Roosevelt books and speeches on Project Gutenberg

Secondary sources

- Beale Howard K. *Theodore Roosevelt and the Rise of America to World Power.* (1956).
- Blum, John Morton *The Republican Roosevelt.* (1954). Series of essays that examine how TR did politics
- Blum, John Morton. *The Progressive Presidents: Roosevelt, Wilson, Roosevelt, Johnson* (1980)
- Brands, H.W. *Theodore Roosevelt* (2001), full biography
- Cooper, John Milton *The Warrior and the Priest: Woodrow Wilson and Theodore Roosevelt.* (1983) a dual biography
- Dalton, Kathleen. *Theodore Roosevelt: A Strenuous Life.* (2002), full biography
- Gould, Lewis L. *The Presidency of Theodore Roosevelt.* (1991)
- Harbaugh, William Henry. *The Life and Times of Theodore Roosevelt.* (1963), full biography
- Keller, Morton, ed., *Theodore Roosevelt: A Profile* (1967) excerpts from TR and from historians.
- McCullough, David. *Mornings on Horseback, The Story of an Extraordinary Family. a Vanished Way of Life, and the Unique Child Who Became Theodore Roosevelt.* (2001) biography to 1884
- Morris, Edmund *The Rise of Theodore Roosevelt*, to 1901 (1979); vol 2: *Theodore Rex 1901-1909.* (2001); Pulitzer prize
- Mowry, George. *The Era of Theodore Roosevelt and the Birth of Modern America, 1900-1912.* (1954) general survey of era
- Mowry, George E. *Theodore Roosevelt and the Progressive Movement.* (2001) focus on 1912
- O'Toole, Patricia. *When Trumpets Call: Theodore Roosevelt After the White House* (2005)
- Pringle, Henry F. *Theodore Roosevelt* (1932; 2nd ed. 1956), full biography
- Putnam, Carleton *Theodore Roosevelt: A Biography, Volume I: The Formative Years* (1958), only volume published, to age 28.
- Rhodes, James Ford Rhodes. *The McKinley and Roosevelt Administrations, 1897-1909* (1922)

Preceded by: Frank S. Black	Governor of New York 1899 - 1901	Succeeded by: Benjamin B. Odell, Jr.
Preceded by: Garret Hobart	Republican Party Vice Presidential Candidate 1900 (won)	Succeeded by: Charles W. Fairbanks
Preceded by: Garret Hobart	Vice President of the United States March 4, 1901 - September 14, 1901	Succeeded by: Charles W. Fairbanks
Preceded by: William McKinley	President of the United States September 14, 1901 - March 3, 1909	Succeeded by: William Howard Taft
Preceded by: William McKinley	Republican Party Presidential Candidate 1904 (won)	Succeeded by: William Howard Taft
Preceded by: –	Progressive Party Presidential Candidate 1912 (lost)	Succeeded by: –

Notes

1. ^ [Thomas A. Bailey, *Presidential Greatness* (1966) p. 308
2. ^ Editors (2006). Month=June&Date=26 "Theodore Roosevelt - The 20th Century Express - "At home and abroad, Theodore Roosevelt was the locomotive President, the man who drew his flourishing nation into the future" ". Retrieved March 26, 2006.
3. ^ "TR's Legacy - The Environment". Retrieved March 6, 2006.
4. ^ Thayer, William Roscoe (1919). *Theodore Roosevelt: An Intimate Biography*, Chapter I, p. 20. Bartleby.com.
5. ^ Roosevelt, Theodore (1913). *Theodore Roosevelt: An Autobiography*, Chapter I, p. 13. Macmillan. ISBN 1-58734-045-3.
6. ^ "The Film & More: Program Transcript Part One". Retrieved March 9, 2006.
7. ^ PBS *American Experience* http://www.pbs.org/wgbh/amex/presidents/26_t_roosevelt/t_roosevelt_early.html
8. ^ *T. R.: The Last Romantic* by H. W. Brands P. 49-50
9. ^ Brands p. 62
10. ^ Thayer, Chapter I, pp. 30, 36.
11. ^ Thayer, Chapter I, p. 37.
12. ^ "The Naval War of 1812 by Theodore Roosevelt".
13. ^ Brands, pp 123-29
14. ^ Brands pp 175-79
15. ^ Thayer, Chapter II, p. 29.
16. ^ Thayer, Chapter V, pp. 4, 6.
17. ^ Thayer, Chapter VI, pp. 1–2.

18. ^ Thayer, Chapter VI, pp. 18–24.
19. ^ Thayer, Chapter VII, pp. 20–26.
20. ^ Thayer, Chapter VIII, p. 7.
21. ^ Thayer, Chapter VIII, p. 19.
22. ^ Thayer, Chapter VIII, pp. 27–28.
23. ^ The Rector and Visitors of the University of Virginia (2005). "Theodore Roosevelt (1901-1909)". Retrieved March 6, 2006.
24. ^ [a] [b] [c] Hanson, David C. (2005). "Theodore Roosevelt: Lion in the White House". Retrieved March 6, 2006.
25. ^ Smith, Ira R. T.; Morris, Joe Alex (1949). *"Dear Mr. President": The Story of Fifty Years in the White House Mail Room*, p. 52. Julian Messner.
26. ^ Kennedy, Robert C. (2005). "'I hear there are some kids in the White House this year'". Retrieved March 6, 2006.
27. ^ Pringle 465-7
28. ^ (Some sources attribute this quote to one of Roosevelt's sons instead.) Thayer, Chapter XIII, p. 7.
29. ^ O'Toole, Patricia (2005) *When Trumpets Call*, p. 67, Simon and Schuster, ISBN 0-684-86477-0
30. ^ Thayer, Chapter XXI, p. 10.
31. ^ Thayer, Chapter XXII, pp. 25–31.
32. ^ Thayer, Chapter XXIII, pp. 4–7.
33. ^ Brands 781-4
34. ^ Larson, Keith (2006). "Theodore Roosevelt". Retrieved March 6, 2006.
35. ^ "The Religious Affiliation of Theodore Roosevelt U.S. President". Retrieved March 7, 2006.
36. ^ Reynolds, Ralph C. (1999). "In God We Trust: All Others Pay Cash". Retrieved March 7, 2006.
37. ^ Matinecock Masonic Historical Society. "History". Retrieved March 12, 2006.
38. ^ Thayer, Chapter XVII, pp. 22–24.
39. ^ Shaw, K.B. & Maiden, David (2006). "Theodore Roosevelt". Retrieved March 7, 2006.
40. ^ Amberger, J Christoph, Secret History of the Sword Adventures in Ancient Martial Arts 1998, ISBN 1-892515-04-0.
41. ^ David H. Burton, *The Learned Presidency* 1988, p 12.
42. ^ The Rector and Visitors of the University of Virginia (2005). "Biography: Impact and Legacy". Retrieved March 7, 2006.
43. ^ "Legacy". Retrieved March 7, 2006.
44. ^ "History of the Teddy Bear". Retrieved March 7, 2006.

Retrieved from "http://en.wikipedia.org/wiki/Theodore_Roosevelt"

- This page was last modified 08:39, 15 July 2006.

Francis Schaeffer Study Center
Mt. Juliet, Tennessee

Western Civilization, Year Four
From 1865 to 1990, Reconstruction to Modern Times
Rob Shearer, Tutor

Week Nine Reading

The Russo-Japanese War

The Russo-Japanese War

From Wikipedia, the free encyclopedia

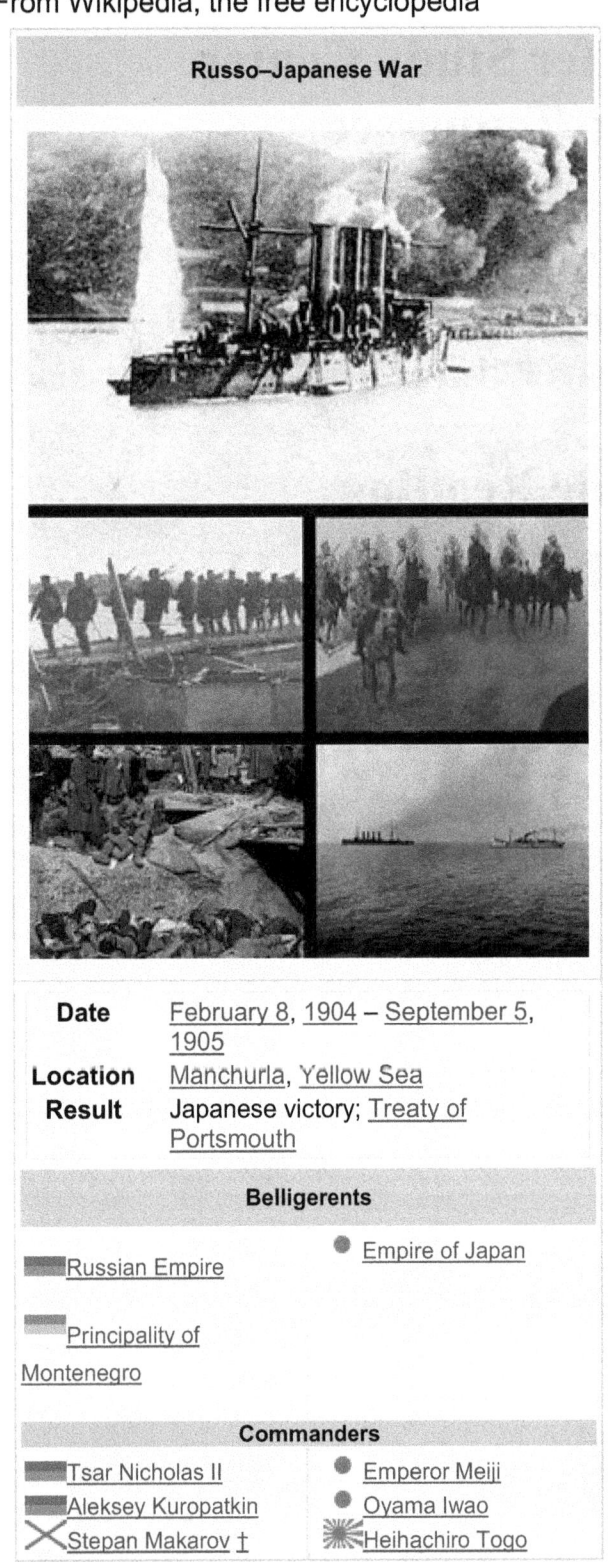

Date	February 8, 1904 – September 5, 1905
Location	Manchuria, Yellow Sea
Result	Japanese victory; Treaty of Portsmouth

Belligerents	
Russian Empire Principality of Montenegro	Empire of Japan

Commanders	
Tsar Nicholas II Aleksey Kuropatkin Stepan Makarov †	Emperor Meiji Oyama Iwao Heihachiro Togo

Year Four Sourcebook, page 144

Summary

The **Russo–Japanese War** (Japanese: 日露戦争; Romaji: Nichi-Ro Sensō; Russian: Русско-японская война *Russko-Yaponskaya Voyna*; simplified Chinese: 日俄 争; traditional Chinese: 日俄戰争; pinyin: Rìézhànzhēng, February 10, 1904 – September 5, 1905) was a conflict that grew out of the rival imperialist ambitions of the Russian Empire and Japanese Empire over Manchuria and Korea. The major theatres of operations were Southern Manchuria, specifically the area around the Liaodong Peninsula and Mukden, and the seas around Korea, Japan, and the Yellow Sea.

The Russians were in constant pursuit of a warm water port on the Pacific Ocean, for their navy as well as for maritime trade. The recently established Pacific seaport of Vladivostok was the only active Russian port that was reasonably operational during the summer season; but Port Arthur would be operational all year. From the end of the First Sino-Japanese War and 1903 negotiations between the Tsar's government and Japan had proved futile. Japan chose war to protect its country by maintaining exclusive dominance in Korea, while all European countries expected Russia would win.

The resulting campaigns, in which the fledgling Japanese military consistently attained victory over the Russian forces arrayed against them, were unexpected by world observers. These victories, as time transpired, would dramatically transform the balance of power in East Asia, resulting in a sober reassessment of Japan's recent entry onto the world stage. The embarrassing string of defeats increased Russian populace's dissatisfaction with the inefficient and corrupt Tsarist government and proved a major cause of the Russian Revolution of 1905.

Contents

1 Origins of the Russo-Japanese war

1.1 Sino-Japanese War (1894-1895)

1.2 Russian Encroachment

1.3 The Boxer Rebellion

1.4 Negotiations

2 War

2.1 Declaration of War

2.2 Campaign of 1904

- 2.2.1 Battle of Port Arthur
- 2.2.2 Battle of Yalu River
- 2.2.3 Blockade of Port Arthur
- 2.2.4 Siege of Port Arthur
- 2.2.5 Fall of Port Arthur
- 2.2.6 Baltic Fleet

2.3 Campaign of 1905

- 2.3.1 Harsh winter and final battles
- 2.3.2 Victory at Tsushima

3 Peace

3.1 Casualties

3.2 Aftermath and consequences

4 Assessment of war results

5 List of battles

6 Art and literature

7 See also

8 Notes

9 References

10 External links

Origins of the Russo-Japanese war

After the Meiji Restoration in 1868, the Meiji government embarked on an endeavor to assimilate Western ideas, technological advances and customs. By the late 19th century, Japan had emerged from isolation and transformed itself into a modernized industrial state in a remarkably short time. The Japanese wished to preserve their sovereignty and to be recognized as an equal with the Western powers.

Russia, a major Imperial power, had ambitions in the East. By the 1890s it had extended its realm across Central Asia to Afghanistan, absorbing local states in the process. The Russian Empire stretched from Poland in the west to the Kamchatka peninsula in the East[1]. With its construction of the Trans-Siberian Railway to the port of Vladivostok, Russia hoped to further consolidate its influence and presence in the region. This was precisely what Japan feared, as they regarded Korea (and to a lesser extent Manchuria) as a protective buffer.

Sino-Japanese War (1894-1895)

The Japanese government regarded Korea, which was geo-politically close to Japan, as an essential part of its national security. The Japanese wanted, at the very least, to keep Korea independent under Japanese influence. Japan's subsequent defeat of China during the war led to the Treaty of Shimonoseki under which China abandoned its own suzerainty over Korea and ceded Taiwan, Pescadores and the Liaodong Peninsula(Port Arthur) to Japan.

However, the Russians, having their own ambitions in the region persuaded Germany and France in applying pressure on Japan. Through the Triple Intervention, Japan relinquished its claim on the Liaodong Peninsula for an increased financial indemnity.

Russian Encroachment

In December 1897, a Russian fleet appeared off Port Arthur. After three months, in 1898, a convention was agreed between China and Russia by which Russia was leased Port Arthur, Talienwan and the surrounding waters. It was further agreed that the convention could be extended by mutual agreement. The Russians clearly believed that would be the case for they lost no time in occupation and in fortifying Port Arthur, their sole warm-water port on the Pacific coast, and of great strategic value. A year later, in order to consolidate their position, the Russians began a new railway from Harbin through Mukden to Port Arthur. The development of the railway was a contributory factor towards the Boxer Rebellion and the railway stations at Tiehling and Lioyang were burnt. The Russian also began to make inroads into Korea, by 1898 they acquired mining and forestry concessions near Yalu and Tumen rivers,[2] causing the Japanese much anxiety.

The Boxer Rebellion

The Russians and Japanese were both part of the eight member international force which was sent into quell the Boxer Rebellion and to relieve the international legations under siege in the Chinese capital. As with other member nations, the Russians sent troops into China, specifically Manchuria to protect its interests.[3] Russia assured other powers that it would vacate the area after the crisis. However, by 1903 the Russian had not yet adhered to any timetable for withdrawal[4] and actually strenthened their position in Manchuria.

Negotiations

The Japanese statesman, Itō Hirobumi, started to negotiate with the Russians. He believed that Japan was too weak to evict Russia militarily, so he proposed giving Russia control over Manchuria in exchange for Japanese control of northern Korea. Meanwhile, Japan and the Britain had signed the Anglo-Japanese Alliance in 1902, the British seeking to restrict naval competition by keeping the Russian Pacific seaports of Vladivostok and Port Arthur from their full use. The alliance with the British meant, in part, that if any nation allied itself with Russia during any war with Japan, then Britain would enter the war on Japan's side. Russia could no longer count on receiving help from either Germany or France without there being a danger of the British involvement with the war. With such an alliance, Japan felt free to commence hostilities, if necessary.

On 28 July 1903, the Japanese Minister at St. Petersburg was instructed to represent his country's view opposing Russia's consolidation plans over Manchuria. Trade-offs followed and the situation was reached on 13 January 1904 whereby Japan proposed a formula of Manchuria being outside her sphere of influence and sought in return a similar statement relating to Russia's discontinuing interest in Korea. By 4 February 1904, no formal reply had been forthcoming and on the 6th February Mr. Kurino Shinichiro, the Japanese Minister, called on the Russian Foreign Minister, Count Lamsdorf, to take his leave.[5] Japan severed diplomatic relations on February 6, 1904.

War

Declaration of War

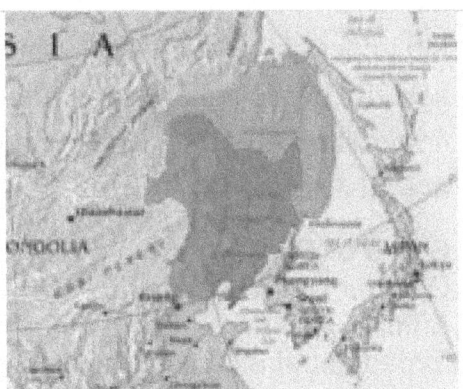

Greater Manchuria, Russian (outer) Manchuria is the lighter red region to the upper right

Japan issued a declaration of war on 8 February 1904. However, three hours before Japan's declaration of war was received by the Russian Government, the Japanese Imperial Navy attacked the Russian Far East Fleet at Port Arthur. Tsar Nicholas II was stunned by news of the attack. He could not believe that Japan could initiate a warlike act without a formal declaration of war, and had been assured by his ministers that the Japanese would not fight. Russia declared war on Japan eight days later.[6] However, the requirement to declare war before commencing hostilities was not made international law until after the war had ended in October 1907, effective from 26 January 1910.[7] Montenegro also declared war against Japan as a gesture of moral support for Russia out of gratefulness for Russian support in Montenegro's struggles against the Ottoman Empire. However, due to logistical reasons and distance, Montenegro's contribution to the war effort was limited to those Montenegrins who served in the Russian armed forces.

Campaign of 1904

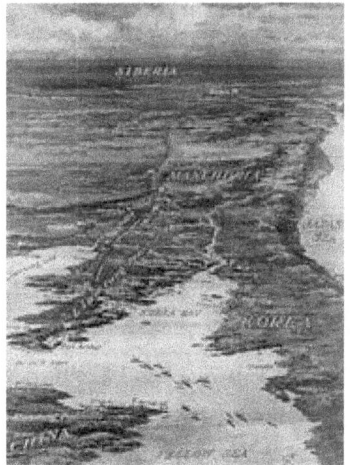

1 Battlefields in the Russo-Japanese War

Port Arthur, on the Liaodong Peninsula in the south of Manchuria, had been fortified into a major naval base by the Imperial Russian Army. Since it needed to control the sea in order to fight a war on the Asian mainland, Japan's first military objective was to neutralize the Russian fleet at Port Arthur.

Battle of Port Arthur
On the night of 8 February 1904, the Japanese fleet under Admiral Heihachiro Togo opened the war with a surprise torpedo boat attack on the Russian ships at Port Arthur.

The attack badly damaged the *Tsesarevich* and *Retvizan*, the heaviest battleships in Russia's far Eastern theater, and the 6,600 ton cruiser *Pallada*. [8] These attacks developed into the Battle of Port Arthur the next morning. A series of indecisive naval engagements followed, in which Admiral Togo was unable to attack the Russian fleet successfully as it was protected by the shore batteries of the harbor, and the Russians were reluctant to leave the harbor for the open seas, especially after the death of Admiral Stepan Osipovich Makarov on 13 April 1904.

However, these engagements provided cover for a Japanese landing near Incheon in Korea. From Incheon the Japanese occupied Seoul and then the rest of Korea. By the end of April, the Imperial Japanese Army under Kuroki Itei was ready to cross the Yalu river into Russian-occupied Manchuria.

Battle of Yalu River

In contrast to the Japanese strategy of rapidly gaining ground to control Manchuria, Russian strategy focused on fighting delaying actions to gain time for reinforcements to arrive via the long Trans-Siberian railway which was at the time incomplete near Irkutsk. On 1 May 1904, the Battle of the Yalu River became the first major land battle of the war, when Japanese troops stormed a Russian position after an unopposed crossing of the river. Japanese troops proceeded to land at several points on the Manchurian coast, and, in a series of engagements, drove the Russians back towards Port Arthur. These battles, including the Battle of Nanshan on 25 May 1904, were marked by heavy Japanese losses from attacking entrenched Russian positions, but the Russians maintained their focus on defending, and did not counterattack.

Blockade of Port Arthur

Year Four Sourcebook, page 150

The Japanese attempted to deny the Russians use of Port Arthur. During the night of 13 February-14 February, the Japanese attempted to block the entrance to Port Arthur by sinking several cement-filled steamers in the deep water channel to the port, but they sank too deep to be effective. Another similar attempt to block the harbor entrance during the night of 3-4 May also failed. In March, the charismatic Vice Admiral Makarov had taken command of the First Russian Pacific Squadron with the intention of breaking out of the Port Arthur blockade.

On 12 April 1904, two Russian pre-dreadnought battleships, the flagship *Petropavlovsk* and the *Pobeda* slipped out of port but struck Japanese mines off Port Arthur. The *Petropavlovsk* sank almost immediately, while the *Pobeda* had to be towed back to port for extensive repairs. Admiral Makarov, the single most effective Russian naval strategist of the war, had perished on the battleship *Petropavlovsk*.

On 15 April 1904, the Russian government made overtures threatening to seize the British war correspondents who were taking the ship *Haimun* into warzones to report for the London-based *The Times* newspaper, citing concerns about the possibility of the British giving away Russian positions to the Japanese fleet.

The Russians learned quickly, and soon employed the Japanese tactic of offensive minelaying. On 15 May 1904, two Japanese battleships, the *Yashima* and the *Hatsuse*, were lured into a recently laid Russian minefield off Port Arthur, each striking at least two mines. The *Hatsue* sank within minutes, taking 450 sailors with her, while the *Yashima* sank while under tow towards Korea for repairs. On June 23, 1904, a breakout attempt by the Russian squadron, now under the command of Admiral Wilgelm Vitgeft failed. By the end of the month, Japanese artillery were firing shells into the harbor.

Siege of Port Arthur

Bombardment during the Siege of Port Arthur

Japan began a long siege of Port Arthur. On 10 August 1904, the Russian fleet again attempted to break out and proceed to Vladivostok, but upon reaching the open sea were confronted by Admiral Togo's battleship squadron. Known to the Russians as the Battle of August 10 [9], but more commonly referred to as the Battle of the Yellow Sea, battleships from both sides exchanged gunfire. The battle had the elements of a decisive battle, though Admiral Togo knew that another Russian battleship fleet would soon be sent to the Pacific. The Japanese had only one battleship fleet and Togo had already lost two battleships to Russian mines. The Russian and Japanese battleships continued to exchange gunfire, until the Russian flagship, the battleship _Tsesarevich_, received a direct hit on the bridge, killing the fleet commander, Admiral Vitgeft. At this, the Russian fleet turned around and headed back into Port Arthur. Though no warships were sunk by either side in the battle, the Russians were now back in port and the Japanese navy still had battleships to meet the new Russian fleet when it arrived.

Fall of Port Arthur

Eventually, the Russian warships at Port Arthur were sunk by the artillery of the besieging army. Attempts to relieve the besieged city by land also failed, and, after the Battle of Liaoyang in late August, the Russians retreated to Mukden (Shenyang). Port Arthur finally fell on 2 January 1905 when the garrison's commanding officer ceded the port to the Japanese without consulting his high command.

Baltic Fleet

Meanwhile, at sea, the Russians were preparing to reinforce the Far East Fleet by sending the Baltic Fleet, under Admiral Zinovy Rozhestvensky The fleet sailed around the world from the Baltic Sea to China via the Cape of Good Hope. The Baltic Fleet would not reach the Far East until May 1905.

On 21 October 1904, while passing by the United Kingdom (an ally of Japan but neutral in this war), vessels of the Baltic Fleet nearly provoked a war in the Dogger Bank incident by firing on British fishing boats that they mistook for enemy torpedo boats.

Campaign of 1905

Retreat of Russian Soldiers after the Battle of Mukden.

Harsh winter and final battles

With the fall of Port Arthur, the Japanese 3rd army was now able to continue northward and reinforce positions south of Russian-held Mukden. With the onset of the severe Manchurian winter, there had been no major land engagements since the Battle of Shaho the previous year. Both sides camped opposite each other along 60 to 70 miles (110 km) of front lines, south of Mukden.

The Russian Second Army under General Oskar Grippenberg, between January 25–29, attacked the Japanese left flank near the town of Sandepu, almost breaking through. This caught the Japanese by surprise. However, without support from other Russian units the attack was stalled, Grippenberg was ordered to halt by Kuropatkin and the battle was inconclusive. The Japanese knew that they needed to destroy the Russian army in Manchuria before Russian reinforcements arrived via the Trans-Siberian railroad.

The Battle of Mukden commenced on February 20, 1905. In the following days Japanese forces proceeded to assault the right and left flanks of Russian forces surrounding Mukden, along a 50-mile (80 km) front. Both sides were well entrenched and were backed with hundreds of artillery pieces. After days of harsh fighting, added pressure from both flanks forced both ends of the Russian defensive line to curve backwards. Seeing they were about to be encircled, the Russians began a general retreat, fighting a series of fierce rearguard actions, which soon deteriorated in the confusion and collapse of Russian forces. On March 10, 1905 after three weeks of fighting, General Kuropatkin decided to withdraw to the north of Mukden.

The retreating Russian Manchurian Army formations disintegrated as fighting units, but the Japanese failed to destroy them completely. The Japanese themselves had suffered large casualties and were in no condition to pursue. Although the battle of Mukden was a major defeat for the Russians it had not been decisive, and the final victory would depend on the navy.

Victory at Tsushima

Japanese battleship *Mikasa*,
the flagship of Admiral Tōgō Heihachirō
at the Battle of Tsushima.

The Russian **Second Pacific Squadron** (the renamed Baltic Fleet) voyaged the unprecedented 18,000 miles (29,000 km) to relieve Port Arthur. The demoralizing news that Port Arthur had fallen reached the fleet while at Madagascar. Admiral Rozhestvensky's only hope now was to reach the port of Vladivostok. There were three routes to Vladivostok, with the shortest and most direct passing through Tsushima Straits between Korea and Japan. However, this was also the most dangerous route as it passed very close to the Japanese home islands.

Admiral Togo was aware of the Russian progress and understood that with the fall of Port Arthur, the Second and Third Pacific Squadrons would try to reach the only other Russian port in the Far East, Vladivostok. Battle plans were laid down and ships were repaired and refitted to intercept the Russian fleet.

The Japanese **Combined Fleet**, which had originally consisted of six battleships, was now down to four (two had been lost to mines), but still retained its cruisers, destroyers, and torpedo boats. The *Second Pacific Squadron* contained eight battleships, including four new battleships of the *Borodino* class, as well as cruisers, destroyers and other auxiliaries for a total of 38 ships.

By the end of May the Second Pacific Squadron was on the last leg of its journey to Vladivostok. They decided to take the shorter, more risky route between Korea and Japan. They travelled at night so they might not be discovered. Unfortunately for the Russians, one of their hospital ships exposed a light, which was sighted by the Japanese armed merchant cruiser *Shinano Maru*. Wireless communication was used to inform Togo's headquarters, where the Combined Fleet was immediately ordered to sortie. Still receiving naval intelligence from scouting forces, the Japanese were able to position their fleet so that they would "cross the T" of the Russian fleet. The Japanese engaged the Russian fleet in the Tsushima Straits on 27 May–28 May 1905. The Russian fleet was virtually annihilated, losing eight battleships, numerous smaller vessels, and more than 5,000 men, while the Japanese lost three torpedo boats and 116 men. Only three Russian vessels escaped to Vladivostok. After the Battle of Tsushima, the Japanese army occupied the entire Sakhalin Islands chain to force the Russians to sue for peace.

Peace

Russian and Japanese Delegates negotiating the Treaty of Portsmouth.

The defeat of the Russian Army and Russian Navy shook Russian confidence. Throughout 1905, the Imperial Russian government was rocked by revolution. Tsar Nicholas II elected to negotiate peace so he could concentrate on internal matters.

U.S. President Theodore Roosevelt offered to mediate, and earned a Nobel Peace Prize for his effort. Sergius Witte led the Russian delegation and Baron Komura, a graduate of Harvard, led the Japanese Delegation. The Treaty of Portsmouth was signed on 5 September 1905[10] in the U.S. naval facility in Portsmouth, New Hampshire. Witte became Russian Prime Minister the same year. However a peace treaty with Montenegro was not signed by the Japanese, and a state of war technically remained with this small European country until its independence from Serbia in 2006 (see List of wars extended by diplomatic irregularity).

Russia recognized Korea as part of the Japanese sphere of influence and agreed to evacuate Manchuria. Japan would annex Korea in 1910, with scant protest from other powers.

Russia also signed over its 25-year leasehold rights to Port Arthur, including the naval base and the peninsula around it. Russia also ceded the southern half of Sakhalin Island to Japan. It was regained by the USSR in 1952 under the Treaty of San Francisco following the Second World War. However, the cessation of Southern Sakhalin to the USSR was not supported by the majority of Japanese politicians.

Casualties

Sources do not agree on a precise number of deaths from the war because of lack of body counts for confirmation. The number of Japanese dead in combat is put at around 47,000 with around 80,000 if disease is included. Estimates of Russian dead range from around 40,000 to around 70,000. The total number of dead is generally stated at around 130,000.[11] China suffered 20,000 collateral deaths, and financially the loss amounted to over 69 million taels worth of silver.

Aftermath and consequences

This was the first major victory of an Asian power over a European one in the modern era. Japan's prestige rose greatly as it began to be considered a modern Great Power. Concurrently, Russia lost virtually its entire *Eastern* and *Baltic* fleets, and also lost international esteem. This was particularly true in the eyes of Germany and Austria-Hungary; Russia was France's and Serbia's ally, and that loss of prestige would have a significant effect on Germany's future when planning for war with France, and Austria-Hungary's war with Serbia.

In the absence of Russian competition and with the distraction of European nations during World War I, combined with the Great Depression which followed, the Japanese military began its efforts to dominate China and the rest of Asia, which would eventually lead to the Second Sino-Japanese War and the Pacific War, theatres of World War II.

In Russia, the defeat of 1905 led in the short term to a reform of the Russian military that allowed it to face Germany in World War I. However, the revolts at home following the war planted the seeds that presaged the Russian Revolution of 1917.

All above dates are believed to be New-Style (Gregorian, not the Julian used in Tsarist Russia: for conformity, where there are two, use the one that reads 13 days "later" than the other).

A lock of Admiral Nelson's hair was given to the Imperial Japanese Navy from the Royal Navy after the war to commemorate the victory of the 1905 Battle of Tsushima; which was in tune with Britain's victory at Trafalgar in 1805. It is still on display at Kyouiku Sankoukan, a public museum maintained by the Japan Self-Defense Force.

Assessment of war results

Japanese soldiers' corpses in a trench, with Russian soldiers looking on.

Russia had lost two of its three fleets. Only its Black Sea Fleet remained, and that had been due to an earlier treaty that had prevented the fleet from leaving the Black Sea. Jakob Meckel, a German military advisor sent to Japan, had a tremendous impact on the development of the Japanese military training, tactics, strategy and organization. His reforms were credited with Japan's overwhelming victory over China in the First Sino-Japanese War of 1894–1895. However, his over-reliance on the use of infantry in offensive campaigns also led to the large number of Japanese casualties in the Russo-Japanese War. The Japanese were on the offensive for most of the war, and used massed infantry (human wave) tactics against defensive positions, which would be the standard by all European armies during World War I. Battles during the Russo-Japanese War were a precursor to trench warfare of World War I, in which machine guns and artillery had taken their toll on Japanese troops.

Military and economic exhaustion affected both countries. Popular discontent in Russia after the war added more fuel to the already simmering Russian Revolution of 1905, an event Nicholas II of Russia had hoped to avoid entirely by taking intransigent negotiating stances prior to coming to the table at all. In ten more years, that discontent would boil over into the Bolshevik Revolution of 1917. In Poland, which Russia partitioned in the late 18th century, and where Russian rule already caused two major uprisings, the population was so restless that an army of 250,000-300,000 - larger than the one facing the Japanese - had to be stationed to put down the unrest.[12] Notably, some political leaders of Polish insurrection movement (in particular, Józef Piłsudski) sent emissaries to Japan to collaborate on sabotage and intelligence gathering within the Russian Empire and even plan a Japan-aided uprising.[13]

Although the war had ended in a victory for Japan, there was a noteworthy gap between Japanese public opinion and the very restrained peace terms which negotiated at the war's end.[14] Widespread discontent spread through the populace upon the announcement of the treaty terms. Riots erupted in major cities in Japan.

Year Four Sourcebook, page 157

Two specific demands, expected from such a costly victory, were especially lacking: territorial gains and monetary reparations to Japan. The peace accord led to feelings of distrust, as the Japanese had intended to retain all of Sakhalin Island, but they were forced to settle for half of it after being pressured by the U.S.

Russia's defeat had been met with shock both in the West and across the Far East, that an Asian country could defeat an established European power in a large military conflict.

Japanese historians consider this war to be a turning point for Japan, and a key to understanding the reasons why Japan may have failed militarily and politically later on. The acrimony was felt at every stratum of Japanese society and it became the consensus within Japan that their nation had been treated as the defeated power during the peace conference. As time went on, this feeling, coupled with the sense of arrogance of becoming a Great Power, grew and added to their growing hostility towards the West and fueled their own militarist and imperialist ambitions, which would cumulate in Japan's invasion of East, Southeast, and South Asia in World War II in an attempt to create their own great colonial empire in the name of creating the Greater East Asia Co-prosperity Sphere. Only five years after the war, Japan de jure annexed Korea as its colonial empire, and invaded Manchuria in the Mukden Incident 21 years after in 1931. As a result, most Chinese historians note the war as a key development of Japanese militarism.

List of battles

1904 Battle of Port Arthur, February 8: naval battle Inconclusive
1904 Battle of Chemulpo Bay, February 9: naval battle Japanese victory
1904 Battle of Yalu River, April 30 to May 1: Japanese victory
1904 Battle of Nanshan, May 25 – May 26, Japanese victory
1904 Battle of Telissu, June 14 – June 15 , Japanese victory
1904 Battle of Motien Pass, July 17, Japanese victory
1904 Battle of Ta-shih-chiao, July 24, Japanese victory
1904 Battle of Hsimucheng, July 31, Japanese victory
1904 Battle of the Yellow Sea, August 10: naval battle Japanese victory strategically/tactically inconclusive
1904 Battle off Ulsan, August 14: naval battle Japanese victory
1904–1905 Siege of Port Arthur, August 19 to January 2: Japanese victory
1904 Battle of Liaoyang, August 25 to September 3: Inconclusive
1904 Battle of Shaho, October 5 to October 17: Inconclusive
1905 Battle of Sandepu, January 26 to January 27: Inconclusive
1905 Battle of Mukden, February 21 to March 10: Japanese victory
1905 Battle of Tsushima, May 27 to 28 May naval battle: Japanese victory

Art and literature

Painting of Admiral Togo
on the bridge of the Japanese battleship Mikasa,
before the Battle of Tsushima in 1905.

The Russo-Japanese War was covered by dozens of foreign journalists who sent back sketches that were turned into lithographs and other reproducible forms. Propaganda images were circulated by both sides and quite a few photographs have been preserved.

Siege of Port Arthur is covered in an excellent historical novel 'Port Arthur' by Alexander Stepanov (1892-1965), who, at the age of 12, lived in the besieged city and witnessed many key events of the siege. He took a personal role in Port Arthur defense by carrying water to front line trenches; was contused; narrowly evaded amputation of both legs while in the hospital. His father, Nikolay Stepanov, commanded one of Russian onshore batteries protecting the harbor; through him Alexander personally knew many top military commanders of the city - generals Stessels, Belikh, Nikitin, Kondratenko, admiral Makarov and many others. The novel itself was written in 1932, based on the author's own diaries and notes of his father; although it might be subject to ideological bias, as anything published in the USSR at that time, it was (and still is) generally considered in Russia one of the best historical novels of Soviet period[15].

The Russo-Japanese War is occasionally alluded to in James Joyce's novel, Ulysses. In the "Eumaeus" chapter, a drunken sailor in a bar proclaims, "But a day of reckoning, he stated crescendo with no uncertain voice—thoroughly monopolizing all the conversation—was in store for mighty England, despite her power of pelf on account of her crimes. There would be a fall and the greatest fall in history. The Germans and the Japs were going to have their little lookin, he affirmed."

The Russo-Japanese War is the setting for the naval strategy computer game Distant Guns developed by Storm Eagle Studios.

The Russo-Japanese War is the setting for the first part of the novel The Diamond Vehicle, in the Erast Fandorin detective series by Boris Akunin.

The Domination series by S.M. Stirling has an alternate Battle of Tsushima where the Japanese use airships to attack the Russian Fleet. This is detailed in the short story "Written by the Wind" by Roland J. Green in the Drakas! anthology.

Notes

1. ^ University of Texas: Growth of colonial empires in Asia
2. ^ S.C.M. Paine, p. 317
3. ^ Connaughton R., p. 7-8.
4. ^ S.C.M. Paine, p. 320.
5. ^ Connaughton, p. 10.
6. ^ Connaughton, p. 34.
7. ^ Yale University: Laws of War: Opening of Hostilities (Hague III); October 18, 1907, Avalon Project at Yale Law School.
8. ^ Shaw, Albert (March, 1904), "The Progress of the World - Japan's Swift Action", *The American Monthly Review of Reviews* (New York: The Review of Reviews Company) **29** (No. 3): 260, <http://books.google.com/books?id=Jr8CAAAAYAAJ&dq=%22Review+of+Reviews%22&lr=&as_brr=1&source=gbs_summary_s&cad=0>
9. ^ Semenov: "Battle of Tsushima"
10. ^ Connaughton, p. 272; "Text of Treaty; Signed by the Emperor of Japan and Czar of Russia," *New York Times.* October 17, 1905.
11. ^ Twentieth Century Atlas - Death Tolls and Casualty Statistics for Wars, Dictatorships and Genocides

12. ^ Abraham Ascher, *The Revolution of 1905: Russia in Disarray*, Stanford University Press, 1994, ISBN 0804723273, Google Print, p.157-158
13. ^ For Polish-Japanese negotiations and relations during the war, see:Bert Edström, *The Japanese and Europe: Images and Perceptions*, Routledge, 2000, ISBN 1873410867, Google Print, p.126-133
    Jerzy Lerski, *A Polish Chapter of the Russio-Japanese War*, Transactions of the Asiatic Society of Japan, III/7 p. 69-96
14. ^ "Japan's Present Crisis and Her Constitution; The Mikado's Ministers Will Be Held Responsible by the People for the Peace Treaty -- Marquis Ito May Be Able to Save Baron Komura," *New York Times*. September 3, 1905.
15. ^ 'Port Arthur' by Alexander Stepanov, published by 'Soviet Russia' in 1978, 'About Author' section

References

Connaughton, R.M., *The War of the Rising Sun and the Tumbling Bear—A Military History of the Russo-Japanese War 1904-5*, London, 1988, ISBN 0-415-00906-5.

Pine, S.C.M., *The Sino-Japanese War of 1894-1895: Perceptions, Power, and Primacy*, 2003, ISBN 0-521-81714-5

Corbett, Sir Julian. *Maritime Operations In The Russo-Japanese War 1904-1905*. (1994) Originally classified, and in two volumnes, ISBN 155-7501-297.

Grant, R., Captain, D.S.O. *Before Port Arthur In A Destroyer*. (The Personal Diary Of A Japanese Naval Officer-Translated from the Spanish Edition by Captain R. Grant, D.S.O. Rifle Brigade). John Murray, Albemarle St. W. (1907).

Hough, Richard A. *The Fleet That Had To Die*. Ballantine Books. (1960).

Jukes, Geoffry. *The Russo-Japanese War 1904–1905*. Osprey Essential Histories. (2002). ISBN 9-78184-17644-67.

Kowner, Rotem (2006). *Historical Dictionary of the Russo-Japanese War*. Scarecrow. ISBN 0-8108-4927-5.

Morris, Edmund (2002). *Theodore Rex*. The Modern Library. ISBN 0-8129-6600-7.

Aleksei Novikov-Priboy|Novikov-Priboy, Aleksei. *Tsushima*. (An account from a seaman aboard the Battleship *Orel* (which was captured at Tsushima). London: George Allen & Unwin Ltd. (1936).

Nish, Ian (1985). *The Origins of the Russo-Japanese War*. Longman. ISBN 0-582-49114-2.

Okamoto, Shumpei (1970). *The Japanese Oligarchy and the Russo-Japanese War*. Columbia University Press.

Pleshakov, Constantine. *The Tsar's Last Armada: The Epic Voyage to the Battle of Tsushima*. ISBN 0-46505-792-6. (2002).

Saaler, Sven und Inaba Chiharu (Hg.). *Der Russisch-Japanische Krieg 1904/05 im Spiegel deutscher Bilderbogen*, Deutsches Institut für Japanstudien Tokyo, (2005).

Seager, Robert. *Alfred Thayer Mahan: The Man And His Letters*. (1977) ISBN 0870-21359-8.

Semenov, Vladimir, Capt. *The Battle of Tsushima*. E.P. Dutton & Co. (1912).

Semenov, Vladimir, Capt. *Rasplata (The Reckoning)*. John Murray, (1910).

Tomitch, V. M. *Warships of the Imperial Russian Navy*. Volume 1, Battleships. (1968).

Warner, Denis & Peggy. *The Tide at Sunrise, A History of the Russo-Japanese War 1904–1905*. (1975). ISBN 0-7146-5256-3.

This page was last modified on 24 June 2008, at 10:33.

Francis Schaeffer Study Center
Mt. Juliet, Tennessee

Western Civilization, Year Four

From 1865 to 1990, Reconstruction to Modern Times

Rob Shearer, Tutor

Week Ten Reading

The Great War

World War I

From Wikipedia, the free encyclopedia

World War I	
Date	28 July 1914–11 November 1918
Location	Europe, Africa and the Middle East (briefly in China and the Pacific Islands)
Casus belli	Assassination of Archduke Franz Ferdinand (28 June) followed by Austrian declaration of war on Serbia (28 July) and Russian mobilisation against Austria-Hungary (29 July).
Result	Allied victory. End of the German Empire, the Russian Empire, the Ottoman Empire, and the Austro-Hungarian Empire. Creation of many new countries in Eastern and Central Europe.

Clockwise from top: Trenches on the Western Front; a British Mark IV tank crossing a trench; Royal Navy battleship HMS *Irresistible* sinking after striking a mine at the Battle of the Dardanelles; a Vickers machine gun crew with gas masks, and German Albatros D.III biplanes

Combatants

Entente Powers:
- Kingdom of Serbia
- Russian Empire
- France
- British Empire
- Italy
- United States

Central Powers:
- Austria-Hungary
- German Empire
- Ottoman Empire
- Bulgaria

Casualties

Military dead: 5,525,000	**Military dead:** 4,386,000
Military wounded: 12,831,500	**Military wounded:** 8,388,000
Military missing: 4,121,000[1]	**Military missing:** 3,629,000[1]

Summary

World War I, also known as the **First World War**, the **Great War** and the **War To End All Wars**, was a global military conflict which took place primarily in Europe from 1914 to 1918. Over 40 million casualties resulted, including approximately 20 million military and civilian deaths. The conflict had a decisive impact on the history of the 20th century.

The Entente Powers, led by France, Russia, the United Kingdom and its colonies and dominions, and later Italy (from 1915) and the United States (from 1917), defeated the Central Powers, led by the Austro-Hungarian, German, and Ottoman Empires. Russia withdrew from the war after the revolution in 1917.

The fighting that took place along the Western Front occurred along a system of trenches, breastworks, and fortifications separated by an area known as no man's land.[2] These fortifications stretched 475 miles (more than 600 kilometres)[2] and defined the war for many. On the Eastern Front, the vast eastern plains and limited rail network prevented a trench warfare stalemate, though the scale of the conflict was just as large as on the Western Front. The Middle Eastern Front and the Italian Front also saw heavy fighting, while hostilities also occurred at sea, and for the first time, in the air.

The war caused the disintegration of four empires: the Austro-Hungarian, German, Ottoman and Russian. Germany lost its colonial empire and states such as Czechoslovakia, Estonia, Finland, Latvia, Lithuania, Poland and Yugoslavia gained independence. The cost of waging the war set the stage for the breakup of the British Empire as well and left France devastated for more than a generation.

World War I marked the end of the world order which had existed after the Napoleonic Wars, and was an important factor in the outbreak of World War II.

- **Contents 1 Causes**
  - 1.1 Arms race
  - 1.2 Plans, distrust and mobilization
  - 1.3 Militarism and autocracy
  - 1.4 Balance of Power
  - 1.5 Economic imperialism
  - 1.6 Trade barriers
  - 1.7 Ethnic and political rivalries
- 2 July crisis and declarations of war
- 3 Chronology
  - 3.1 Opening hostilities
    - 3.1.1 Confusion among the Central Powers
    - 3.1.2 African campaigns
    - 3.1.3 Serbian campaign
    - 3.1.4 German forces in Belgium and France
    - 3.1.5 Asia and the Pacific
  - 3.2 Early stages
    - 3.2.1 Trench warfare begins
  - 3.3 Naval war
  - 3.4 Southern theatres
    - 3.4.1 Ottoman Empire
    - 3.4.2 Italian participation
    - 3.4.3 War in the Balkans
    - 3.4.4 Fighting in India
  - 3.5 Eastern Front
    - 3.5.1 Initial actions
    - 3.5.2 Ukrainian oppression
    - 3.5.3 Russian Revolution
  - 3.6 1917–1918
    - 3.6.1 Entry of the United States
    - 3.6.2 German Spring Offensive of 1918
    - 3.6.3 New states under war zone
    - 3.6.4 Allied victory: summer and autumn 1918
  - 3.7 End of war
- 4 Soldiers' experiences
- 5 Prisoners of war
- 6 War crimes
  - 6.1 Armenian Genocide
  - 6.2 Rape of Belgium
- 7 Economics and manpower issues
- 8 Technology
- 9 Opposition to the war
- 10 Aftermath
  - 10.1 Peace treaties
  - 10.2 New national identities
  - 10.3 Social trauma
- 11 Other names
- 12 Historical era
- 13 See also
  - 13.1 Media
- 14 Notes
- 15 References
- 16 Maps
  - 16.1 Western Front
    - 16.1.1 American Operations

Causes

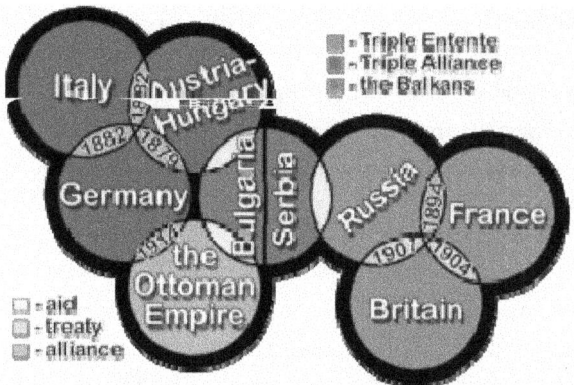

A graphic depiction of the state of international relations in pre-WWI Europe.
Italy came in on the side of France and Britain in April 1915.

On the 28 June 1914, Gavrilo Princip, a Bosnian Serb student, killed Archduke Franz Ferdinand, heir to the Austro-Hungarian throne, in Sarajevo. Princip was a member of Young Bosnia, a group whose aims included the unification of the South Slavs and independence from Austria-Hungary. The assassination in Sarajevo set into motion a series of fast-moving events that eventually escalated into full-scale war. Austria-Hungary demanded action by Serbia to punish those responsible, and when Austria-Hungary deemed Serbia had not complied, declared war. Major European powers were at war within weeks because of overlapping agreements for collective defense and the complex nature of international alliances.

Arms race

The naval race between Britain and Germany was intensified by the 1906 launch of HMS Dreadnought —a revolutionary craft whose size and power rendered previous battleships obsolete. Britain also maintained a large naval lead in other areas particularly over Germany and Italy. Paul Kennedy pointed out both nations believed Alfred Thayer Mahan's thesis of command of the sea as vital to great nation status; experience with guerre de course would prove Mahan wrong.

David Stevenson described the arms race as "a self-reinforcing cycle of heightened military preparedness." David Herrmann viewed the shipbuilding rivalry as part of a general movement in the direction of war. Niall Ferguson, however, argued Britain's ability to maintain an overall lead signified this was not a factor in the oncoming conflict.

The cost of the arms race was felt in both Britain and Germany. The total arms spending by the six Great Powers (Britain, Germany, France, Russia, Austria-Hungary and Italy) increased by 50% between 1908 and 1913.[3]

Plans, distrust and mobilization

Closely related is the thesis adopted by many political scientists that the mobilization plans of Germany, France and Russia automatically escalated the conflict. Fritz Fischer emphasized the inherently aggressive nature of the Schlieffen Plan, which outlined a two-front strategy. Fighting on two fronts meant Germany had to eliminate one opponent quickly before taking on the other. It called for a strong right flank attack, to seize Belgium and cripple the French army by pre-empting its mobilization. After the attack, the German army would rush east by railroad and quickly destroy the slowly mobilizing Russian forces.

France's Plan XVII envisioned a quick thrust into the Ruhr Valley, Germany's industrial heartland, which would in theory cripple Germany's ability to wage a modern war.

Russia's Plan XIX foresaw a mobilization of its armies against both Austria-Hungary and Germany.

All three plans created an atmosphere in which speed was one of the determining factors for victory. Elaborate timetables were prepared; once mobilization had begun, there was little possibility of turning back. Diplomatic delays and poor communications exacerbated the problems.

Also, the plans of France, Germany and Russia were all biased toward the offensive, in clear conflict with the improvements of defensive firepower and entrenchment.[4]

Militarism and autocracy

President Woodrow Wilson of the United States and others blamed the war on militarism.[5] Some argued that aristocrats and military élites had too much power in countries such as Germany, Russia, and Austria-Hungary. War was thus a consequence of their desire for military power and disdain for democracy. This theme figured prominently in anti-German propaganda. Consequently, supporters of this theory called for the abdication of rulers such as Kaiser Wilhelm II, as well as an end to aristocracy and militarism in general. This platform provided some justification for the American entry into the war when the Russian Empire surrendered in 1917.

Wilson hoped the League of Nations and disarmament would secure a lasting peace. He also acknowledged that variations of militarism, in his opinion, existed within the British and French Empires.

There was some validity to this view, as the Allies consisted of Great Britain and France, both democracies, fighting the Central Powers, which included Germany, Austro-Hungary, and the Ottoman Empire. Russia, one of the Allied Powers, was an empire until 1917, but it was opposed to the subjugation of Slavic peoples by Austro-Hungary.

Against this backdrop, the view of the war as one of democracy versus dictatorship initially had some validity, but lost credibility as the conflict dragged on.

Balance of Power

Political cartoon depicting the tangled web of European alliances.

One of the goals of the foreign policies of the Great Powers in the pre-war years was to maintain the 'Balance of Power' in Europe. This evolved into an elaborate network of secret and public alliances and agreements. For example, after the Franco-Prussian war (1870–71), Britain seemed to favor a strong Germany, as it helped to balance its traditional enemy, France. After Germany began its naval construction plans to rival that of Britain, this stance shifted. France, looking for an ally to balance the threat created by Germany, found it in Russia. Austria-Hungary, facing a threat from Russia, sought support from Germany.

When the Great War broke out, these treaties only partially determined who entered the war on which side. Britain had no treaties with France or Russia, but entered the war on their side. Italy had a treaty with both Austria-Hungary and Germany, yet did not enter the war with them; Italy later sided with the Allies. Perhaps the most significant treaty of all was the initially *defensive* pact between Germany and Austria-Hungary, which Germany in 1909 extended by declaring that Germany was bound to stand with Austria-Hungary even if it had started the war.[6]

Economic imperialism

Vladimir Lenin asserted that imperialism was responsible for the war. He drew upon the economic theories of Karl Marx and English economist John A. Hobson, who predicted that unlimited competition for expanding markets would lead to a global conflict.[7] This argument was popular in the wake of the war and assisted in the rise of Communism. Lenin argued that the banking interests of various capitalist-imperialist powers orchestrated the war.[8]

Trade barriers

Cordell Hull, American Secretary of State under Franklin Roosevelt, believed that trade barriers were the root cause of both World War I and World War II. In 1944, he helped design the Bretton Woods Agreements to reduce trade barriers and eliminate what he saw as the cause of the conflicts.

Ethnic and political rivalries

A Balkan war between Austria-Hungary and Serbia was considered inevitable, as Austria-Hungary's influence waned and the Pan-Slavic movement grew. The rise of ethnic nationalism coincided with the growth of Serbia, where anti-Austrian sentiment was perhaps most fervent. Austria-Hungary had occupied the former Ottoman province of Bosnia-Herzegovina, which had a large Serb population, in 1878. It was formally annexed by Austria-Hungary in 1908. Increasing nationalist sentiment also coincided with the decline of the Ottoman Empire. Russia supported the Pan-Slavic movement, motivated by ethnic and religious loyalties and a rivalry with Austria dating back to the Crimean War. Recent events such as the failed Russian-Austrian treaty and a century-old dream of a warm water port also motivated St. Petersburg.[9]

Myriad other geopolitical motivations existed elsewhere as well, for example France's loss of Alsace and Lorraine in the Franco-Prussian War helped create a sentiment of irredentist *revanchism* in that country. France eventually allied itself with Russia, creating the likelihood of a two-front war for Germany.

July crisis and declarations of war

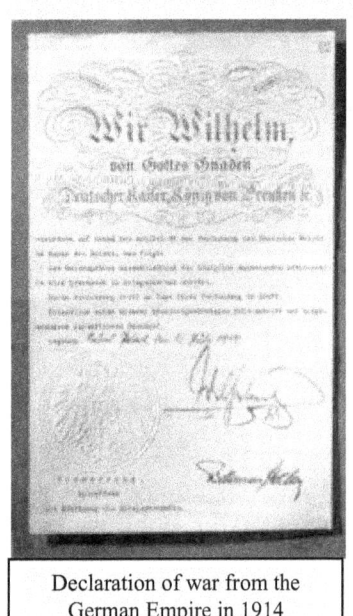

Declaration of war from the German Empire in 1914

The Austro-Hungarian government used the assassination of Archduke Franz Ferdinand as a pretext to deal with the Serbian question, supported by Germany. On 23 July 1914, an ultimatum was sent to Serbia with demands so extreme that it was rejected. The Serbians, relying on support from Russia, instead ordered mobilization. In response to this, Austria-Hungary issued a declaration of war on 28 July. Initially, Russia ordered partial mobilization, directed at the Austrian frontier. On 31 July, after the Russian General Staff informed the Czar that partial mobilization was logistically impossible, a full mobilization was ordered. The Schlieffen Plan, which relied on a quick strike against France, could not afford to allow the Russians to mobilize without launching an attack. Thus, the Germans declared war against Russia on 1 August and on France two days later. Next, Germany violated Belgium's neutrality by the German advance through it to Paris, and this brought the British Empire into the war. With this, five of the six

European powers were now involved in the largest continental European conflict since the Napoleonic Wars.[10]

Chronology

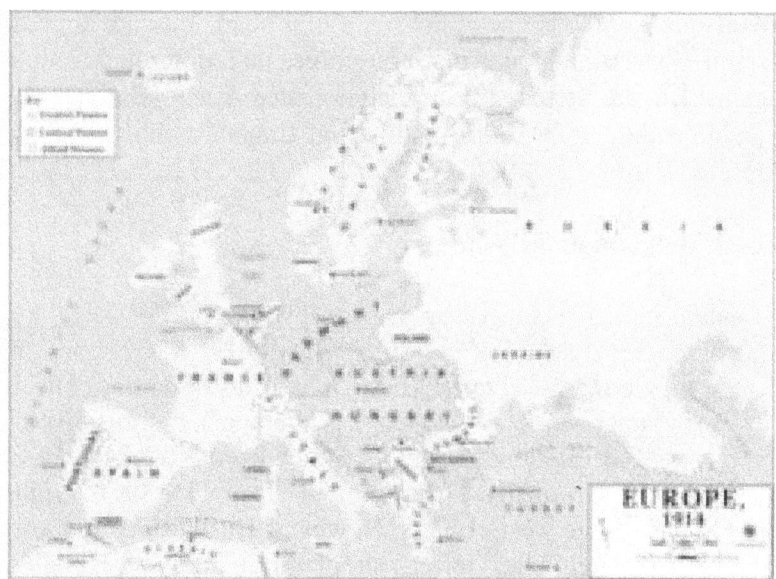

European military alliances in 1914; Central Powers purplish-red, Entente Powers grey and neutral countries yellow

Opening hostilities

Confusion among the Central Powers

The strategy of the Central Powers suffered from miscommunication. Germany had promised to support Austria-Hungary's invasion of Serbia, but interpretations of what this meant differed. Austro-Hungarian leaders believed Germany would cover its northern flank against Russia. Germany, however, envisioned Austria-Hungary directing the majority of its troops against Russia, while Germany dealt with France. This confusion forced the Austro-Hungarian Army to divide its forces between the Russian and Serbian fronts.

African campaigns

Some of the first clashes of the war involved British, French and German colonial forces in Africa. On 7 August, French and British troops invaded the German protectorate of Togoland. On 10 August German forces in South-West Africa attacked South Africa; sporadic and fierce fighting continued for the remainder of the war.

Serbian campaign

The Serbian army fought the Battle of Cer against the invading Austrians, beginning on 12 August, occupying defensive positions on the south side of the Drina and Sava rivers. Over the next two weeks Austrian attacks were thrown back with heavy losses, which marked the first major Allied victory of the war and dashed Austrian hopes of a swift victory. As a result, Austria had to keep sizable forces on the Serbian front, weakening their efforts against Russia. Serbian troops then defeated Austro-Hungarian forces at the Battle of Kolubara, leading to 240,000 Austro-Hungarian casualties. The Serbian Army lost 170,000 troops.

German forces in Belgium and France

Initially, the Germans had great success in the Battle of the Frontiers (14 August – 24 August). Russia, however, attacked in East Prussia and diverted German forces intended for the Western Front. Germany defeated Russia in a series of battles collectively known as the First Battle of Tannenberg (17 August – 2 September), but this diversion exacerbated problems of insufficient speed of advance from rail-heads not foreseen by the German General Staff. Originally, the Schlieffen Plan called for the right flank of the German advance to pass to the west of Paris. However, the capacity and low speed of horse-drawn transport hampered the German supply train, allowing French and British forces to finally halt the German advance east of Paris at the First Battle of the Marne (5 September – 12 September), thereby denying the Central Powers a quick victory and forcing them to fight a war on two fronts. The German army had fought its way into a good defensive position inside France and had permanently incapacitated 230,000 more French and British troops than it had lost itself. Despite this, communications problems and questionable command decisions cost Germany the chance for an early victory.

Asia and the Pacific

New Zealand occupied German Samoa (later Western Samoa) on 30 August. On 11 September the Australian Naval and Military Expeditionary Force landed on the island of Neu Pommern (later New Britain), which formed part of German New Guinea. Japan seized Germany's Micronesian colonies and after Battle of Tsingtao, the German coaling port of Qingdao, in the Chinese Shandong peninsula. Within a few months, the Allied forces had seized all the German territories in the Pacific.

Early stages

In the trenches: Infantry with gas masks, Ypres, 1917

Trench warfare begins

Military tactics before World War I had failed to keep pace with advances in technology. It demanded the building of impressive defence systems, which out-of-date tactics could not break through for most of the war. Barbed wire was a significant hindrance to massed infantry advances. Artillery, vastly more lethal than in the 1870s, coupled with machine guns, made crossing open ground very difficult. The Germans introduced poison gas; it soon became used by both sides, though it never proved decisive in winning a battle. Its effects were brutal, however, causing slow and painful death, and poison gas became one of the most-feared and best-remembered horrors of the war. Commanders on both sides failed to develop tactics for breaking through entrenched positions without heavy casualties. In time, however, technology began also to yield new offensive weapons, such as the tank. Britain and France were its primary users; the Germans employed captured Allied tanks and small numbers of their own design.

After the First Battle of the Marne, both Entente and German forces began a series of outflanking maneuvers, in the so-called 'Race to the Sea'. Britain and France soon found themselves facing entrenched German forces from Lorraine to Belgium's Flemish coast. Britain and France sought to take the offensive, while Germany defended the occupied territories; consequentially, German trenches were generally much better constructed than those of their enemy. Anglo-French trenches were only intended to be 'temporary' before their forces broke through German defenses. Both sides attempted to break the stalemate using scientific and technological advances. In April 1915, the Germans used chlorine gas for the first time (in violation of the Hague Convention), opening a 6 kilometres (4 mi) hole in the Allied lines when British and French colonial troops retreated. Canadian soldiers closed the breach at the Second Battle of Ypres. At the Third Battle of Ypres, Canadian forces took the village of Passchendaele.

A French assault on German positions. Champagne, France, 1917.

On 1 July 1916, the first day of the Battle of the Somme, the British Army endured the bloodiest day in its history, suffering 57,470 casualties and 19,240 dead. Most of the casualties occurred in the first hour of the attack. The entire offensive cost the British Army almost half a million dead.

Neither side proved able to deliver a decisive blow for the next two years, though protracted German action at Verdun throughout 1916, combined with the Entente's

Year Four Sourcebook, page 173

failure at the Somme, brought the exhausted French army to the brink of collapse. Futile attempts at frontal assault, a rigid adherence to an ineffectual method, came at a high price for both the British and the French *poilu* (infantry) and led to widespread mutinies, especially during the Nivelle Offensive.

Canadian troops advancing behind a British Mark II tank at the Vimy Ridge.

Throughout 1915–17, the British Empire and France suffered more casualties than Germany, due both to the strategic and tactical stances chosen by the sides. At the strategic level, while the Germans only mounted a single main offensive at Verdun, the Allies made several attempts to break through German lines. At the tactical level, the German defensive doctrine was well suited for trench warfare, with a relatively lightly defended "sacrificial" forward position, and a more powerful main position from which an immediate and powerful counter-offensive could be launched. This combination usually was effective in pushing out attackers at a relatively low cost to the Germans. In absolute terms, of course, the cost in lives of men for both attack and defense was astounding.

Around 800,000 soldiers from the British Empire were on the Western Front at any one time. 1,000 battalions, occupying sectors of the line from the North Sea to the Orne River, operated on a month-long four-stage rotation system, unless an offensive was underway. The front contained over 9,600 kilometres (5,965 mi) of trenches. Each battalion held its sector for about a week before moving back to support lines and then further back to the reserve lines before a week out-of-line, often in the Poperinge or Amiens areas.

In the Battle of Arras under British command during the 1917 campaign, the only military success was the capture of Vimy Ridge by Canadian forces under Sir Arthur Currie and Julian Byng. It provided the allies with a great military advantage and had a lasting impact on the war. Vimy is considered by many historians to be one of the founding myths of Canada.

Naval war

A battleship squadron of the Hochseeflotte at sea.

At the start of the war, the German Empire had cruisers scattered across the globe, some of which were subsequently used to attack Allied merchant shipping. The British Royal Navy systematically hunted them down, though not without some embarrassment from its inability to protect allied shipping. For example, the German detached light cruiser Emden, part of the East-Asia squadron stationed at Tsingtao, seized or destroyed 15 merchantmen, as well as sinking a Russian cruiser and a French destroyer. However, the bulk of the German East-Asia squadron—consisting of the armoured cruisers *Scharnhorst* and *Gneisenau*, light cruisers *Nürnberg* and *Leipzig* and two transport ships—did not have orders to raid shipping and was instead underway to Germany when it encountered elements of the British fleet. The German flotilla, along with *Dresden*, sank two armoured cruisers at the Battle of Coronel, but was almost completely destroyed at the Battle of the Falkland Islands in December 1914, with only *Dresden* escaping.[11]

Soon after the outbreak of hostilities, Britain initiated a naval blockade of Germany. The strategy proved effective, cutting off vital military and civilian supplies, although this blockade violated generally accepted international law codified by several international agreements of the past two centuries. A blockade of stationed ships within a three mile (5 km) radius was considered legitimate, however Britain mined international waters to prevent any ships from entering entire sections of ocean, causing danger to even neutral ships. Since there was limited response to this tactic, Germany expected a similar response to its unrestricted submarine warfare.

The 1916 Battle of Jutland (German: *Skagerrakschlacht*, or "Battle of the Skagerrak") developed into the largest naval battle of the war, the only full-scale clash of battleships during the war. It took place on 31 May–1 June 1916, in the North Sea off Jutland. The Kaiserliche Marine's High Seas Fleet, commanded by Vice Admiral Reinhard Scheer, squared off against the Royal Navy's Grand Fleet, led by Admiral Sir John Jellicoe. The engagement was a standoff, as the Germans, outmaneuvered by the larger British fleet, managed to escape and inflicted more damage to the British fleet than they received. Strategically, however, the British asserted their control of the sea, and the bulk of the German surface fleet remained confined to port for the duration of the war.

German U-boats attempted to cut the supply lines between North America and Britain. The nature of submarine warfare meant that attacks often came without warning, giving the crews of the merchant ships little hope of survival. The United States launched a protest, and Germany modified its rules of engagement. After the infamous sinking of the passenger ship RMS *Lusitania* in 1915, Germany promised not to target passenger liners, while Britain armed its merchant ships. Finally, in early 1917 Germany adopted a policy of unrestricted submarine warfare, realizing the Americans would eventually enter the war. Germany sought to strangle Allied sea lanes before the U.S. could transport a large army overseas.

The U-boat threat lessened in 1917, when merchant ships entered convoys escorted by destroyers. This tactic made it difficult for U-boats to find targets, which significantly lessened losses; after the introduction of hydrophone and depth charges, accompanying destroyers might actually attack a submerged submarine with some hope of success. The convoy system slowed the flow of supplies, since ships had to wait as convoys were assembled. The solution to the delays was a massive program to build new freighters. Troop ships were too fast for the submarines and did not travel the North Atlantic in convoys.

The First World War also saw the first use of aircraft carriers in combat, with HMS *Furious* launching Sopwith Camels in a successful raid against the Zeppelin hangars at Tondern in July 1918, as well as blimps for antisubmarine patrol.[12]

Southern theatres

Ottoman Empire

The Ottoman Empire joined the Central Powers in the war, the secret Ottoman-German Alliance having been signed in August 1914. It threatened Russia's Caucasian territories and Britain's communications with India via the Suez Canal. The British and French opened overseas fronts with the Gallipoli (1915) and Mesopotamian campaigns. In Gallipoli, the Turks successfully repelled the British, French and Australian and New Zealand Army Corps (ANZACs). In Mesopotamia, by contrast, after the disastrous Siege of Kut (1915–16), British Imperial forces reorganised and captured Baghdad in March 1917. Further to the west, in the Sinai and Palestine Campaign, initial British setbacks were overcome when Jerusalem was captured in December 1917. The Egyptian Expeditionary Force, under Field Marshal Edmund Allenby, broke the Ottoman forces at the Battle of Megiddo in September 1918.

Russian armies generally had the best of it in the Caucasus. *Vice-Generalissimo* Enver Pasha, supreme commander of the Turkish armed forces, was ambitious and dreamed of conquering central Asia. He was, however, a poor commander. He launched an offensive against the Russians in the Caucasus in December 1914 with 100,000 troops; insisting on a frontal attack against mountainous Russian positions in winter, he lost 86% of his force at the Battle of Sarikamis.

The Russian commander from 1915 to 1916, General Yudenich, drove the Turks out of most of the southern Caucasus with a string of victories.

In 1917, Russian Grand Duke Nicholas assumed command of the Caucasus front. Nicholas planned a railway from Russian Georgia to the conquered territories, so that fresh supplies could be brought up for a new offensive in 1917. However, in March 1917, (February in the pre-revolutionary Russian calendar), the Czar was overthrown in the February Revolution and the Russian Caucasus Army began to fall apart. In this situation, the army corps of Armenian volunteer units realigned themselves under the command of General Tovmas Nazarbekian, with Dro as a civilian commissioner of the Administration for Western Armenia. The front line had three main divisions: Movses Silikyan, Andranik and Mikhail Areshian. Another regular unit was under Colonel Korganian. There were Armenian partisan guerrilla detachments (more than 40,000[13]) accompanying these main units.

The Arab Revolt was a major cause of the Ottoman Empire's defeat. The revolts started with the Battle of Mecca by Sherif Hussain of Mecca with the help of Britain in June 1916, and ended with the Ottoman surrender of Damascus. Fakhri Pasha the Ottoman commander of Medina showed stubborn resistance for over two and half years during the Siege of Medina.

Along the border of Italian Libya and British Egypt, the Senussi tribe, incited and armed by the Turks, waged a small-scale guerilla war against Allied troops. According to Martin Gilbert's *The First World War*, the British were forced to dispatch 12,000 troops to deal with the Senussi. Their rebellion was finally crushed in mid-1916.

Italian participation

Italy had been allied with the German and Austro-Hungarian Empires since 1882 as part of the Triple Alliance. However, the nation had its own designs on Austrian territory in Trentino, Istria and Dalmatia. Rome had a secret 1902 pact with France, effectively nullifying its alliance.[14] At the start of hostilities, Italy refused to commit troops, arguing that the Triple Alliance was defensive in nature, and that Austria-Hungary was an aggressor. The Austro-Hungarian government began negotiations to secure Italian neutrality, offering the French colony of Tunisia in return. However, Italy then joined the Entente in April 1915 and declared war on Austria-Hungary in May. Fifteen months later, it declared war on Germany.

Difficult Progress In the Alps

Militarily, the Italians had numerical superiority. This advantage, however, was lost, not only because of the difficult terrain in which fighting took place, but also because of the strategies and tactics employed. Generalissimo Luigi Cadorna insisted on attacking the Isonzo front. Cadorna, a staunch proponent of the frontal assault, had dreams of breaking into the Slovenian plateau, taking Ljubljana and threatening Vienna. It was a Napoleonic plan, which had no realistic chance of success in an age of barbed wire, machine guns, and indirect artillery fire, combined with hilly and mountainous terrain. Cadorna unleashed eleven offensives (Battles of the Isonzo) with total disregard for his men's lives. The Italians also went on the offensive to relieve pressure on other Allied fronts. On the Trentino front, the Austro-Hungarians took advantage of the mountainous terrain, which favoured the defender. After an initial strategic retreat, the front remained largely unchanged, while Austrian Kaiserschützen and Standschützen and Italian Alpini engaged in bitter hand-to-hand combat throughout the summer. The Austro-Hungarians counter-attacked in the Altopiano of Asiago, towards Verona and Padua, in the spring of 1916 (*Strafexpedition*), but made little progress.

Beginning in 1915, the Italians mounted eleven offensives along the Isonzo River, north-east of Trieste. All eleven offensives were repelled by the Austro-Hungarians, who held the higher ground. In the summer of 1916, the Italians captured the town of Gorizia. After this minor victory, the front remained static for over a year, despite several Italian offensives. In the autumn of 1917, thanks to the improving situation on the Eastern front, the Austrians received large numbers of reinforcements, including German Stormtroopers and the elite Alpenkorps. The Central Powers launched a crushing offensive on 26 October 1917, spearheaded by the Germans. They achieved a victory at Caporetto. The Italian army was routed and retreated more than 100 km (60 miles). They were able to reorganise and stabilize the front at the Piave River. In 1918, the Austro-Hungarians repeatedly failed to break through, in a series of battles on the Asiago Plateau, finally being decisively defeated in the Battle of Vittorio Veneto in October of that year. Austria-Hungary surrendered in early November 1918.

War in the Balkans

Faced with Russia, Austria-Hungary could spare only one third of its army to attack Serbia. After suffering heavy losses, the Austrians briefly occupied the Serbian capital, Belgrade. Serbian counterattacks, however, succeeded in driving them from the country by the end of 1914. For the first ten months of 1915, Austria-Hungary used most of its military reserves to fight Italy. German and Austro-Hungarian diplomats, however, scored a coup by convincing Bulgaria to join in attacking Serbia. The Austro-Hungarian provinces of Slovenia, Croatia and Bosnia provided troops for Austria-Hungary, invading Serbia as well as fighting Russia and Italy. Montenegro allied itself with Serbia.

Serbia was conquered in a little more than a month. The attack began in October, when the Central Powers launched an offensive from the north; four days later the Bulgarians joined the attack from the east. The Serbian army, fighting on two fronts and facing certain defeat, retreated into Albania, halting only once, to make a stand against the Bulgarians. The Serbs suffered defeat near modern day Gnjilane in Kosovo, forces being evacuated by ship to Greece.

In late 1915, a Franco-British force landed at Salonica in Greece, to offer assistance and to pressure the government to declare war against the Central Powers. Unfortunately for the Allies, the pro-German King Constantine I dismissed the pro-Allied government of Eleftherios Venizelos, before the allied expeditionary force could arrive.

The Salonica Front proved static; it was joked that Salonica was the largest German prisoner of war camp of the war. Only at the end of the conflict were the Entente powers able to break through, which was after most of the German and Austro-Hungarian troops had been withdrawn. The Bulgarians suffered their only defeat of the war, at the battle of Dobro Pole, but days later, they decisively defeated British and Greek forces at the battle of Doiran, avoiding occupation. Bulgaria signed an armistice on 29 September 1918.

Fighting in India

Although the conflict in India cannot be explicitly said to have been a part of the First World War, it can certainly be said to have been significant in terms of the wider strategic context. The British attempt to subjugate the tribal leaders who had rebelled against their British overlords drew away much needed troops from other theaters, in particular, of course, the Western Front, where the real decisive victory would be made.

The reason why some Indian and Afghani tribes rose up simply came down to years of discontent which erupted, probably not coincidentally, during the First World War. It is likely that the tribal leaders were aware that Britain would not be able to field the required men, in terms of either number or quality. They underestimated, however, the strategic importance placed on India by the British; despite being located far away from the epicenter of the conflict, it provided a bounty of men for the fronts. Its produce was also needed for the British war effort and many trade routes running to other profitable areas of the Empire ran through India. Therefore, although the British were not able to send the men that they wanted, they were able to send enough to resist the revolt of the tribesmen through a gradual but effective counter-guerilla war. The fighting continued into 1919 and in some areas lasted even longer. See also Third Anglo-Afghan War.

Eastern Front

Initial actions

While the Western Front had reached stalemate, the war continued in the East. Initial Russian plans called for simultaneous invasions of Austrian Galicia and German East Prussia. Although Russia's initial advance into Galicia was largely successful, they were driven back from East Prussia by Hindenburg and Ludendorff at Tannenberg and the Masurian Lakes in August and September 1914. Russia's less developed industrial base and ineffective military leadership was instrumental in the events that unfolded. By the spring of 1915, the Russians had retreated into Galicia, and in May the Central Powers achieved a remarkable breakthrough on Poland's southern frontiers. On 5 August they captured Warsaw and forced the Russians to withdraw from Poland. This became known as the "Great Retreat" in Russia and the "Great Advance" in Germany.

Russian Revolution

Vladimir Illyich Lenin

Dissatisfaction with the Russian government's conduct of the war grew, despite the success of the June 1916 Brusilov offensive in eastern Galicia. The success was undermined by the reluctance of other generals to commit their forces to support the victory. Allied and Russian forces revived only temporarily with Romania's entry into the war on 27 August. German forces came to the aid of embattled Austrian units in Transylvania and Bucharest fell to the Central Powers on 6 December. Meanwhile, unrest grew in Russia, as the Tsar remained at the front. Empress Alexandra's increasingly incompetent rule drew protests and resulted in the murder of her favourite, Rasputin, at the end of 1916.

In March 1917, demonstrations in St Petersburg culminated in the abdication of Tsar Nicholas II and the appointment of a weak Provisional Government. It shared power with the socialists of the Petrograd Soviet. This arrangement led to confusion and chaos both at the front and at home. The army became increasingly ineffective.

The war and the government became more and more unpopular. Discontent led to a rise in popularity of the Bolshevik party, led by Vladimir Lenin. He promised to pull Russia out of the war and was able to gain power. The triumph of the Bolsheviks in November was followed in December by an armistice and negotiations with Germany. At first, the Bolsheviks refused to agree to the harsh German terms. But when Germany resumed the war and marched with impunity across Ukraine, the new government acceded to the Treaty of Brest-Litovsk on 3 March 1918. It took Russia out of the war and ceded vast territories, including Finland, the Baltic provinces, parts of Poland and Ukraine to the Central Powers.

The publication by the new Bolshevik government of the secret treaties signed by the Tsar was hailed across the world, either as a great step forward for the respect of the will of the people, or as a dreadful catastrophe which could destabilise the world. The existence of a new type of government in Russia led to the reinforcement in many countries of Communist parties.

After the Russians dropped out of the war, the Entente no longer existed. The Allied powers led a small-scale invasion of Russia. The intent was primarily to stop Germany from exploiting Russian resources and, to a lesser extent, to support the Whites in the Russian Civil War. Troops landed in Archangel (see North Russia Campaign) and in Vladivostok.

1917–1918

In the trenches: Royal Irish Rifles in a communications trench on the first day on the Somme, 1 July 1916

Events of 1917 proved decisive in ending the war, although their effects were not fully felt until 1918. The British naval blockade began to have a serious impact on Germany. In response, in February 1917, the German General Staff convinced Chancellor Theobald von Bethmann Hollweg to declare unrestricted submarine warfare, with the goal of starving Britain out of the war. Tonnage sunk rose above 500,000 tons per month from February to July. It peaked at 860,000 tons in April. After July, the reintroduced convoy system became extremely effective in neutralizing the U-boat threat. Britain was safe from starvation and German industrial output fell.

The victory of Austria-Hungary and Germany at the Battle of Caporetto led the Allied at the Rapallo Conference to form the Supreme Allied Council to coordinate planning. Previously, British and French armies had operated under separate commands.

In December, the Central Powers signed an armistice with Russia. This released troops for use in the west. Ironically, German troop transfers could have been greater if their territorial acquisitions had not been so dramatic. With German reinforcements and new American troops pouring in, the final outcome was to be decided on the Western front. The Central Powers knew that they could not win a protracted war, but they held high hopes for a quick offensive. Furthermore, the leaders of the Central Powers and the Allies became increasingly fearful of social unrest and revolution in Europe. Thus, both sides urgently sought a decisive victory.

Entry of the United States

An American doughboy, circa: 1918

President Wilson before Congress, announcing the break in official relations with Germany on 3 February 1917

The United States originally pursued a policy of isolationism, avoiding conflict while trying to broker a peace. This resulted in increased tensions with both Berlin and London. When a German U-boat sank the British liner *Lusitania* in 1915, with 128 Americans aboard, the U.S. President Woodrow Wilson vowed that "America was too proud to fight" and demanded an end to attacks on passenger ships. Germany complied. Wilson unsuccessfully tried to mediate a settlement. He repeatedly warned that America would not tolerate unrestricted submarine warfare, in violation of international law and American ideas of human rights. Wilson was under pressure from former president Theodore Roosevelt, who denounced German acts as "piracy."[15] Other factors contributing to the U.S. entry into the war include German sabotage of both Black Tom in Jersey City, NJ, and the Kingsland Explosion in what is now Lyndhurst, NJ.

In January 1917, after the German Naval staff pressured the Kaiser, Germany resumed unrestricted submarine warfare. Britain's secret "Room 40" cryptography group had decrypted the German diplomatic code, and discovered a proposal from Berlin (the famed Zimmermann Telegram) to Mexico to join the war as Germany's ally against the United States. The proposal suggested that Mexico should declare war against the United States and enlist Japan as an ally; this would prevent America from joining the Allies and deploying troops to Europe, which would give the Germans more time for their unrestricted submarine warfare program to strangle Britain's vital war supplies. In return, the Germans would promise Mexico support in reclaiming Texas, New Mexico and Arizona.[16]

After the British revealed the telegram to the Americans, Woodrow Wilson was still reluctant to abandon neutrality but released the captured telegram as a way of supporting his proposed plan to arm American merchant ships. After submarines sank seven American merchant ships and the publication of the Zimmerman telegram, Wilson called for war on Germany, which the U.S. Congress declared on 6 April 1917.[17]

The United States was never formally a member of the Allies but became a self-styled "Associated Power". America had a small army, but it drafted four million men and by summer 1918 was sending 10,000 fresh soldiers to France every day. Germany had miscalculated that it would be many more months before they would arrive or that the arrival could be stopped by U-boats.[18]

The United States Navy sent a battleship group to Scapa Flow to join with the British Grand Fleet, destroyers to Queenstown, Ireland and submarines to help guard convoys. Several regiments of U.S. Marines were also dispatched to France. The British and French wanted American units used to reinforce their troops already on the battle lines and not waste scarce shipping on bringing over supplies. The Americans rejected the first proposition and accepted the second. General John J. Pershing, American Expeditionary Force (AEF) commander, refused to break up American units to be used as reinforcements for British Empire and French units (though he did allow African American combat units to be used by the French). AEF doctrine called for the use of frontal assaults, which had been discarded by that time by British Empire and French commanders because of the large loss of life sustained throughout the war.[19]

German Spring Offensive of 1918

German General Erich Ludendorff drew up plans (codenamed Operation Michael) for the 1918 offensive on the Western Front. The Spring Offensive sought to divide the British and French forces with a series of feints and advances. The German leadership hoped to strike a decisive blow before significant U.S. forces arrived. Before the offensive began, Ludendorff decided to leave the

For most of World War I, Allied forces were stalled at trenches on the Western Front elite Eighth Army in Russia and transferred over only a small portion of the German forces to the west.

Operation Michael opened on 21 March 1918. British forces were attacked near Amiens. Ludendorff wanted to split the British and French armies. German forces achieved an unprecedented advance of 60 kilometers (40 miles). For the first time since 1914, the maneuver was successful on the battlefield.

British and French trenches were penetrated using novel infiltration tactics, also named *Hutier* tactics, after General Oskar von Hutier. Attacks had been characterised by long artillery bombardments and massed assaults. However, in the Spring Offensive, the German Army used artillery only briefly and infiltrated small groups of infantry at weak points. They attacked command and logistics areas and bypassed points of serious resistance. More heavily armed infantry then destroyed these isolated positions. German success relied greatly on the element of surprise.

The front moved to within 120 kilometers (75 mi) of Paris. Three heavy Krupp railway guns fired 183 shells on the capital, causing many Parisians to flee. The initial offensive was so successful that Kaiser Wilhelm II declared 24 March a national holiday. Many Germans thought victory was near. After heavy fighting, however, the offensive was halted. Lacking tanks or motorised artillery, the Germans were unable to consolidate their gains. The sudden stop was also a result of the four AIF (Australian Imperial Forces) divisions that were "rushed" down, thus doing what no other army had done and stopping the German advance in its tracks. While during that time the first Australian division was hurriedly sent north again to stop the second German break through.

British 55th (West Lancashire) Division troops blinded by tear gas during the Battle of Estaires, 10 April 1918.

American divisions, which Pershing had sought to field as an independent force, were assigned to the depleted French and British Empire commands on 28 March. A Supreme War Council of Allied forces was created at the Doullens Conference on 5 November 1917.[20] General Foch was appointed as supreme commander of the allied forces. Haig, Petain and Pershing retained tactical control of their respective armies; Foch would assume a coordinating role, rather than a directing role and the British, French and U.S. commands operated largely independently.[20]

Following Operation Michael, Germany launched Operation Georgette against the northern English channel ports. The Allies halted the drive with limited territorial gains for Germany. The German Army to the south then conducted Operations Blücher and Yorck, broadly towards Paris. Operation Marne was launched on 15 July, attempting to encircle Reims and beginning the Second Battle of the Marne. The resulting Allied counterattack marked their first successful offensive of the war.

By 20 July, the Germans were back at their Kaiserschlacht starting lines, having achieved nothing. Following this last phase of the war in the West, the German Army never again regained the initiative. German casualties between March and April 1918 were 270,000, including many highly trained stormtroopers.

Meanwhile, Germany was falling apart at home. Anti-war marches become frequent and morale in the army fell. Industrial output was 53% of 1913 levels.

New states under war zone

In 1918, the internationally recognized Democratic Republic of Armenia and Democratic Republic of Georgia bordering the Ottoman Empire, and the not-recognized Centrocaspian Dictatorship and South West Caucasian Republic were established.

In 1918, the Dashnaks of Armenian national liberation movement declared the Democratic Republic of Armenia (DRA) through the Armenian Congress of Eastern Armenians (unified form of Armenian National Councils) after the dissolution of Transcaucasian Democratic Federative Republic. Tovmas Nazarbekian become the first Commander-in-chief of DRA. Enver Pasha ordered the creation of a new army to be named the Army of Islam. He ordered the Army of Islam into DRA, with the goal of taking Baku on the Caspian Sea. This new offensive was strongly opposed by the Germans. In early May 1918, the Ottoman army attacked the newly declared DRA. Although the Armenians managed to inflict one defeat on the Ottomans at the Battle of Sardarapat, the Ottoman army won a later battle and scattered the Armenian army. The Republic of Armenia was forced to sign the Treaty of Batum in June 1918.

Allied victory: summer and autumn 1918

American engineers returning from the front during the Battle of Saint-Mihiel in September 1918

The Allied counteroffensive, known as the Hundred Days Offensive, began on 8 August 1918. The Battle of Amiens developed with III Corps Fourth British Army on the left, the First French Army on the right, and the Australian and Canadian Corps spearheading the offensive in the centre. It involved 414 tanks of the Mark IV and Mark V type, and 120,000 men. They advanced 12 kilometers (7 miles) into German-held territory in just seven hours. Erich Ludendorff referred to this day as the "Black Day of the German army". Supply problems caused the offensive to lose momentum. British units had encountered problems when all but seven tanks and trucks ran out of fuel. On 15 August General Haig called a halt and began planning a new offensive in Albert.

The Second Battle of the Somme began on 21 August. The Third and Fourth British Armies and the American II Corps pushed the Second German Army back over a

55 kilometer (34 mile) front. By 2 September, the Germans were back to the Hindenburg Line, their starting point in 1914.

The Allied attack on the Hindenburg Line began on 26 September. 260,000 American soldiers went "over the top". All initial objectives were captured; the U.S. 79th Infantry Division, which met stiff resistance at Montfaucon, took an extra day to capture its objective. The U.S. Army stalled because of supply problems because its inexperienced headquarters had to cope with large units and a difficult landscape. At the same time, French units broke through in Champagne and closed on the Belgian frontier. The most significant advance came from Commonwealth units, as they entered Belgium (liberation of Ghent). The German army had to shorten its front and use the Dutch frontier as an anchor to fight rear-guard actions. This probably saved the army from disintegration but was devastating for morale.

By October, it was evident that Germany could no longer mount a successful defense. They were increasingly outnumbered, with few new recruits. Rations were cut. Ludendorff decided, on 1 October, that Germany had two ways out — total annihilation or an armistice. He recommended the latter at a summit of senior German officials. Allied pressure did not let up.

Meanwhile, news of Germany's impending military defeat spread throughout the German armed forces. The threat of mutiny was rife. Admiral Reinhard Scheer and Ludendorff decided to launch a last attempt to restore the "valor" of the German Navy. Knowing the government of Max von Baden would veto any such action, Ludendorff decided not to inform him. Nonetheless, word of the impending assault reached sailors at Kiel. Many rebelled and were arrested, refusing to be part of a naval offensive which they believed to be suicidal. Ludendorff took the blame—the Kaiser dismissed him on 26 October. The collapse of the Balkans meant that Germany was about to lose its main supplies of oil and food. The reserves had been used up, but the Americans kept arriving at the rate of 10,000 per day.[21]

With power coming into the hands of new men in Berlin, further fighting became impossible. With 6 million German casualties, Germany moved toward peace. Prince Max von Baden took charge of a new government. Negotiations with President Wilson began immediately, in the vain hope that better terms would be offered than with the British and French. Instead Wilson demanded the abdication of the Kaiser. There was no resistance when the social democrat Philipp Scheidemann on 9 November declared Germany to be a republic. Imperial Germany was dead; a new Germany had been born: the Weimar Republic.[22]

End of war

This photograph was taken after reaching an agreement for the armistice that ended World War I. The location is in the forest of Compiègne. Foch is second from the right. The train carriage seen in the background, where the armistice was signed, would prove to be the setting of France's own armistice in June 1940. When the WWII armistice was signed, Hitler had the rail car taken back to Berlin where it was destroyed when allied aircraft bombed the city.

The collapse of the Central Powers came swiftly. Bulgaria was the first to sign an armistice on September 29, 1918 at Saloniki.[23] On October 30, the Ottoman Empire capitulated at Mudros.[24]

On October 24 the Italians began a push which rapidly recovered territory lost after the Battle of Caporetto. This culminated in the Battle of Vittorio Veneto, which marked the end of the Austro-Hungarian Army as an effective fighting force. The offensive also triggered the disintegration of Austro-Hungarian Empire. During the last week of October declarations of independence were made in Budapest, Prague and Zagreb. On October 29, the imperial authorities asked Italy for an armistice. But the Italians continued advancing, reaching Trento, Udine and Trieste. On November 3 Austria-Hungary sent a flag of truce to ask for an Armistice. The terms, arranged by telegraph with the Allied Authorities in Paris, were communicated to the Austrian Commander and accepted. The Armistice with Austria was signed in the Villa Giusti, near Padua, on November 3. Austria and Hungary signed separate armistices following the overthrow of the Habsburg monarchy.

Following the outbreak of the German Revolution, a republic was proclaimed on 9 November. The Kaiser fled to the Netherlands. On November 11 an armistice with Germany was signed in a railroad carriage at Compiègne. At 11 a.m. on November 11, 1918 — the eleventh hour of the eleventh day of the eleventh month — a ceasefire came into effect. Opposing armies on the Western Front began to withdraw from their positions. Canadian George Lawrence Price is traditionally regarded as the last soldier killed in the Great War: he was shot by a German sniper and died at 10:58.[25]

A formal state of war between the two sides persisted for another seven months, until signing of the Treaty of Versailles with Germany on June 28, 1919. Later treaties with Austria, Hungary, Bulgaria and the Ottoman Empire were signed. However, the latter treaty with the Ottoman Empire was followed by strife (the Turkish Independence War) and a final peace treaty was signed between the Allied Powers and the country that would shortly become the Republic of Turkey, at Lausanne on July 24, 1923.

Some war memorials date the end of the war as being when the Versailles treaty was signed in 1919; by contrast, most commemorations of the wars end concentrate on the armistice of November 11, 1918. Legally the last formal peace treaties were not signed until the Treaty of Lausanne. Under its terms, the Allied forces abandoned Constantinople on the 23rd of August, 1923.

Soldiers' experiences

The soldiers of the war were initially volunteers but increasingly were conscripted into service. Books such as *All Quiet on the Western Front* detail the mundane time and intense horror of soldiers that fought the war but had no control of the experience they existed in. William Henry Lamin's experience as a front line soldier is detailed in his letters posted in real time (plus 90 years) in a blog [1], as if it were a technology available at the time.

War crimes

Rape of Belgium

In Belgium, German troops, in fear of French and Belgian guerrilla fighters, or *francs-tireurs*, massacred townspeople in Andenne (211 dead), Tamines (384 dead), and Dinant (612 dead). The victims included women and children. On 25 August 1914, the Germans set fire to the town of Leuven, burned the library containing about 230,000 books, killed 209 civilians and forced 42,000 to evacuate. These actions brought worldwide condemnation.[32]

Economics and manpower issues

Gross Domestic Product (GDP) increased for three Allies (Britain, Italy, and U.S.), but decreased in France and Russia, in neutral Netherlands and in the main three Central Powers. The shrinkage in GDP in Austria, Russia, France, and the Ottoman Empire reached 30 to 40%. In Austria, for example, most of the pigs were slaughtered and, at war's end, there was no meat.

All nations had increases in the government's share of GDP, surpassing fifty percent in both Germany and France and nearly reaching fifty percent in Britain. To pay for purchases in the United States, Britain cashed in its massive investments in American railroads and then began borrowing heavily on Wall Street. President Wilson was on the verge of cutting off the loans in late 1916, but allowed a massive increase in U.S. government lending to the Allies. After 1919, the U.S. demanded repayment of these loans, which, in part, were funded by German reparations, which, in turn, were supported by American loans to Germany. This circular system collapsed in 1931 and the loans were never repaid.

One of the most dramatic effects was the expansion of governmental powers and responsibilities in Britain, France, the United States, and the Dominions of the British Empire. In order to harness all the power of their societies, new government ministries and powers were created. New taxes were levied and laws enacted, all designed to bolster the war effort; many of which have lasted to this day.

At the same time, the war strained the abilities of the formerly large and bureaucratised governments such as in Austria-Hungary and Germany. Here, however, the long-term effects were clouded by the defeat of these governments.

Families were altered by the departure of many men. With the death or absence of the primary wage earner, women were forced into the workforce in unprecedented numbers. At the same time, industry needed to replace the lost laborers sent to war. This aided the struggle for voting rights for women.

As the war slowly turned into a war of attrition, conscription was implemented in some countries. This issue was particularly explosive in Canada and Australia. In the former it opened a political gap between French-Canadians — who claimed their true loyalty was to Canada and not the British Empire — and the Anglophone majority who saw the war as a duty to both Britain and Canada. Prime Minister Robert Borden pushed through a Military Service Act, provoking the Conscription Crisis of 1917. In Australia, a sustained pro-conscription campaign by Prime Minister Billy Hughes, caused a split in the Australian Labor Party and Hughes formed the Nationalist Party of Australia in 1917 to pursue the matter. Nevertheless, the labour movement, the Catholic Church, and Irish nationalist expatriates successfully opposed Hughes' push, which was rejected in two plebiscites.

In Britain, rationing was finally imposed in early 1918, limited to meat, sugar, and fats (butter and oleo), but not bread. The new system worked smoothly. From 1914 to 1918 trade union membership doubled, from a little over four million to a little over eight million. Work stoppages and strikes became frequent in 1917–18 as the unions expressed grievances regarding prices, alcohol control, pay disputes, fatigue from overtime and working on Sundays and inadequate housing. Conscription put into uniform nearly every physically fit man, six of ten million eligible. Of these, about 750,000 lost their lives and 1,700,000 were wounded. Most deaths were to young unmarried men; however, 160,000 wives lost husbands and 300,000 children lost fathers.[33]

Britain turned to her colonies for help in obtaining essential war materials whose supply had become difficult from traditional sources. Geologists, such as Albert Ernest Kitson, were called upon to find new resources of precious minerals in the African colonies. Kitson discovered important new deposits of manganese, used in munitions production, in the Gold Coast.[34]

Technology

French Nieuport 17 C.1 fighter, 1917

The First World War began as a clash of 20th century technology and 19th century tactics, with inevitably large casualties. By the end of 1917, however, the major armies, now numbering millions of men, had modernised and were making use of telephone, wireless communication, armoured cars, tanks and aircraft. Infantry formations were reorganised, so that 100-man companies were no longer the main unit of maneuver. Instead, squads of 10 or so men, under the command of a junior NCO, were favoured. Artillery also under went a revolution.

In 1914, cannons were positioned in the front line and fired directly at their targets. By 1917, indirect fire with guns (as well as mortars and even machine guns) was commonplace, using new techniques for spotting and ranging, notably aircraft and (often overlooked) field telephone. Counter-battery missions became commonplace, also, and sound detection was used to locate enemy batteries.

Germany was far ahead of the Allies in utilizing heavy indirect fire. She employed 150 and 210 mm howitzers in 1914 when the typical French and British guns were only 75 and 105 mm. The British had a 6 inch (152 mm) howitzer, but it was so heavy it had to be assembled for firing. Germans also fielded Austrian 305 mm and 420 mm guns, and already by the beginning of the war had inventories of various calibers of *Minenwerfer* ideally suited for trench warfare.[35]

Russian Ilya Muromets the world's first strategic bomber, 1913

Much of the combat involved trench warfare, where hundreds often died for each yard gained. Many of the deadliest battles in history occurred during the First World War. Such battles include Ypres, the Marne, Cambrai, the Somme, Verdun, and Gallipoli. The Haber process of nitrogen fixation was employed to provide the German forces with a constant supply of gunpowder, in the face of British naval blockade. Artillery was responsible for the largest number of casualties and consumed vast quantities of explosives. The large number of head-wounds caused by exploding shells and fragmentation forced the combatant nations to develop the modern steel helmet, led by the French, who introduced the Adrian helmet in 1915. It was quickly followed by the Brodie helmet, worn by British Imperial and U.S. troops, and in 1916 by the distinctive German *Stahlhelm*, a design, with improvements, still in use today.

Year Four Sourcebook, page 189

There was chemical warfare and small-scale strategic bombing, both of which were outlawed by the 1907 Hague Conventions. Both were of limited tactical effectiveness.

The widespread use of chemical warfare was a distinguishing feature of the conflict. Gases used included chlorine, mustard gas and phosgene. Only a small proportion of total war casualties were caused by gas. Effective countermeasures to gas attacks were quickly created, such as gas masks.

The most powerful land-based weapons were railway guns weighing hundreds of tons apiece. These were nicknamed Big Berthas, even though the namesake was not a railway gun. Germany developed the Paris Gun, able to bombard Paris from over 100 km (60mi), though shells were relatively light at 94 kilograms (210 lb). While the Allies had railway guns, German models severely out-ranged and out-classed them.

Fixed-wing aircraft were first used militarily by the Italians in Libya 23 October 1911 during the Italo-Turkish War for reconnaissance, soon followed by the dropping of grenades and aerial photography the next year. By 1914 the military utility was obvious. They were initially used for reconnaissance and ground attack. To shoot down enemy planes, anti-aircraft guns and fighter aircraft were developed. Strategic bombers were created, principally by the Germans and British, though the former used Zeppelins as well.

Towards the end of the conflict, aircraft carriers were used for the first time, with HMS *Furious* launching Sopwith Camels in a raid against the Zepplin hangars at Tondern in 1918.

German U-boats (submarines) were deployed after the war began. Alternating between restricted and unrestricted submarine warfare in the Atlantic, they were employed by the Kaiserliche Marine in a strategy to deprive the British Isles of vital supplies. The deaths of British merchant sailors and the seeming invulnerability of U-boats led to the development of depth charges (1916), hydrophones (passive sonar, 1917), blimps, hunter-killer submarines (HMS *R 1*, 1917), ahead-throwing weapons, and dipping hydrophones (the latter two both abandoned in 1918). To extend their operations, the Germans proposed supply submarines (1916). Most of these would be forgotten in the interwar period until World War II revived the need.

Trenches, machineguns, air reconnaissance, barbed wire, and modern artillery with fragmentation shells helped bring the battle lines of World War I to a stalemate. The British sought a solution with the creation of the tank and mechanised warfare. The first tanks were used during the Battle of the Somme on 15 September 1916. Mechanical reliability became an issue, but the experiment proved its worth. Within a year, the British were fielding tanks by the hundreds and showed their potential during the Battle of Cambrai in November 1917, by breaking the Hindenburg Line, while combined arms teams captured 8000 enemy soldiers and 100 guns. Light automatic weapons also were introduced, such as the Lewis Gun and Browning automatic rifle.

Manned observation balloons, floating high above the trenches, were used as stationary reconnaissance platforms, reporting enemy movements and directing artillery. Balloons commonly had a crew of two, equipped with parachutes.[36] In the event of an enemy air attack, the crew could parachute to safety. At the time, parachutes were too heavy to be used by pilots of aircraft (with their marginal power output) and smaller versions would not be developed until the end of the war; they were also opposed by British leadership, who feared they might promote cowardice.[37] Recognised for their value as observation platforms, balloons were important targets of enemy aircraft. To defend against air attack, they were heavily protected by antiaircraft guns and patrolled by friendly aircraft. Blimps and balloons contributed to air-to-air combat among aircraft, because of their reconnaissance value, and to the trench stalemate, because it was impossible to move large numbers of troops undetected. The Germans conducted air raids on England during 1915 and 1916 with airships, hoping to damage British morale and cause aircraft to be diverted from the front lines. The resulting panic took several squadrons of fighters from France.[38]

Another new weapon, flamethrowers, were first used by the German army and later adopted by other forces. Although not of high tactical value, they were a powerful, demoralizing weapon and caused terror on the battlefield. It was a dangerous weapon to wield, as its heavy weight made operators vulnerable targets.

Opposition to the war

The trade union and socialist movements had long voiced their opposition to a war, which they argued, meant only that workers would kill other workers in the interest of capitalism. Once war was declared, however, the vast majority of socialists and trade unions backed their governments. The exceptions were the Bolsheviks and the Italian Socialist Party, and individuals such as Karl Liebknecht, Rosa Luxemburg and their followers in Germany. There were also small anti-war groups in Britain and France. Other opposition came from conscientious objectors - some socialist, some religious - who refused to fight. In Britain 16,000 people asked for conscientious objector status. Many suffered years of prison, including solitary confinement and bread and water diets. Even after the war, in Britain many job advertisements were marked "No conscientious objectors need apply". Many countries jailed those who spoke out against the conflict. These included Eugene Debs in the United States and Bertrand Russell in Britain.

Aftermath

The Newfoundland Memorial at Beaumont Hamel

No other war had changed the map of Europe so dramatically — four empires disappeared: the German, Austro-Hungarian, Ottoman and the Russian. Four defunct dynasties, the Hohenzollerns, the Habsburg, Romanovs and the Ottomans together with all their ancillary aristocracies, all fell after the war. Belgium was badly damaged, as was France with 1.4 million soldiers dead, not counting other casualties. Germany and Russia were similarly affected. The war had profound economic consequences. In addition, a major influenza epidemic that started in Western Europe in the latter months of the war, killed millions in Europe and then spread around the world. Overall, the Spanish flu killed at least 50 million people.[39][40]

Peace treaties

After the war, the Allies imposed a series of peace treaties on the Central Powers. The 1919 Versailles Treaty, which Germany was kept under blockade until she signed, ended the war. It declared Germany responsible for the war and required Germany to pay enormous war reparations and awarding territory to the victors. Unable to pay them with exports (a result of territorial losses and postwar recession),[41] she did so by borrowing from the United States, until the reparations were suspended in 1931. The "Guilt Thesis" became a controversial explanation of events in Britain and the United States. The Treaty of Versailles caused enormous bitterness in Germany, which nationalist movements, especially the Nazis, exploited. (See Dolchstosslegende). The treaty contributed to one of the worst economic collapses in German history, sparking runaway inflation in the 1920s.

The Ottoman Empire was to be partitioned by the Treaty of Sèvres in 1920. The treaty, however, was never ratified by the Sultan and was rejected by the Turkish republican movement. This led to the Turkish Independence War and, ultimately, to the 1923 Treaty of Lausanne.

Austria-Hungary was also partitioned, largely along ethnic lines. The details were contained in the Treaty of Saint-Germain and the Treaty of Trianon.

New national identities

Poland reemerged as an independent country, after more than a century. Yugoslavia and Czechoslovakia were entirely new nations. Russia became the Soviet Union and lost Finland, Estonia, Lithuania and Latvia, which became independent countries. The Ottoman Empire was soon replaced by Turkey and several other countries in the Middle East.

Some people think that the Allies opened the way to more colonization with their policy, because with it the Allies could colonise territories owned by the Ottoman Empire and Austro-Hungarian Empire, by making them independent.

Postwar colonization in the Ottoman Empire led to many future problems still unresolved today. Conflict between mostly Jewish colonists and the existing, mostly Muslim, population intensified, probably exacerbated by the Holocaust, which stimulated Jewish migration and encouraged the new immigrants to fight for survival, a homeland, or both. However, any new homeland for immigrants would cause hardships for the existing population, especially if the former displaced the latter. The United Nations partitioned Palestine in 1947 with Jewish but not Arab and Muslim approval. After the creation of the state of Israel, a series of wars broke out between Israel and its neighbors, Egypt, Jordan, and Syria, in addition to unrest from the Palestinian population and terrorist activity by Palestinians and others reaching to Iran and beyond. Lasting peace in the region remains an elusive goal almost a century later.

In the British Empire, the war unleashed new forms of nationalism. In Australia and New Zealand the Battle of Gallipoli became known as those nations' "Baptism of Fire". It was the first major war in which the newly established countries fought and it was one of the first times that Australian troops fought as Australians, not just subjects of the British Crown. Anzac Day, commemorating the Australian and New Zealand Army Corps, celebrates this defining moment.

This effect was even greater in Canada. Canadians proved they were a nation and not merely subjects of a distant empire. Indeed, following Vimy, many Canadians began to refer to Canada as a nation "forged from fire". Canadians had proved themselves on the same battlefield where the British and French had previously faltered, and were respected internationally for their accomplishments. Canada entered the war as a Dominion of the British Empire, but when the war came to a close, Canada emerged as a fully independent nation. Canadian diplomats played a significant role in negotiating the Versailles Treaty. Canada was an independent signatory of the treaty, whereas other Dominions were represented by Britain. Canadians commemorate the war dead on Remembrance Day. In French Canada, however, the Conscription Crisis left bitterness in its wake.

Social trauma

The experiences of the war led to a collective trauma for all participating countries. The optimism of the 1900s was gone and those who fought in the war became known as the Lost Generation. For the next few years, much of Europe mourned. Memorials were erected in thousands of villages and towns. The soldiers returning home from World War I suffered greatly from the horrors they had witnessed. Called shell shock at the time, many returning veterans suffered from post-traumatic stress disorder.

The social trauma caused by years of fighting manifested itself in different ways. Some people were revolted by nationalism and its results. They began to work toward a more internationalist world, supporting organisations such as the League of Nations. Pacifism became increasingly popular. Others had the opposite reaction, feeling that only strength and military-might could be relied upon in a chaotic and inhumane world. Anti-modernist views were an outgrowth of the many changes taking place in society. The rise of Nazism and fascism included a revival of the nationalist spirit and a rejection of many post-war changes. Similarly, the popularity of the *Dolchstosslegende* ("backstab") was a testament to the psychological state of defeated Germany and was a rejection of responsibility for the conflict. The myth of betrayal became common and the aggressors came to see themselves as victims. The popularity of the '*Dolchstosslegende* myth played a significant role in the outbreak of World War II and the Holocaust. A sense of disillusionment and cynicism became pronounced, with nihilism growing in popularity. This disillusionment for humanity found a cultural climax with the Dadaist artistic movement. Many believed the war heralded the end of the world as they had known it, including the collapse of capitalism and imperialism. Communist and socialist movements around the world drew strength from this theory and enjoyed a level of popularity they had never known before. These feelings were most pronounced in areas directly or harshly affected by the war.

Lt. Col. John McCrae of Canada

In May 1915, during the Second Battle of Ypres, Lieutenant Colonel John McCrae, M.D., of Guelph, Ontario, Canada wrote the memorable poem *In Flanders Fields* as a salute to those who perished in the Great War. Published in *Punch* on December 8, 1918, it is still recited today, especially on Remembrance Day and Memorial Day.[42][43]

Other names for the war

Before World War II, the war was also known as *The Great War, The War to End All Wars, The Kaiser's War, The War of the Nations* and *The War in Europe*. In France and Belgium it was sometimes referred to as *La Guerre du Droit* (*the War for Justice*) or *La Guerre Pour la Civilisation / de Oorlog tot de Beschaving* (*the War to Preserve Civilization*), especially on medals and commemorative monuments. The term used by official histories of the war in Britain and Canada is *The First World War*, while American histories generally use the term *World War I*.

German biologist and philosopher Ernst Haeckel wrote this shortly after the start of the war:

> There is no doubt that the course and character of the feared "European War"...will become the first world war the full sense of the word.
>
> *Indianapolis Star* September 20, 1914[44]

This is the first known instance of the term *First World War*, which previously had been dated to 1931 for the earliest usage. The term was used again near the end of the war. English journalist Charles à Repington (1858–1925) wrote:

> [*Diary entry, September 10, 1918*]: We discussed the right name of the war. I said the we called it now *The War*, but that this could not last. The Napoleonic War was *The Great War*. To call it *The German War* was too much flattery for the Boche. I suggested *The World War* as a shade better title, and finally we mutually agreed to call it *The First World War* in order to prevent the millennium folk from forgetting that the history of the world was the history of war.
>
> "The First World War, 1914–1918" (1920)[45]

In many European countries, it appears the current usage is tending back to calling it *The Great War / la Grande Guerre / de Grote Oorlog / der Große Krieg*, because of the growing historical awareness that, of the two 20th century world wars, the 1914–1918 conflict caused more social, economic and political upheaval. It was also one of the prime factors in the outbreak of the Second World War.

Notes

1. ^ a b Evans, David. Teach yourself, the First World War, Hodder Arnold, 2004.p.188
2. ^ a b Ashworth, Tony. *Trench warfare 1914–1918*, pp3–4. 2000: Macmillan Press, London.
3. ^ Fromkin, David (2004). "Chapter 15: Europe Goes to the Brink", *Europe's Last Summer: Who Started the Great War in 1914?*. New York: Alfred A. Knopf, 94. ISBN 0-375-72575-X.
4. ^ Snyder, Jack. *Ideology of the Offensive*. Ithaca: Cornell University Press, 1984; Dupuy, Trevor N., Colonel, USA (rtd). *Numbers Predictions, and War*. Philadelphia: Bobbs-Merrill, 1979.
5. ^ 30 October 1918 in Herbert Hoover, *Ordeal of Woodrow Wilson* p. 47
6. ^ Fromkin, David (2004). "Chapter 45: What Did Not Happen", *Europe's Last Summer: Who Started the Great War in 1914?*. New York: Alfred A. Knopf, 266–267. ISBN 0-375-72575-X.
7. ^ "Imperialism" (1902) fordham.edu website
8. ^ 1917 pamphlet "Imperialism: The Highest Stage of Capitalism"
9. ^ Web reference
10. ^ Joll, James. *The Origins of the First World War*, 2nd ed. (Harlow, 1992), pp. 10–38
11. ^ John M. Taylor, "Audacious Cruise of the Emden", The Quarterly Journal of Military History, Volume 19, Number 4, Summer 2007, pp. 39–47
12. ^ Price, Alfred. *Aircraft* versus *the Submarine*. (London: Wiliam Kimber, 1973).
13. ^ Boghos Nubar the president of the "Armenian National Assembly" declared to Paris Peace Conference, 1919 through a letter to French Foreign Office - December 3, 1918
14. ^ Triple Alliance
15. ^ H. W. Brands, *T. R.* (1997) p. 756.

16. ^ Barbara Tuchman, *The Zimmerman Telegram*
17. ^ (see: *Woodrow Wilson declares war on Germany* on Wikisource).
18. ^ William John Wilgus, *Transporting the A. E. F. in Western Europe, 1917–1919* p. 52
19. ^ Allan Reed Millett and Williamson Murray, *Military Effectiveness*, Routledge, p.143
20. ^ *a b* van Courtland Moon, John Ellis. "United States Chemical Warfare Policy in World War II: A Captive of Coalition Policy?" (JSTOR), *The Journal of Military History*, Vol. 60, No. 3. (Jul., 1996), pp. 495-511. Retrieved 14 October 2007.
21. ^ Stevenson, *Cataclysm* (2004) p 383.
22. ^ Stevenson, *Cataclysm* (2004) ch 17.
23. ^ 1918 Timeline
24. ^ 1918 Timeline
25. ^ | The 28th (North-west) Battalion Canadian Corps
26. ^ Geo G. Phillimore and Hugh H. L. Bellot, "Treatment of Prisoners of War", *Transactions of the Grotius Society* Vol. 5, (1919), pp. 47–64.
27. ^ Niall Ferguson, *The Pity of War* (1999) p 368-9 for data.
28. ^ Richard B. Speed, III. *Prisoners, Diplomats and the Great War: A Study in the Diplomacy of Captivity* (1990); Ferguson, *The Pity of War* (1999) ch 13; Desmond Morton, *Silent Battle: Canadian Prisoners of War in Germany, 1914-1919* 1992
29. ^ The Mesopotamia campaign. British National Archives. Retrieved on 2007-03-10.
30. ^ Stolen Years: Australian Prisoners of War. Men of Kut *Driven along like beasts*. Australian War Memorial. Retrieved on 2007-03-10.
31. ^ 1.5 estimate retrieved from here. Data collected by the International Center for Transitional Justice
32. ^ Keegan, John. The First World War. 1998. pp82–83
33. ^ Havighurst p.134-5.
34. ^ John Frederick Norman Green, 'Obituary: Albert Ernest Kitson', *Geological Society, Quarterly Journal* no 94, 1938, p. CXXVI
35. ^ Mosier, John (2001). "Germany and the Development of Combined Arms Tactics", *Myth of the Great War: How the Germans Won the Battles and How the Americans Saved the Allies*. New York: Harper Collins, 42–48. ISBN 0-06-019676-9.
36. ^ Winter, Denis. *First of the Few*.
37. ^ Winter?
38. ^ Winter? Johnson, *Story of Air Fighting*?
39. ^ NAP
40. ^ Influenza Report
41. ^ Keynes, J.M. *The Economic Consequences of the Peace* (New York : Harcourt, 1920).
42. ^ John McCrae (from Historica)
43. ^ John McCrae (from the Canadian Encyclopedia)
44. ^ "The Yale Book of Quotations" (2006) Yale University Press, edited by Fred R. Shapiro
45. ^ "The Yale Book of Quotations" (2006) Yale University Press, edited by Fred R. Shapiro

References

- American Battle Monuments Commission (1938). *American armies and battlefields in Europe : a history, guide, and reference book.* U.S.G.P.O.. Selected photos available online through the Washington State Library's Classics in Washington History collection
- American Battle Monuments Commission (1938). *American armies and battlefields in Europe : a history, guide, and reference book.* U.S.G.P.O.. Maps available online through the Washington State Office of the Secretary of State's Washington History collection
- (1993) *Army art of World War I.* U.S. Army Center of Military History : Smithsonian Institution, National Museum of American History. Prints available online through the Washington State Library's Classics in Washington History collection
- Coffman, Edward M. *The War to End All Wars: The American Military Experience in World War I* (1998)
- Cruttwell, C. R. M. F. *A History of the Great War, 1914–1918* (1934), general military history
- Ellis, John and Mike Cox. *The World War I Databook: The Essential Facts and Figures for All the Combatants* (2002)
- Esposito, Vincent J. *The West Point Atlas of American Wars: 1900–1918* (1997), despite the title covers entire war; online maps from this atlas
- Falls, Cyril. *The Great War* (1960), general military history
- Fussell, Paul. *The Great War and Modern Memory* (1975), on literature
- Gray, Edwyn A. *The U-Boat War, 1914–1918* (1994)
- Haber, L. F. *The Poisonous Cloud: Chemical Warfare in the First World War* (1986)
- Halpern, Paul G. *A Naval History of World War I* (1995)
- Hardach, Gerd. *The First World War 1914–1918* (1977), economics
- Henig, Ruth *The Origins of the First World War* (2002)
- Herrmann, David G. *The Arming of Europe and the Making of the First World War*(1996)
- Herwig, Holger H. *The First World War: Germany and Austria-Hungary 1914–1918* (1996)
- Higham, Robin and Dennis E. Showalter, eds. *Researching World War I: A Handbook* (2003), historiography, stressing military themes
- Howard, Michael. *The First World War* (2002), short (175 pp) general military history
- Hubatsch, Walther. *Germany and the Central Powers in the World War, 1914–1918* (1963)
- Joll, James. *The Origins of the First World War* (1984)
- Keegan, John. *The First World War* (1999), general military history
- Kennedy, David M. *Over Here: The First World War and American Society* (1982), covers politics & economics & society
- Kennett, Lee B. *The First Air War, 1914–1918* (1992)
- Lee, Dwight E. ed. *The Outbreak of the First World War: Who Was Responsible?* (1958), readings from multiple points of view
- Lyons, Michael J. *World War I: A Short History* (2nd Edition), Prentice Hall, (1999)
- Morton, Desmond, and J. L. Granatstein *Marching to Armageddon: Canadians and the Great War 1914–1919* (1989)
- Pope, Stephen and Wheal, Elizabeth-Anne, eds. *The Macmillan Dictionary of the First World War* (1995)

- Robbins, Keith. *The First World War* (1993), short overview
- Silkin, Jon. ed. *The Penguin Book of First World War Poetry* (2nd ed. 1997)
- Stevenson, David. *Cataclysm: The First World War As Political Tragedy* (2004), major reinterpretation, 560pp
- Stevenson, David. *The First World War and International Politics* (2005)
- Stokesbury, James. *A Short History of World War I* (1981)
- Strachan, Hew. *The First World War: Volume I: To Arms* (2004): the major scholarly synthesis. Thorough coverage of 1914; Also: *The First World War* (2004): a 385pp version of his multivolume history
- Taylor, A. J. P. *The First World War: An Illustrated History*, Hamish Hamilton, 1963
- Tuchman, Barbara. *The Guns of August*, tells of the opening diplomatic and military manoeuvres
- Tucker, Spencer, ed. *The Encyclopedia of World War I: A Political, Social, and Military History* (5 vol 2005), online at eBook.com
- Tucker, Spencer, ed. *European Powers in the First World War: An Encyclopedia* (1999)
- Venzon, Anne ed. *The United States in the First World War: An Encyclopedia* (1995)
- Winter, J. M. *The Experience of World War I* (2nd ed 2005), topical essays; well illustrated
- van der Vat, Dan. *The Atlantic Campaign.* (1988). Connects submarine and antisubmarine operations between wars, and suggests a continuous war
- Price, Alfred, Dr. *Aircraft* versus *the Submarine*. Deals with technical developments, including the first dipping hydrophones

---

- This page was last modified 14:45, 16 October 2007.
- Wikipedia® is a registered trademark of the Wikimedia Foundation, Inc., a U.S. registered 501(c)(3) tax-deductible nonprofit charity.

This Page is intentionally blank

(actually, it **WAS** blank, but then I added this text, so now it's not blank anymore, but it had to be inserted so that the next chapter will start on a right-hand page – aren't you glad you asked?)

Text of the GNU Free Documentation License

From Wikipedia, the free encyclopedia

Version 1.2, November 2002

> Copyright (C) 2000,2001,2002 Free Software Foundation, Inc.
> 51 Franklin St, Fifth Floor, Boston, MA 02110-1301 USA
> Everyone is permitted to copy and distribute verbatim copies
> of this license document, but changing it is not allowed.

0. PREAMBLE

The purpose of this License is to make a manual, textbook, or other functional and useful document "free" in the sense of freedom: to assure everyone the effective freedom to copy and redistribute it, with or without modifying it, either commercially or noncommercially. Secondarily, this License preserves for the author and publisher a way to get credit for their work, while not being considered responsible for modifications made by others.

This License is a kind of "copyleft", which means that derivative works of the document must themselves be free in the same sense. It complements the GNU General Public License, which is a copyleft license designed for free software.

We have designed this License in order to use it for manuals for free software, because free software needs free documentation: a free program should come with manuals providing the same freedoms that the software does. But this License is not limited to software manuals; it can be used for any textual work, regardless of subject matter or whether it is published as a printed book. We recommend this License principally for works whose purpose is instruction or reference.

1. APPLICABILITY AND DEFINITIONS

This License applies to any manual or other work, in any medium, that contains a notice placed by the copyright holder saying it can be distributed under the terms of this License. Such a notice grants a world-wide, royalty-free license, unlimited in duration, to use that work under the conditions stated herein. The "Document", below, refers to any such manual or work. Any member of the public is a licensee, and is addressed as "you". You accept the license if you copy, modify or distribute the work in a way requiring permission under copyright law.

A "Modified Version" of the Document means any work containing the Document or a portion of it, either copied verbatim, or with modifications and/or translated into another language.

A "Secondary Section" is a named appendix or a front-matter section of the Document that deals exclusively with the relationship of the publishers or authors of the Document to the Document's overall subject (or to related matters) and contains nothing that could fall directly within that overall subject. (Thus, if the Document is in part a textbook of mathematics, a Secondary Section may not explain any mathematics.) The relationship could be a matter of historical connection with the subject or with related matters, or of legal, commercial, philosophical, ethical or political position regarding them.

The "Invariant Sections" are certain Secondary Sections whose titles are designated, as being those of Invariant Sections, in the notice that says that the Document is released under this License. If a section does not fit the above definition of Secondary then it is not allowed to be designated as Invariant. The Document may contain zero Invariant Sections. If the Document does not identify any Invariant Sections then there are none.

The "Cover Texts" are certain short passages of text that are listed, as Front-Cover Texts or Back-Cover Texts, in the notice that says that the Document is released under this License. A Front-Cover Text may be at most 5 words, and a Back-Cover Text may be at most 25 words.

A "Transparent" copy of the Document means a machine-readable copy, represented in a format whose specification is available to the general public, that is suitable for revising the document straightforwardly with generic text editors or (for images composed of pixels) generic paint programs or (for drawings) some widely available drawing editor, and that is suitable for input to text formatters or for automatic translation to a variety of formats suitable for input to text formatters. A copy made in an otherwise Transparent file format whose markup, or absence of markup, has been arranged to thwart or discourage subsequent modification by readers is not Transparent. An image format is not Transparent if used for any substantial amount of text. A copy that is not "Transparent" is called "Opaque".

Examples of suitable formats for Transparent copies include plain ASCII without markup, Texinfo input format, LaTeX input format, SGML or XML using a publicly available DTD, and standard-conforming simple HTML, PostScript or PDF designed for human modification. Examples of transparent image formats include PNG, XCF and JPG. Opaque formats include proprietary formats that can be read and edited only by proprietary word processors, SGML or XML for which the DTD and/or processing tools are not generally available, and the machine-generated HTML, PostScript or PDF produced by some word processors for output purposes only.

The "Title Page" means, for a printed book, the title page itself, plus such following pages as are needed to hold, legibly, the material this License requires to appear in the title page. For works in formats which do not have any title page as such, "Title Page" means the text near the most prominent appearance of the work's title, preceding the beginning of the body of the text.

A section "Entitled XYZ" means a named subunit of the Document whose title either is precisely XYZ or contains XYZ in parentheses following text that translates XYZ in another language. (Here XYZ stands for a specific section name mentioned below, such as "Acknowledgements", "Dedications", "Endorsements", or "History".) To "Preserve the Title" of such a section when you modify the Document means that it remains a section "Entitled XYZ" according to this definition.

The Document may include Warranty Disclaimers next to the notice which states that this License applies to the Document. These Warranty Disclaimers are considered to be included by reference in this License, but only as regards disclaiming warranties: any other implication that these Warranty Disclaimers may have is void and has no effect on the meaning of this License.

2. VERBATIM COPYING

You may copy and distribute the Document in any medium, either commercially or noncommercially, provided that this License, the copyright notices, and the license notice saying this License applies to the Document are reproduced in all copies, and that you add no other conditions whatsoever to those of this License. You may not use technical measures to obstruct or control the reading or further copying of the copies you make or distribute. However, you may accept compensation in exchange for copies. If you distribute a large enough number of copies you must also follow the conditions in section 3.

You may also lend copies, under the same conditions stated above, and you may publicly display copies.

3. COPYING IN QUANTITY

If you publish printed copies (or copies in media that commonly have printed covers) of the Document, numbering more than 100, and the Document's license notice requires Cover Texts, you must enclose the copies in covers that carry, clearly and legibly, all these Cover Texts: Front-Cover Texts on the front cover, and Back-Cover Texts on the back cover. Both covers must also clearly and legibly identify you as the publisher of these copies. The front cover must present the full title with all words of the title equally prominent and visible. You may add other material on the covers in addition. Copying with changes limited to the covers, as long as they preserve the title of the Document and satisfy these conditions, can be treated as verbatim copying in other respects.

If the required texts for either cover are too voluminous to fit legibly, you should put the first ones listed (as many as fit reasonably) on the actual cover, and continue the rest onto adjacent pages.

If you publish or distribute Opaque copies of the Document numbering more than 100, you must either include a machine-readable Transparent copy along with each Opaque copy, or state in or with each Opaque copy a computer-network location from which the general network-using public has access to download using public-standard network protocols a complete Transparent copy of the Document, free of added material. If you use the latter option, you must take reasonably prudent steps, when you begin distribution of Opaque copies in quantity, to ensure that this Transparent copy will remain thus accessible at the stated location until at least one year after the last time you distribute an Opaque copy (directly or through your agents or retailers) of that edition to the public.

It is requested, but not required, that you contact the authors of the Document well before redistributing any large number of copies, to give them a chance to provide you with an updated version of the Document.

4. MODIFICATIONS

You may copy and distribute a Modified Version of the Document under the conditions of sections 2 and 3 above, provided that you release the Modified Version under precisely this License, with the Modified Version filling the role of the Document, thus licensing distribution and modification of the Modified Version to whoever possesses a copy of it. In addition, you must do these things in the Modified Version:

A. Use in the Title Page (and on the covers, if any) a title distinct from that of the Document, and from those of previous versions (which should, if there were any, be listed in the History section of the Document). You may use the same title as a previous version if the original publisher of that version gives permission.

B. List on the Title Page, as authors, one or more persons or entities responsible for authorship of the modifications in the Modified Version, together with at least five of the principal authors of the Document (all of its principal authors, if it has fewer than five), unless they release you from this requirement.

C. State on the Title page the name of the publisher of the Modified Version, as the publisher.

D. Preserve all the copyright notices of the Document.

E. Add an appropriate copyright notice for your modifications adjacent to the other copyright notices.

F. Include, immediately after the copyright notices, a license notice giving the public permission to use the Modified Version under the terms of this License, in the form shown in the Addendum below.

G. Preserve in that license notice the full lists of Invariant Sections and required Cover Texts given in the Document's license notice.

H. Include an unaltered copy of this License.

I. Preserve the section Entitled "History", Preserve its Title, and add to it an item stating at least the title, year, new authors, and publisher of the Modified Version as given on the Title Page. If there is no section Entitled "History" in the Document, create one stating the title, year, authors, and publisher of the Document as given on its Title Page, then add an item describing the Modified Version as stated in the previous sentence.

J. Preserve the network location, if any, given in the Document for public access to a Transparent copy of the Document, and likewise the network locations given in the Document for previous versions it was based on. These may be placed in the "History" section. You may omit a network location for a work that was published at least four years before the Document itself, or if the original publisher of the version it refers to gives permission.

K. For any section Entitled "Acknowledgements" or "Dedications", Preserve the Title of the section, and preserve in the section all the substance and tone of each of the contributor acknowledgements and/or dedications given therein.

L. Preserve all the Invariant Sections of the Document, unaltered in their text and in their titles. Section numbers or the equivalent are not considered part of the section titles.

M. Delete any section Entitled "Endorsements". Such a section may not be included in the Modified Version.

N. Do not retitle any existing section to be Entitled "Endorsements" or to conflict in title with any Invariant Section.

O. Preserve any Warranty Disclaimers.

If the Modified Version includes new front-matter sections or appendices that qualify as Secondary Sections and contain no material copied from the Document, you may at your option designate some or all of these sections as invariant. To do this, add their titles to the list of Invariant Sections in the Modified Version's license notice. These titles must be distinct from any other section titles.

You may add a section Entitled "Endorsements", provided it contains nothing but endorsements of your Modified Version by various parties--for example, statements of peer review or that the text has been approved by an organization as the authoritative definition of a standard.

You may add a passage of up to five words as a Front-Cover Text, and a passage of up to 25 words as a Back-Cover Text, to the end of the list of Cover Texts in the Modified Version. Only one passage of Front-Cover Text and one of Back-Cover Text may be added by (or through arrangements made by) any one entity. If the Document already includes a cover text for the same cover, previously added by you or by arrangement made by the same entity you are acting on behalf of, you may not add another; but you may replace the old one, on explicit permission from the previous publisher that added the old one.

The author(s) and publisher(s) of the Document do not by this License give permission to use their names for publicity for or to assert or imply endorsement of any Modified Version.

5. COMBINING DOCUMENTS

You may combine the Document with other documents released under this License, under the terms defined in section 4 above for modified versions, provided that you include in the combination all of the Invariant Sections of all of the original documents, unmodified, and list them all as Invariant Sections of your combined work in its license notice, and that you preserve all their Warranty Disclaimers.

The combined work need only contain one copy of this License, and multiple identical Invariant Sections may be replaced with a single copy. If there are multiple Invariant Sections with the same name but different contents, make the title of each such section unique by adding at the end of it, in parentheses, the name of the original author or publisher of that section if known, or else a unique number. Make the same adjustment to the section titles in the list of Invariant Sections in the license notice of the combined work.

In the combination, you must combine any sections Entitled "History" in the various original documents, forming one section Entitled "History"; likewise combine any sections Entitled "Acknowledgements", and any sections Entitled "Dedications". You must delete all sections Entitled "Endorsements."

6. COLLECTIONS OF DOCUMENTS

You may make a collection consisting of the Document and other documents released under this License, and replace the individual copies of this License in the various documents with a single copy that is included in the collection, provided that you follow the rules of this License for verbatim copying of each of the documents in all other respects.

You may extract a single document from such a collection, and distribute it individually under this License, provided you insert a copy of this License into the extracted document, and follow this License in all other respects regarding verbatim copying of that document.

7. AGGREGATION WITH INDEPENDENT WORKS

A compilation of the Document or its derivatives with other separate and independent documents or works, in or on a volume of a storage or distribution medium, is called an "aggregate" if the copyright resulting from the compilation is not used to limit the legal rights of the compilation's users beyond what the individual works permit. When the Document is included in an aggregate, this License does not apply to the other works in the aggregate which are not themselves derivative works of the Document.

If the Cover Text requirement of section 3 is applicable to these copies of the Document, then if the Document is less than one half of the entire aggregate, the Document's Cover Texts may be placed on covers that bracket the Document within the aggregate, or the electronic equivalent of covers if the Document is in electronic form. Otherwise they must appear on printed covers that bracket the whole aggregate.

8. TRANSLATION

Translation is considered a kind of modification, so you may distribute translations of the Document under the terms of section 4. Replacing Invariant Sections with translations requires special permission from their copyright holders, but you may include translations of some or all Invariant Sections in addition to the original versions of these Invariant Sections. You may include a translation of this License, and all the license notices in the Document, and any Warranty Disclaimers, provided that you also include the original English version of this License and the original versions of those notices and disclaimers. In case of a disagreement between the translation and the original version of this License or a notice or disclaimer, the original version will prevail.

If a section in the Document is Entitled "Acknowledgements", "Dedications", or "History", the requirement (section 4) to Preserve its Title (section 1) will typically require changing the actual title.

9. TERMINATION

You may not copy, modify, sublicense, or distribute the Document except as expressly provided for under this License. Any other attempt to copy, modify, sublicense or distribute the Document is void, and will automatically terminate your rights under this License. However, parties who have received copies, or rights, from you under this License will not have their licenses terminated so long as such parties remain in full compliance.

10. FUTURE REVISIONS OF THIS LICENSE

The Free Software Foundation may publish new, revised versions of the GNU Free Documentation License from time to time. Such new versions will be similar in spirit to the present version, but may differ in detail to address new problems or concerns. See http://www.gnu.org/copyleft/.

Each version of the License is given a distinguishing version number. If the Document specifies that a particular numbered version of this License "or any later version" applies to it, you have the option of following the terms and conditions either of that specified version or of any later version that has been published (not as a draft) by the Free Software Foundation. If the Document does not specify a version number of this License, you may choose any version ever published (not as a draft) by the Free Software Foundation.

How to use this License for your documents

To use this License in a document you have written, include a copy of the License in the document and put the following copyright and license notices just after the title page:

Copyright (c) YEAR YOUR NAME.

Permission is granted to copy, distribute and/or modify this document

under the terms of the GNU Free Documentation License, Version 1.2

or any later version published by the Free Software Foundation;

with no Invariant Sections, no Front-Cover Texts, and no Back-Cover Texts.

A copy of the license is included in the section entitled "GNU

Free Documentation License".

If you have Invariant Sections, Front-Cover Texts and Back-Cover Texts, replace the "with...Texts." line with this:

with the Invariant Sections being LIST THEIR TITLES, with the

Front-Cover Texts being LIST, and with the Back-Cover Texts being LIST.

If you have Invariant Sections without Cover Texts, or some other combination of the three, merge those two alternatives to suit the situation.

If your document contains nontrivial examples of program code, we recommend releasing these examples in parallel under your choice of free software license, such as the GNU General Public License, to permit their use in free software.

www.ingramcontent.com/pod-product-compliance
Lightning Source LLC
Chambersburg PA
CBHW081836170426
43199CB00017B/2741